Regulating Code

Information Revolution and Global Politics

William J. Drake and Ernest J. Wilson III, editors

Regulating Code: Good Governance and Better Regulation in the Information Age

Ian Brown and Christopher T. Marsden

The MIT Press
Cambridge, Massachusetts
London, England

MIT Press books may be purchased at special quantity discounts for business or sales promotional use. For information, please email special_sales@mitpress.mit.edu or write to Special Sales Department, The MIT Press, 55 Hayward Street, Cambridge, MA 02142.

This book was set in Stone Sans and Stone Serif by Toppan Best-set Premedia Limited, Hong Kong. Printed and bound in the United States of America.

Library of Congress Cataloging-in-Publication Data

Brown, Ian, Dr.
Regulating code : good governance and better regulation in the information age / Ian Brown and Christopher T. Marsden.
    p.   cm. — (Information revolution and global politics)
Includes bibliographical references and index.
ISBN 978-0-262-01882-1 (hardcover : alk. paper)
1. Computer networks—Law and legislation.   2. Programming languages (Electronic computers)   3. Internet—Law and legislation.   4. Information policy.   I. Marsden, Christopher T.   II. Title.
K564.C6B76   2013
338.9'26—dc23
2012029444

10 9 8 7 6 5 4 3 2 1

Contents

Acknowledgments

Ian Brown thanks his research assistant at Oxford University, Jon Penney, and his research sponsor EPSRC (grant EP/G002606/1).

Both Chris and Ian are grateful to the reviewers of the manuscript for this book: Trisha Meyer, Yana Breindl, Axel Arnbak, Andre Oboler, and the anonymous reviewers at MIT Press. All errors and omissions remain our own responsibility.

Chris Marsden thanks Dr. Tiew Han for keeping his wife, Kenza, able to function despite a calamitous period of ill health as this book was being finalized in Melbourne; Andrew Kenyon at the University of Melbourne for his hospitality when Chris was an academic visitor there in that period; and Kenza for putting up with him during the last frenetic weeks of February 2012. Truly it was the longest February in many years.

The ideas in this book fermented for many years, notably during a walk with his coauthor by the Thames on a summer day in 2008 that led to the inspiration for the 2008 GiKii paper that started the "prosumer interoperability" idea germinating. He also benefited from many conversations over many years with Internet lawyers, scientists, and sages. The main venues for this process were the TPRC conferences in Arlington, Virginia; the Ruschlikon conferences in Switzerland; the Wharton colloquia in Philadelphia; Oxford media conventions; symposia at Columbia University and the Organization for Economic Cooperation and Development; discussions in Brussels; and various other venues on the U.S. West and East Coasts. If this book is the adequate result of the best of ideas from the United States and Europe, then it is thanks to illuminating discussions with these and other colleagues. He also thanks his colleagues at Essex, notably dearly departed Kevin Boyle, for encouraging the unthinkable. Bill Drake was the most honest of series editors and an inspiration throughout the writing process.

Chris Marsden dedicates his contribution to this book to his family, who endured throughout the period of its gestation, and especially his mother, who taught the value of patience and durability.

Introduction: Regulating the Information Giants

Governments and their regulatory agencies, those "weary giants of flesh and steel" (Barlow 1996), have spent the past two decades playing catch-up with the rapidly changing technologies and uses of the Internet. Few would now follow Barlow in claiming that governments have no legitimate claim to sovereignty in cyberspace, but many government agencies are still feeling their way in regulating this new global ecosystem (Brynjolfsson, Smith, and Hu 2003).

In this book, we conduct a comparative analysis of hard cases that best illustrate the state exercise of regulatory power in this new domain, as well as forbearance from regulation, to enhance the production of public goods such as fully functioning markets and security, and the protection of fundamental democratic rights (Stiglitz 1999). Our focus is the regulatory shaping of "code"—the technologies that underpin the Internet—to achieve more efficient outcomes, drawing out lessons for more economically effective and socially just regulation of the Internet.

Broad political attention began being paid to the Internet around 1993 with Berners-Lee's World Wide Web popularized by the release of Mosaic as the first widely adopted browser (Kahin and Abbate 1995) and the Clinton-Gore electoral campaign policy toward what was then touted as the "information superhighway." This book addresses the third decade of Internet regulation, not the libertarian first decade (1993–2002) or the re-regulatory middle decade (2003–2012), that followed the dot-com bust and state security imperative driven by the 9/11 terrorist attacks on the United States.

This introduction sets out the terms of our research engagement with these topical and critical issues for all Internet users. We use *code* in the sense of Joel Reidenberg (1998) and Lawrence Lessig's foundational work

(1999, 2006), referring to the technical environment of the Internet, resting on the architecture of computer hardware and software code. Our goal is to examine regulation of and on the Internet from both a technologically advanced and a sophisticated regulatory perspective.

While code predominantly regulates the user experience of the Internet, governments as well as self-regulatory standards significantly influence that environment (Pattberg 2005). We use *regulation* here in the widest sense to refer to the control of the online environment, whether exercised by code, government, self-regulatory standards, or private actors' commercial imperatives exercised largely through contract law as terms of use. Later chapters refer to legal regulation and its effect in "regulating" code, unless we specifically refer to "code regulating" user behavior.

To give a concrete example of the interplay of code with legal regulation, this book was coauthored on an Apple iMac, Macbook, iPad, and Sony laptop, in Google Documents and Dropbox as online sharing tools, viewed through variously Microsoft Internet Explorer, Google Chrome, the open source Firefox, and Apple's Safari browsers, with additional word processing on both Apple and Microsoft software, in various countries across Europe, North America, Asia, Australasia, and Africa. The terms of use of these systems were set by those various companies, with privacy policies influenced by national privacy standards and laws but mediated by individual browser functionality and settings. Some concepts were discussed with "friends" on Facebook and Google+ social networks, with their own terms of use, privacy, and copyright policies, as well as standards for taking down illegal or offensive material. (We promised MIT Press that the book's contents are neither illegal nor obscene.) We are thus addressing the web of technical, legal, market, and social standards that Internet users constantly inhabit.

A serious discussion of Internet regulation needs to examine the deficiencies and benefits of technical, political, legal, and economic solutions (Bauer, Obar, and Koh 2011) based on a mix of self-, co-, and state regulatory approaches. The first two approaches have been widely used in the fast-moving technical environment of the Internet in an effort to build on the expertise of and gain buy-in from technology companies. Using extended case studies in durable and intractable policy controversies, we analyze the costs and benefits of this responsive regulation, set alongside the coordination disincentives and legitimacy gaps that inevitably accompany such a transient regulatory arrangement. These include the reform initiatives by the Obama and Barroso administrations in Washington and Brussels, whose policies institutionalized a somewhat more consensual transatlantic (if not trans-Pacific) basis for Internet regulation.

In this introduction, we first briefly describe the regulatory challenges that the Internet's code and market development presents before examining the regulatory goals of the creation of public goods, including the protection and extension of human rights, and a competitive market for innovation. In the following chapter, we examine in more depth the interoperability challenges of the Internet and introduce our five case studies, chosen for their development of both code and more traditional regulatory solutions.

We have included a glossary at the end of the book with definitions of the many acronyms, abbreviations, and terms that pervade discussions of Internet technology and regulation.

Regulation and the Internet's Unique Challenges

The public Internet has been a faster-developing, more innovative environment than almost any other sector of the economy and society over the past two decades. Software and information management has pervaded other sectors to such an extent that discrete analysis of the Internet is becoming much more difficult, as digital information exchange diffuses throughout the economy and society. But supporting the Internet's capacity for rapid innovation remains a central goal of states, with great potential for future social and public benefits (Lessig 1999; Benkler 2006; Zittrain 2008).

The Internet presents a series of often fast-moving targets to regulators, with rapid churn in some market sectors. Interoperability makes Internet markets particularly susceptible to both failure and remedy as they tip toward a dominant product, firm, or standard. These tipping characteristics are not confined to economic markets but apply to public goods including privacy, security, and freedom of speech—in part as a response to the extraordinary forces that shape the adoption and switching between different products and services on the Internet.

The scalability of the generative Internet and personal computer (PC) ecosystem (Zittrain 2006) means that small companies and communities of programmers can evolve from minnows to whales in a few years, writing code that will work on multiple devices, networks, and programs due to their interoperable standards (the Internet is a network of about forty thousand autonomous networks [Haddadi et al., 2009]). But firms such as Microsoft, Apple, SAP, Intel, Cisco, and Google have all used their control of a particular product to redefine markets in their favor, often by both vertical integration and the establishment of semi- or wholly proprietary standards (Coates 2011).

Many technology companies grew quickly from humble beginnings to dominate their markets. They outlived their original "host body" (IBM as the "host" for Microsoft's DOS as the operating system for its PC; Facebook and Google originally "hosted" more or less willingly by their universities, respectively, Harvard and Stanford) or find new uses for their unique proposition. Google used search to master online advertising; Skype found a use as a more popular voice alternative to Windows products, and was eventually acquired in 2011 for more than $8 billion by Microsoft.

Market forces can (though rarely do) quickly return these markets toward equilibrium and beyond, to a different type of failure, with a different dominant standard (Wu 2003a). For example, social networks have developed out of user-created Usenet discussions and bulletin boards in the 1980s and 1990s, seeing increasingly socially responsible self-regulation by the emerging commercial actors such as AOL, Microsoft, Yahoo, MySpace, and Bebo by the mid-2000s, followed by the supplanting of these actors in the West by the enormously popular Facebook since 2008. Facebook grew from nothing in 2004 to become the second most popular destination Web site in the world by 2012. As a result, regulatory conditions have changed, as has the coding of the architecture of the social networks to which users entrust their personal information.

Facebook's policies toward sharing of personal data are both shaped by and reshape existing laws, regulations, and social mores regarding personal data. Its rival Google also both creates and responds to regulation in its markets, whether in its dominant search advertising market or its own social network Orkut (most popular in Brazil), its failed social network Buzz, and its relaunch into social networking, Google+. One could point to more established companies such as Microsoft or Intel to explore the "plumbing" of the Internet and its terminal devices, cases we return to in examining the layered model for Internet design in the next chapter.

National economies retain significantly different online market conditions and regulation in spite of the homogenizing force of U.S. information giants. Hence, no matter how heroic the internal or even external view of companies such as Facebook, Microsoft, or Google, their totalizing tendency as a result of their strong corporate culture (whether "Windows Everywhere" or "Don't Be Evil") is susceptible to regulatory response and—after often painful maturation processes—corporate adaptation to legal reality in their host markets. Hence, Google felt obliged to move their search engine from mainland China to Hong Kong in mid-2010, after facing hacking attacks and having failed to supplant the dominance of Chinese government-supported Baidu. Skype decided not to directly enter the Chinese market, instead setting up a joint venture, TOM-Skype, that could comply with government requests to install a back door into its proprietary encrypted voice over Internet protocol (VOIP) peer-to-peer (P2P) messaging service. In Europe, Microsoft finally settled its antitrust suit with the European Commission in late 2009 and introduced a mandated choice for users of Internet browser (after a $1 billion fine in the case).

Such use of the software and service giants' own market power to exert the regulatory remedy preferred by national lawmakers is becoming commonplace—requiring rewriting of the code of Facebook, Google, Skype, and Microsoft to force the companies into obedience to legal norms. This is a regulatory technique that is not unique to the Internet but can be uniquely appropriate to these information goods.

Ambitious and profit-maximizing companies still have social responsibilities toward their users as citizens as well as economic exploitation as users (Marsden 2008). Claims that mobile, grid, or cloud computing or social networking are technological advances that outweigh the value of protection of users' personal data, or that broadband networks are overloaded such that Internet service providers (ISPs[1]) must censor their subscribers' Internet use, should be met by governments with well-informed skepticism, and subjected to rigorous examination.

Path dependency and network effects can have long-term effects in code solutions and raise a serious regulatory problem when dealing with

---

1. While *ISP* is capable of multiple legal definitions, we generally use it to refer to suppliers of access for consumers to the Internet (Marsden 2012).

communication networks. Historically this is illustrated by the dominance of the internal combustion engine for automobiles, or the decision to adopt alternating current for the electricity grid, both decisions made a century ago (North 1990).

The TCP/IP communications protocols underlying the Internet create an ecosystem of transport, physical links, network, data link, operating systems, and applications and content, which is different from other network utilities due to its fragmented but interoperable characteristics and its private ownership by a patchwork of companies. This leads to serious issues of cybersecurity and dependence of governments on private solutions to fundamental security threats (Pfleeger and Pfleeger 2006).

The millennium or "Y2K" bug showed how much effort can be required to make fundamental changes to entrenched technical systems, as does the snail's-pace adoption of IPv6 (the new Internet addressing standard). That makes Internet regulation a critical current policy for governments, as well as a particularly complex challenge that cannot be entirely left to a rapidly maturing industry to design without oversight. Maintaining unstudied indifference or attempting to retrofit telecoms or utilities regulation onto the fundamentally different Internet environment are not workable solutions, as we will see.

If the information giants and governments are often tied together in a security bargain that may resemble those of other critical infrastructure such as electricity, telecoms, or rail networks, the insurgents can be almost invisible and anonymous. Many regulators woke up relatively slowly to regulation via technology, which is powerful but faces a fundamental constraint: the widespread availability of general-purpose PCs combined with the ability of a small number of open source programmers to undermine regulatory intent. If regulators fail to address regulatory objects, then the regulatory object can grow until its social adoption overwhelms the attempt to regulate. An example is the use of peer-to-peer file sharing, developed in the 1990s both to share music and more generally to help distribute multimedia files more efficiently in the absence of wider deployment of multicasting protocols. The P2P prototypes quickly grew into more powerful tools of file sharing (e.g., Napster to KaZaA to BitTorrent, which we examine in chapter 4) as courts and regulators struggled to catch up.

While regulation can be slow and ill adapted to rapid technological change, mainstream user behavioral change is also slower than potential technological change. For example, the extended debate over regulation of the Internet addressing system could be changed dramatically by a technologically-simple replacement of the domain name system (Crowcroft 2009). User adoption and entrenched interests make such a transition very unlikely.

Code changes quickly, user adoption more slowly, legal contracting and judicial adaptation to new technologies slower yet, and regulation through legislation slowest of all. This is not to criticize regulation by law, but to point out that law reform typically follows technological change at a measured pace. That was true of legal responses to earlier network technologies such as the railways as much as it is to the Internet.

Public Goods, Interoperability, and Human Rights

Corporate social responsibility (International Standards Organization 2009; Porter and Kramer 2006), information to create transparency, and better governance are tools for achieving a wider and deeper array of global public goods (Kaul, Grunberg, and Stern 1999). The outcomes of information, commercialization, and regulation are critically supported by the rule of law, education, and health care. The public Internet is a vast public library, as well as a bookshop, recording store, and open public space connected to many private Internet spaces (Stalla-Bourdillon 2010). By some estimates "private" intranets may be ten times larger than the public Internet—analogous to private property compared to that in public hands. Several authors have warned against private enclosure of the public Internet space, which Boyle (2008) refers to as "enclosing the commons of the mind."

We come "to praise the Internet, not to bury it." In this book we are not attempting to persuade the regulatory Samson to bring down the temple, or the thwarted Google to salt the land. Instead our analysis aims to identify policies that will encourage both competition and creation of public goods in a balanced public policy that shapes network effects toward social ends—not to turn "Microserf" or Google millionaires into billionaires without social responsibility, but equally not to destroy the sublimity of the Internet (Mosco 2004) and rebuild it in the image of the automobile industry or energy utilities. Some multinational commercial Internet providers have recognized the need to provide consistency in their application of law (Global Network Initiative 2011), though others have been challenged for the uses of their technology to aid repressive regimes (Morozov 2011).

There is a public interest in Internet regulation, but this does not naturally coalesce with either elected or authoritarian politicians' view of the national interest as expressed in some of the unworkable laws that continue to be applied, such as draconian court orders under English defamation law. The Internet is a global network, however splintered by national controls, and national responses must be cognizant of that technological reality, not least due to the indirect innovation costs and welfare losses of inappropriate intervention (however one defines that on behalf of individuals).

Regulators need to be made aware that their actions can and almost certainly will have unintended consequences. As Hall et al. (2011, 5) state, "More recent history of government interaction with the Internet has been unhappy. Various governments have made ham-fisted attempts to impose censorship or surveillance, while others have defended local telecommunications monopolies or have propped up other industries that were disrupted by the Internet." They also explain that there is "remarkably little reliable information about the size and shape of the Internet infrastructure or its daily operation. . . . The opacity also hinders research and development of improved protocols, systems and practices by making it hard to know what the issues really are and harder yet to test proposed solutions."

The public interest is not always well represented by the government or corporate interest, especially in as dynamic and generation dividing a set of technologies as those considered here. Although we do not adopt a government-bashing libertarianism (despite its manifest attractions in terms of consistency and the manifold examples of the incompetence of governments in their attempts at regulation), we recognize the insights of public choice analysis (Moe 1997, counterbalanced by North 1990) that government is all too easily captured by self-interested lobbyists, not least in security and copyright policies.

We do not engage in attacks on the straw man of Anglo-Saxon Internet libertarianism, as that debate is, to all intents and purposes, over (Goldsmith and Wu 2006), though U.S. companies dominate the European Internet environment. Nor do we fall easily into China bashing when the regulatory lens moves toward censorship issues, though clearly Chinese government policies toward information autonomy and freedom are much more restrictive than those of U.S. or European governments (Boyle 2001). Culturally specific regulatory responses by governments eager to impose their existing worldview on their new generation of Internet users are prone to fail, whether that be the security backdoor into TOM-Skype or the Australian government's attempt to impose mandatory Web site blocking, an approach abandoned by the Clinton administration in 1997. Governments are frequent failures in learning lessons from regulatory history.

Regulation is not always reactive and outmoded. The Internet grew out of both strategic government investments in research under open standards, as well as regulatory decisions designed to maintain an open network architecture (Ungerer 2000; Cannon 2003; Coates 2011).

Free/open source software has had a powerful regulatory influence because its mere availability can sometimes constrain monopolistic commercial behavior: it does not need to succeed always and everywhere to have a very significant impact. For example, widespread use of Mozilla's open source Firefox browser prevented Microsoft from extending its Internet Explorer/Information Server dominance through proprietary extensions to HTML and HTTP.

Is this a significant constraint on the monopolist? Can we say that competition policy that permits market entry can permit the market to tip back to equilibrium, or is it just regulatory theater? How can we distinguish which network effects are totally entrenching and which can be regulated by traditional ex post regulatory tools? Regulators need to understand both the detail of this process, and how they can use it to effectively regulate the resulting global information giants. We explore this issue further in chapter 2, as well as in the case studies.

Human rights concerns have also become more critical, reflecting the mass adoption of the Internet in countries with serious democratic deficits, notably in the Middle East and North Africa. The concerns far predate the Arab Spring of 2011, and the regulatory debate has been well rehearsed in the United States and Europe since the birth of the commercial Internet.

Freedom of expression is a fundamental right that balances its jurisprudential limits only against those of other fundamental rights, such as privacy and freedom from racial discrimination or violence against the person, and must be balanced carefully against rights to private property including copyright (Leader 1982; *Scarlet* v. *SABAM* 2011). Its defense has been partially limited by torts such as defamation and trespass in private common law intended to prevent abuse of free speech (Wright 2001; Cornford 2008).

Boyle (2001) has, for instance, condemned Chinese Internet censorship yet decried promiscuous hate speech under U.S. First Amendment standards and tried to strike a middle ground in calling for "new efforts to establish codes of conduct about harmful content on . . . this marvellous medium."

In 2011, universal Internet access was declared a human right by a report presented to the United Nations General Assembly (La Rue 2011), while regional human rights bodies (Council of Europe 2011b) and national law (Bits of Freedom 2011) gave effect to that broad concern, notably by declaring best practices in preventing Internet filtering from harming freedom of expression. Viviane Reding, the European Commission vice president who is responsible for human rights, declared, "Copyright protection (Article 17 (2) of the EU Charter of Fundamental Rights) can never be a justification for eliminating freedom of expression (Article 11(1) of the EU Charter of Fundamental Rights) or freedom of information. That is why for me, blocking the Internet is never an option" (2012, paragraph 3). We examine the reality of these changes more closely in chapters 5 and 7.

Our Approach: Hard Cases

In this introduction, we have emphasized that the Internet environment is dynamic and complex and that its interdependence and interoperability are both its innovative strength and its inherent security weakness. We also introduced the regulatory concept that code determines many online transactions, an idea elaborated in the 1990s by Reidenberg (1998) and Lessig (1999). Lessig (1999, 2006) explained to critics who accused him of doomsaying that many users would choose to adopt the information giants' solutions that are more tethered, favoring security, simplicity, and ease of use over adaptability. Zittrain (2006) called this "generativity," or the ability to reprogram (or "hack" in the best sense of the word) the device to create new uses.

Code is no more neutral than regulation, with each subject to monopoly and capture by commercial interests. However, recent regulatory development through competition law and human rights policy discourse has created a more fertile environment for code solutions that support competition and efficiency—broadly defined to include social welfare—and users' human rights to privacy and freedom of expression. The claims of interoperability and fundamental rights are central to our examination of hard cases, and their solution by code and other forms of regulation (Wu 2003a, 2003b).

In our interdisciplinary analysis of five hard cases, we aim to shed significant new light on these questions. In the next two chapters, we explain in more detail the environment we examine, our approach to its analysis, and why hard cases can provide more interesting answers than a one-size-fits-all slogan to the future regulation of code.

1   Mapping the Hard Cases

We described in the Introduction the problems and challenges of regulating the Internet, given the dynamism of markets and the even greater dynamism of code, whether closed or open.

The claim that regulation can serve both economic and social efficiency and human rights goals is hardly novel (Mill 1869; Teubner 1986; Brownsword 2005; Brownsword and Yeung 2008). But we argue that the growing societal importance of the Internet makes the policy challenge increasingly important and that we need to reject simple magic bullet solutions based on study of one discipline (whether computer science, law, or economics), one industry sector (telecommunications or free software), or one solution (self-regulation or government control). Examining the claim that solutions can combine such disparate tools (regulation and code) and aims (efficiency and human rights) is the aim of our case study examinations in this book.

In this chapter, we explain our methodology. First, we assess the standard analyses of Internet regulation. We then explain how regulation of this virtual environment is best approached by examining the protocol stack rather than geographical approaches and assessing regulatory intervention according to the code solution or solutions used. However, following Shannon (1948, 1949), we reject a technologically determinist view of code as an efficient stand-alone solution and examine the predominant justifications for various regulatory systems, classified as broadly supported by economic or rights-based regulation (Lessig 1999; Balleisen and Moss 2010).

In the following section, we explore a particularly promising recent approach, multistakeholder governance. Its importance for our analysis is that it introduces both user rights and technical solution advocates into the otherwise frequently closed government-corporate regulatory discussion. Whatever the practical flaws of the previously researched practices of multistakeholder Internet regulation, it is rapidly becoming an element in regulatory design (Drake and Wilson 2008; DeNardis 2009).

Finally, we briefly outline our case studies, as well as our approach to their analysis. The case studies cover both fundamental rights-based Internet fields (censorship, privacy, copyright) and information infrastructures that are attracting increasing regulatory attention (social networking sites and network neutrality).

Standard Approaches to Internet Regulation

There are three existing conflicting approaches to Internet regulation from a technical and legal policy perspective: continued technological and market-led self-regulation, reintroduction of state-led regulation, and multistakeholder coregulation.

The first, self-regulation, holds that from technical and economic perspectives, self-regulation and minimal state involvement are most efficient in dynamic innovative industries such as the Internet. This is challenged by three factors: technological, competition, and democratic. Technology is never neutral in its social impact (Reed 2007; Dommering 2006). Network and scale effects are driving massive concentration in information industries (Zittrain 2008; Wu 2010). And voters will not allow governments to ignore the social impact of this ubiquitous medium.

The second explanation holds that from the legal policy perspective, governments need to reassert their sovereignty. It states that code and other types of self-regulation critically lack constitutional checks and balances for private citizens, including appeal against corporate action to prevent access or remove materials (Frydman and Rorive 2002; Goldsmith and Wu 2006). According to this explanation, government should at least reserve statutory powers to oversee self-regulation to ensure the effective application of due process and attention to fundamental rights in the measures taken by private actors.

However, it may also be argued that government regulation has serious legitimacy deficits, with as much government as market failure in Internet regulation to date, with overregulation evident in "censorship" (MacKinnon 2012). There has been widespread industry capture of regulators and legislators in, for instance, copyright law (Horten 2011). Incumbents lobby to protect and introduce new barriers to entry with regulatory or legislative approval, as in a perceived failure to enforce or approve network neutrality legislation (Marsden 2010). There has been continued exclusion of wider civil society from the formal policy discussion, where official views do not permit easy representation of new noncorporate technical or user rights lobbies (Mueller 2010).

The view that traditional regulation fails to embrace new multistakeholder discussion has partly been justified by states criticizing the extremely tenuous chain of accountability of participants within international fora to nongovernmental organization stakeholders. Former French president Sarkozy, host of the eG8 meeting in 2011, stated in relation to Internet governance (Poullet 2007) that "governments are the only legitimate representatives of the will of the people in our democracies. To forget this is to take the risk of democratic chaos and hence anarchy" (Howard 2011).

The civil society argument leads to the third multistakeholder coregulatory position: that formally inclusive multistakeholder coregulation—reintroducing both state and citizen—is the approach that has the best chance to reconcile market failures and constitutional legitimacy failures in self-regulation (Collins 2010; Marsden 2011).

Though intended to increase inclusiveness by representation beyond the government-business dialogue, there are significant questions as to the effectiveness, accountability, and legitimacy of civil society groups in representing the public interest. There is a body of work on Internet governance specifically addressing legitimacy gaps and development challenges in global institutions from an international political economy perspective (Mueller 2010; Drake and Wilson 2008).

Given the legitimacy gap in multistakeholder interaction, it is unsurprising that the approach so far has been to conduct conversations rather than make law in such fora, reflecting the "unconference" approach of Internet innovators (in which agendas are collaboratively determined by participants at the beginning of a meeting). Cynicism is at least partly justified (Morozov 2011).

Coregulation has been extensively discussed in European law (Senden 2005; Hüpkes 2009), including in Internet regulatory debates (Lievens, Dumortier, and Ryan 2006; Frydman, Hennebel, and Lewkowicz 2008) and in relation to data protection governance (Raab 1993). Coregulation is even more familiar to Australian regulatory scholars since the term entered common use in about 1989 (Marsden 2011), with the term applied to codes of conduct for industry sectors (Palmera 1989; McKay 1994; Grabowsky 1995; Sinclair 1997) including the Internet (Chen 2002). Adoption of the term in the United States has been slow, with *coregulatory* in legal terms referring to state-federal division of competencies (Noam 1983). However, both Balleisen (Balleisen and Eisner 2009; Balleisen 2010) and Weiser (2009, 2010) have made extensive claims for coregulation to be adopted more frequently.

We assess these counterpoints in chapters 3 through 7 in empirically grounded, multidisciplinary case studies of five difficult areas—what we refer to as *hard cases*. Previous legal work has tended to examine the Internet from a position reflecting the technology's unregulated origins (Post 2009), even in debunking the borderless "Wild West" mythology of the early libertarian paradigm (Lessig 2006; Goldsmith and Wu 2006; Zittrain 2008). They equally have tended to be U.S.-centric. This debate has been effectively ended in favor of realistic pragmatic viewpoints (Reidenberg 1993, 2005; Goldsmith and Wu 2006; Wu 2010).

Regulatory and political economy work has concentrated on single issues or themes, such as the domain name system or privacy issues. There has been significant analysis in individual issue areas, notably the Internet Corporation for Assigned Names and Numbers, or ICANN (Mueller 2002) and Internet standard setting (Camp and Vincent 2004). Holistic examinations have tended to be compendia, such as Marsden (2000), Thierer and Crews (2003), and Brown (2013), or examine the Internet from development or other political economy perspectives (Cowhey, Aronson, and Abelson, 2009).

Our approach takes a multidisciplinary perspective from both computer science and law, following Kahin and Abbate (1995), Berman and Weitzner (1995), and Lessig and Resnick (1998). We cover European as well as U.S. regulation and policy, and in the following section explain why a geographically specific attempt to regulate will largely fail to achieve optimal code and regulatory solutions.

Geographies of Internet Regulation

It is not feasible to map Internet regulation as a patchwork of national networks where international regulatory discussion centers on areas with overlapping jurisdictions or unclear jurisdiction. This comparison of Internet regulation with the Law of the Sea or medieval mercantile law (Lex Mercatoria as Lex Informatica: Reidenberg 1998) is untenable in practice; unlike maritime transactions, Internet transactions commonly take place in real time in multiple jurisdictions, potentially using the same computer software worldwide (Lessig 1999; Murray 2006). China or Iran may be able to maintain their own hermetically sealed intranets despite the economic and social losses associated with such self-imposed isolation (in which China and Iran both have an unfortunate historical inheritance), but interconnecting with the Internet will lead to contamination of that drastic solution. Longer-term Internet control by authoritarian regimes is likely to be more subtle (Morozov 2011).

That is not to say the Internet is unregulable or that such a status should be assumed. However, to state that any country can effectively create a wall (like a naval blockade) around its domestic Internet appears empirically to be an exaggeration (Clayton, Murdoch, and Watson 2006), as with the Law of Space.

A further difference with traditional trade in goods is in the nature of those "goods": information goods are often media or speech products that carry an explicit political or ideological message. Even dramatic attempts at national disconnection by repressive regimes during national uprisings in Burma and Egypt failed to prevent information exchange with the wider world.

For over a decade, governments have been able to require crude filtering of content to users based on geography. The imposition of sanctions on U.S. Internet host Yahoo! by the French courts in 2001 could not block all French users from accessing content that was illegal in France but legal in the United States. It was intended to restrict the vast majority of ordinary nonexpert users who did not have the ability or incentive to disguise their location (Reidenberg 2004, 2005; Goldsmith and Wu 2006). Expert witnesses told the French court that users could be blocked with about 70 percent effectiveness, although one witness later retracted this opinion (Laurie 2000).

The idea that one can map Internet regulation based on the location of bits is therefore superficially attractive but essentially a technologically determined attempt to reintroduce physical jurisdictional boundaries (Bender 1998). Ultimately the Internet's highly connected nature has enabled at least sophisticated users to route around censorship, protected by encryption, which we explore in more depth in the next chapter.

If Internet transactions cannot be regulated in the same way as physical goods transactions, a second suggestion is that they be mapped using their nearest physical analog: the geography of their routing through servers. The problem here is significant and can be stated simply: the Internet remains largely a "dumb" network that routes packets without examining their contents. This lies behind the so-called end-to-end nature of the Internet: "intelligence" lies in end nodes such as PCs and smart phones, not between these nodes in network routers (Saltzer, Clark, and Reed 1984; Clark and Blumenthal 2011).

Though attempts are being made to "see" inside the packets to check their compliance with the law (as we will see in the chapter 7), governments still cannot very effectively act as customs officials and stop, check, deport, or import packets (Burk 1999; Marsden 2010). Though this is a technological possibility in Internet design, it would create a significantly different environment where, for instance, the anonymity of senders was removed or at least heavily penalized (Deibert et al. 2008, 2010; Johnson et al. 2003).

Early analysts viewed technical and geographical challenges to existing regulatory functions (Johnson and Post 1996) as insurmountable obstacles to regulation. Later analysis demonstrated that there was much greater interdependence between the allegedly global and unregulable Internet and national rules (Thierer and Crews 2003; Marsden 2000).

The ability of the state to seize physical assets and interrogate evidence (such as data on servers) is at the center of national enforcement (Brown, Edwards, and Marsden 2009), as well as traditional state censorship. Our selection of hard cases is an attempt to investigate the gaps where full state regulation is unfeasible, unwieldy, or unnecessary. A strong working assumption of our research is that many such institutions will map not to geographical boundaries but to sectoral or technical realms (Bar et al. 2000; Barnes 2000).

National law does not create effective solutions to prevent code-based problems, but a better solution may be a combination of a pooling of sovereignty to create global standards in support of effective code and protection of users' rights. There has been a growing realization that the Internet presents a complex series of challenges to existing laws, but that a nuanced and interdependent (if complex) relationship has emerged between existing nationally based legal systems and a global (or at least multipolar) Internet architecture based on code.

The role of state sovereignty has been reintroduced by both the Internet's mass adoption and by government desires to reintroduce substantial monitoring and other functions to maintain state security. These were particularly driven by the September 11, 2001, terrorist attacks in the United States and subsequent attacks in Bali, Madrid, London, and elsewhere (Ball and Webster 2003), and the growing scourge of virus writers, spammers, fraudsters, child pornographers, and pedophiles using the Internet (Brown, Edwards, and Marsden 2006).

The Internet is not a novelty in regulatory discussion (and was not at the time of much initial surveying in this field; Kahin and Nesson 1997). But its relatively fast and technologically dynamic development means that there is likely to remain a governance gap between what the technologists and advanced users know of the medium and political responses, as with many other advanced technologies (Brownsword 2005). Internet regulatory history is partial or incomplete, as the issue areas were either neglected by regulators for Internet-specific reasons as technically forbidding (as with many Internet security problems) or because of forbearance based on the desire to avoid harming self-regulatory mechanisms (Price and Verhulst 2004; Priest 1997) and to ensure the continued competitiveness advantages of rapid Internet deployment and development. Regulation has lagged Internet development.

Regulating Through Code

A more technical view can provide a different perspective. Engineers designed the Internet, and its content, services, and applications sit on the infrastructure. Therefore the logic of the infrastructure's design can provide a basis to assess what is different about the Internet for regulatory purposes: its code (Reidenberg 1998; Lessig 1999; Werbach 1997). This suggests that we explore the Internet from the perspective of those who designed its standards, whether the basic standards of the Internet Protocol (IP) itself and its end-to-end design (Clark and Blumenthal 2011), the motives and (limited) policy purposes behind the refinement of that design, or the particular applications that interact directly with the content layer

(Berners-Lee and Fischetti 2000). Internet self-regulation emerges from that technical perspective.

Problems of both a regulatory and disciplinary nature remain. The lack of interaction between (most) engineers and (most) social scientists mean that the technology is often as unsuitable for wider societal goals as the law is unsuitable for many practical enforcement processes (de Sola Pool 1983).

A technical view of mapping begins with the classic open systems interconnect (OSI) "layers model," which was adapted to represent the stack of protocols that enable end-to-end signaling of communications traffic (Werbach 2002). There are cross-cutting issues that affect the stack as a whole, examples such as digital rights management (DRM) and security. Content and applications and their regulation sit atop the Internet's deeper architecture, which is typically represented by the "protocol stack."

We can illustrate the stack as an iceberg, with the content as the visible layer above the water and the technical layers submerged from sight for nonexpert users, as shown in figure 1.1:

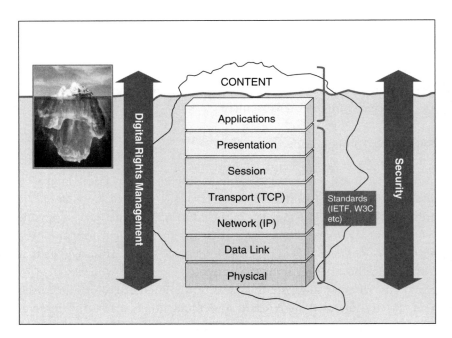

Figure 1.1
Graphically representing content sitting above the standards iceberg

There are rules written into the entirety of the protocol layers "iceberg" (Wright 2006) that affect users' perspectives of how to receive and share content or how to ensure the security of their use and enjoyment of that content.

The technical infrastructure provides the underpinning of the content layer, and design choices in those layers underpinning content have a significant influence on the content itself (Reidenberg 2005; Lessig 1999). We selected case studies that have a significant material impact on the content layer, including those that may be located further from the end user's visibility. For example, the relatively anonymous end-to-end nature of the Internet facilitates the transmission of unsolicited commercial e-mail (spam). Laws restricting this content cannot be effective for most consumers without also enlisting the support and deployment of services deployed outside the user's own computer (Clark 2005; Brown, Edwards, and Marsden 2006) through some level of classification and filtering at other points in the network.

The hard case studies that we analyze in later chapters demonstrate the links between core protocols and content regulation in the areas of data protection, network neutrality, censorship, copyright, and social networks. For instance, DRM and security affect content consumption but can also be embedded within architectures and hardware. This type of joined-up thinking between content-based laws and architectural principles runs through our logical analysis of the case studies. It explains in large measure governments' acknowledgment of the futility of attempts to regulate using law alone.

For a road traffic comparison, one cannot enforce fundamental changes in road users' behavior without the support of automobile manufacturers, transport planners, as well as suppliers, pedestrians, bicyclists, and environmental groups. Instrumental regulation-led description of the Internet must acknowledge the underlying architecture in the same way as road traffic rules and conventions must acknowledge the environment in which they operate (safety rules do not permit bicycling at night without lights, for instance).

Though one does not have to understand every element in design to implement a rule, or every protocol in the layers model, it is essential to understand the system fundamentals. The end-to-end IP-based Internet is by definition an interoperable and technically neutral regime on which many open standards result in open source products or services for use without charge, protected by copyright licences (such as the General Public License) that require any derivative software to be freely available and modifiable (EC 2011a). In such a regime, anyone can design based on publicly and freely available protocols and software and interoperate with anyone else properly deploying the same protocols with the same rules. This open interoperability gives enormous practical advantages, which resulted in the development of the public Internet as it is widely experienced today.

Economic and Human Rights Justifications for Regulation

Code is not designed in a bubble by automatons, and it is not consumed in a bubble. Inherited regulation from other mass and personal media is relevant—an instance of regulatory path dependence.

Internet regulation can be discussed from the perspective of, for instance, laws relating to copyright, child protection, or freedom of speech. These are reflected in differing systems of regulation converging on the Internet, for instance, telecommunications, mass media, or information technology law. A growing body of analysis has focused on the interdependence of the various environments merging on the Internet and the question of regulatory divergence or convergence (Zittrain 2006; Schulz and Held 2001; Tambini, Danilo, and Marsden 2007).

We can somewhat simplify differing regulatory approaches into two types: those based on human rights such as child protection and freedom of speech and those based on economic efficiency (competition policy and competitiveness: for instance, infrastructure regulation, often characterized as technocratic in character). Although economics (Laffont and Tirole 2001) and human rights (Murray and Klang 2005) approaches to Internet regulation may have different emphases, there can be common ground (Lessig 1999; Ogus 1994). We show a schematic of the approaches and their predominant justifications in table 1.1.

Copyright is a particularly controversial issue in digital markets, where works can be perfectly reproduced, adapted, and redistributed at almost no marginal cost. It is primarily categorized in Anglo-American political discourse as an economic issue, while acknowledging authors' moral rights and the speech rights–based debate surrounding technical protection measures that can stop users from taking advantage of copyright exceptions.

Table 1.1
Representative regulatory systems and their predominant justification

Human rights intervention	Economic and competition frameworks
Freedom of expression	Digital rights management and trusted computing
Social network regulation	Personal Internet security
Consumer protection regulation	Network neutrality rules
Child protection blocking	Copyright and associated rights
Data protection	Telecoms infrastructure regulation

Though control over key infrastructure may be placed in the field of economic issues, these have fundamental impacts on users' rights and responsibilities.

These distinctions help us begin to sketch some of the fundamental rights problems in Internet regulation and develop our analysis. In looking for hard cases, we focused on copyright, data protection, censorship through filtering or technical blocking, social networking, and Internet service provider (ISP) network regulation. Competition policy and government aid (e.g., to the digitally excluded or marginalized) are a matter of particular relevance given that the returns to scale in digital industries are very high, tending to a high degree of concentration in each industry (Noam 2011).

The transdisciplinary approach that Clark et al. (2002, 2005) urge also offers a more holistic approach to regulatory design. The approach of using interlocking analysis taken from geographical, substantive, and disciplinary examination of the Internet is that most commonly used by legal and social scientific analysts of Internet regulation. We conduct our case studies with this approach in mind, along with a focus on human rights and due process, and economic analysis, which creates more effective regulation when married with technically efficient uses of code. We return to the wider benefits and changes of this approach in the concluding chapter.

Internet Regulation and Multistakeholders

Government and industry acting together is not the whole of the Internet story, whose unique regulatory characteristic lies in the two sides of the citizen's separate role. First, the citizen is increasingly involved in formal decision making and informal lobbying in the international and national system: consider the Congress of Non Governmental Organisations in the U.N. system, or the role of the EU Economic and Social Committee, or at a national level, the influence of single-issue lobbies such as environmentalists or human rights groups (Baird 2002; Hoffman 2005).

This pluralism is increased in the Internet regulatory map by the influence of "Netheads": highly influential and often stridently independent Internet engineers and technologists, who play a significant role in the standards and other regulatory processes (Cerf 1994; Lessig 1999; Gould 2000, Kahin and Abbate 1995), particularly in the infrastructure technology but also in content, applications and services. The Internet Technical Advisory Committee to the Organization for Economic Cooperation and Development (OECD) is an example we return to in the concluding chapter.

We need to unpack the term *governance* for computer scientists and lawyers, who are more comfortable with the term *regulation*, whether in its narrower legal enforcement sense (Baldwin et al. 1998) or the broad Lessigian architectural concept we outlined in the Introduction. Previous work has analyzed regulation on a continuum from state regulation to coregulation and regulated self-regulation to self-regulation, and on to standard setting and regulation by individual communities and by norm setting (Posner 1984; Ogus 1994; Leiner et al. 1998; Gaines and Kimber 2001), which matches the soft law negotiation process in which governance can be placed (Senden 2005). *Self-regulation* is defined broadly as a rule or the formation of norms: it exercises a function that shapes or controls the behavior of actors in that environment, which may include software code (Pitofsky 1998; Lemley 1999).

The term *governance* began to be used widely in political science literature in the 1990s to describe intermediate forms of self-regulation in the post–Cold War globalization literature (Pierre 2000). It emerged from the study of the firm in organizational theory (Williamson 1975, 1985, 1994). The term appears to have been first used in its political science meaning in Jones and Hesterly (1993) and has since developed a specific meaning in analysis of European federal-state politics (Kohler-Koch and Eising 1999). Governance is further discussed in much of the political science literature in terms of networks and informal rule-making institutions, such as multinational corporations and—particularly relevant for Internet governance—standard-setting organizations (Christou and Simpson 2009).

Practitioners and academics have adopted varying definitions of Internet governance (see Working Group on Internet Governance 2005 and Reding 2005) that fall into what might be termed minimalist (Mueller, Mathiason, and McKnight 2004) and maximalist (Drake 2005) areas. We use the term *Internet regulation* to refer to the range of public-private interactions covering substantive national and regional-plurilateral rules and practices governing specific Internet topics (Scott 2004; Marsden 2000; Grewlich 1999), similar to the broad use in Zysman and Weber (2000), noting that *governance* is a yet broader term that encompasses the institutional politics surrounding such regulation, including regimes with no enforcement powers at all, not even by norms, which therefore fall outside legal analysis (U.N. Economic and Social Council 2006).

Three paradigmatic examples of multistakeholder governance have previously been identified and widely studied in the Internet literature: the Internet Governance Forum (IGF), ICANN, and the newer regulatory issue of user-generated content. First, in the U.N. system, the IGF (created out of the World Summit on the Information Society) has enabled a highly influential type of civil society involvement in its activities. It as yet has no formal membership and no formal enforcement powers. Its "dynamic coalitions" formulate and publish opinions that have some political soft power, given the high degree of stakeholder involvement in the discussions. The presence of national government representatives at high levels in the IGF process demonstrates its importance and potential for precedent setting, as does its continued existence from 2006 with an annual mandate until 2015.

The idea that roles and responsibilities in the global and highly dynamic environment enabled by the Internet can be allocated on a temporary and contingent basis according to inclusive and nonhierarchical relationships is of course not new. Roles have often shifted among government, corporations, and civil society, but it appears that the United Nations is underwriting a more durable multistakeholder relationship in regard to Internet governance. This is a novel and fascinating attempt to achieve global dialogue around responsibilities in Internet regulation and was thought to represent a significant new networked governance paradigm (MacLean 2004; Murray 2006). However, the lack of significant influence and perceived marginalization of civil society over governance outcomes has led many academic analysts to doubt its real impact (Mueller 2010, Kleinwächter 2011).

The second example is that of ICANN, a coregulatory institution created by the U.S. government and contracted as a private corporation "responsible for managing and coordinating the Domain Name System (DNS) to ensure that every address is unique and that all users of the Internet can find all valid addresses." Domain names are an essential resource for effectively using the Internet: without such addresses and related numbers, it is difficult for other users to locate your computer (Kahn and Cerf 1999). The DNS is therefore a classic global public good (Kaul, Grunberg, and Stern 1999).

ICANN has been the main international organization charged with legitimising the user's role in Internet coregulation (Machill and Ahlert 2001), including through an attempt to introduce Internet voting in elections to the board (Mueller 2000, 2002; Froomkin 2000). It has also introduced an elaborate consultation and governance structure, but much of the debate has reinforced observers' views that civil society is marginalized in favor of governments, particularly the U.S. government (Komaitis 2010; Mueller 2010). In 2009, the Joint Project Agreement between the U.S. Department of Commerce and ICANN was replaced with an "affirmation of commitments" that reinforces ICANN's status as a nonprofit, multistakeholder organization with a bottom-up policy development process (Marsden 2011).

A third multistakeholder example concerns user-generated or Web 2.0 content (O'Reilly 2005; OECD 2007). Self-regulated communities of users and distributors of content, including peer-to-peer (P2P) networks such as KaZaA (Karagiannis, Rodriguez, and Papagiannaki 2005), and communities such as Facebook, Twitter, and YouTube, are transforming the Internet experience. Online communities have hundreds of millions of members regulated through a combination of the community's conditions or terms of use, general law (including, for instance, libel and copyright law)—the technical means for users to self-regulate, by, for instance, rating and labeling content; as well as reviewing and choosing to set content or users as trusted friends or otherwise (Marsden et al. 2006, 2008).

Radically different models of user control, rating, and filtering are enabled by such networks, though their relations to formal regulation and law are contingent on corporate whim (Berners Lee 2000; Benkler 2002, 2006; Braman and Lynch 2003; Braman 2009). These creators are also adopting new royalty-free licensing for their content, whether software that is collaboratively developed and freely distributed (the General Public License, for instance, for the Linux operating system) or content (e.g., via the Creative Commons project, which has created standard licenses to allow the sharing and "remixing" of content; Guadamuz 2009).

These three examples demonstrate the potential but also the perilous existence and relevance of less formal multistakeholder approaches and governance, as opposed to legal regulation with enforceable mechanisms and accountability. The importance of multistakeholder partnership as a fundamentally participatory approach to Internet policy is contested by its critics and, even more so, its supporters, who claim to have been marginalized and treated as symbolic, rhetorical, but powerless partners with corporations and governments in international standard setting. Our case study selection examines this paradigm more closely to assess whether governments' symbolic embrace of multistakeholder processes is reflected in genuine partnership in regulatory discussions.

Institutional Analysis of Internet Regulation

The growth of firms and other market institutions (Hodgson 1988) is explained by transaction cost analysis and intellectual property rights and other nondisclosure by protection of information outside those institutions (Stiglitz 1985). When one combines the two in information technologies, which are both disproportionately strategic and tend to market failure on a global scale, one has the ingredients for a compelling market failure scenario.

Where information communication technology has become the primary driver of growth, the intervention of governments in markets increasingly bears the hallmark of these institutionally based strategic analyses. To put it bluntly, who regulates information giants such as Microsoft, Facebook, and Google, and in whose interests? We cannot analyze the legal environment and software code in Internet regulation without considering the relationships of government, business, and users in civil society.

McCahery et al. (1996, 2) set out three "primary and interrelated concerns" in their study of regulation with a globalization agenda:

• Institutional response to dynamic economic change

• The "functional policy concern" regarding the utility and geometry of regulation

• The democratic deficit, resulting from the institutional (i.e., constitutional) underdevelopment of the regimes formed to regulate international economic actors

These questions of how, where, and with what tools to regulate in an increasingly complex and interdependent environment are vital:

• How do regulatory institutions respond to dynamic change in economic conditions?

• How are these governance reforms influenced by political (social, cultural, and ideological) and economic factors?

• To what extent do national and regional regulators diverge in their response to global technological factors?

These questions are part of the research hypothesis addressed in the school of institutional analysis termed the *new institutional economics*. The new institutionalism recognizes an increased complexity of both political and economic markets and the interaction between the two. The sociological version of institutionalism analyzes the mode of action constrained by normative, moral, and cognitive boundaries (Blom-Hansen 1997). Whereas economic institutionalism places microlevel motivations as the driver of change, sociological institutionalism adopts a macrolevel approach.

North (1990) acknowledges the contribution of sociological institutionalism within his concentration on historical institutional path dependency and thus provides a broader explanation of the incremental development of policy. This contrasts with the public choice variant of economic institutionalism (Moe 1997), in which the microfoundations of theory place too limited a role on institutions and actors. North begins from a view that acknowledges the economic compromises and failures of existing markets and public choice from an assumption that the individual pursues self-interest in a more economically rational and determinist approach.

North explains: "It is no accident that economic models of the polity developed in the public choice literature make the state into something like the mafia . . . the traditional public choice literature is clearly not the whole story" (140). He then explains why the parameters of investigation must be broadened from the narrowly neoclassical economic to encompass prior institutional structures and practices: "Informal constraints matter. We need to know much more about culturally derived norms of behavior and how they interact with formal rules to get better answers to such issues" (140).

Public choice has a weakness beyond the overly simplistic reliance on economic resources: it reveals taxpayer preferences where mobility is assumed (thus competition between geographically fixed regulatory jurisdictions) rather than the total electorate, and therefore policy "dictated by the private preferences of a narrow, arbitrarily identified class of itinerant at-the-margin consumers or investors . . . competition can force the pursuit of policies . . . removed from the public interest" (McCahery 1996, 15). This can lead to a deregulatory race to the bottom in which protections for nonmobile and vulnerable citizens are regressively removed. As McCahery puts it: "Competition influences results traditionally thought to lie in the discretion of sovereign regulators" (13).

Critics of public choice indicate that government actors are not necessarily efficiency maximizers in a narrow monetary sense (Tiebout 1956) and can resist races to the bottom. However, this potential for capture by regulated interests, notably large corporate lobbies, is an essential insight that we use throughout our analysis.

The Case Studies

This brings us to our five case studies, to each of which we dedicate a chapter. They address the topics of privacy; copyrights; censors; social networking; and smart pipes. The first three are case studies in fundamental rights with economic implications. The final two are studies of the most innovative platforms to develop new markets and protect those fundamental rights. They are also in a period of regulatory flux, yet with significant regulatory development in the past five years such that it is possible to draw some conclusions. We deliberately omitted search, whose development was critically dependent on further antitrust activity in Brussels and Washington. Furthermore, the concerns with multistakeholder representation and procedural justice that we explore in other case studies have been recently developed extensively in the search engine case (Zittrain 2008; Deibert et al. 2010).

Privacy Privacy and data protection is a well-studied field—not least because it has proven difficult for legislators and regulators to keep up with the rapid pace of change in Internet technologies that gather, process, and share data related to individuals. Most existing data protection legislation focuses on the behavior of governments and companies as they process the data. In chapter 3, we assess more recent attempts to shape the development of Internet technologies in an effort to improve the efficacy of regulation by embedding privacy by design into new systems.

Copyright As the Internet and digital duplication tools have lowered the marginal cost of reproduction and distribution of digital works toward zero, copyright has increasingly come into conflict with decades-old consumer behavioral norms about the use of copyrighted works. Rights holders have persuaded governments around the world to target new copyright regulation at personal computers, media devices, and Internet service providers (ISPs). In particular, new legal protection has been given to digital locks that restrict access to protected works; more recently some governments have placed requirements on ISPs to police the behavior of their users. The potential sanctions range from warning letters, through restrictions on connection speed, to disconnection. In chapter 4, we assess the outcome and broader lessons of these attempts to regulate the technology underlying the control of creative works.

Censors The debate over control of harmful and illegal material on the public Internet has developed from early debates in the United States over online obscenity leading to the Communications Decency Act 1996, through totalitarian regimes' great firewalls including China's 2009 "Green Dam" project, to democracies' self-regulatory actions, such as the U.K. Cleanfeed/Child Abuse Image Content system. Recent moves in Europe have stepped away from a decade-old self-regulatory approach toward a coregulatory approach in which ISPs and government agencies cooperate. ISP-level filtering of inadvertent viewing of illegal material is becoming mandatory, with definitions widened from child pornography to hate speech to extreme speech and then copyright (McIntyre 2013). The institutionalization of this new state-sanctioned and audited approach presents significant new challenges to freedom of expression and has led to calls for an Internet bill of rights in the European Parliament, U.S. Congress, and elsewhere (Reding 2012).

Social networking sites The mass take-up of social networking tools has heightened concerns over privacy, copyright, and child protection and created a generic center for regulatory activity that raises new questions about the scope and focus of Internet regulation. With over 1 billion Facebook users, regulators' concerns over ordinary citizens' use of the Internet have led to specific regulatory instruments that address the risks of such use (Facebook 2012; Office of the Data Protection Commissioner Ireland 2011). Chapter 6 builds on the literature and regulatory proceedings to assess the extent to which the more conventional issues-based regulatory instruments are being supplemented by generic social networking regulation.

Smart pipes Network openness is under reconsideration as never before, with increasing partitioning of the Internet, partly driven by security concerns, which is leading many ISPs to add capabilities to their routers to filter, inspect, and prioritize network traffic to a much greater degree than previously possible. This policy field displays both a plurality of market actors (content and carriage disguises the various interests within and between those sectors, such as mobile networks and vertically integrated actors) and a profusion of formal (state and supranational) and informal (standard-setting) regulators. It exhibits advanced examples of regulatory capture, especially in the more static and matured regulatory environment of telecoms. In chapter 7, many of the features of earlier case studies, from content industries (copyright and privacy) and networks (surveillance and cryptography policy, security policy), come together.

We address these key questions in each of the substantive case studies:

• Who were the key stakeholders (traditional and multistakeholder), and how far were they involved in policy debates, organizational design, and operational issues associated with the regulatory processes or institutions adopted? What was the institutional political economy (Mueller 2010)?

• How far did solutions have source, process, or outcome legitimacy (Weber and Grosz 2009), including human rights compliance, in the outcome? What influence did fundamental rights have in policy design? This exploration is based on both documents relating to design and later judgments of human rights bodies (e.g., national parliamentary scrutiny committees, Council of Europe).

• How effective is the current and developing code solution? How might it have developed differently under different regulatory conditions?

In the next chapter, we assess examples of both code created by "prosumers" (active users who are sharing and producing content, rather than passively consuming it—notably hackers) and economic regulation through competition law in more detail and construct a matrix for the individual case studies. In each case study, we examine whether governments have moved from sledgehammer prohibition-based, enforcement-oriented regulation, to smarter regulation that works technically, with some degree of outcome legitimacy in terms of goals. These might, for instance, support the creation of public goods and disruptive innovation in markets. A smart solution in terms of code and regulation would provide effectiveness in enforcement (whether by law or code), technical efficiency (in an engineering sense) and legitimacy, transparency, and accountability (to allay rights-based concerns). Unsurprisingly, the outcomes are likely to be trade-offs among these goals.

By analyzing and contrasting our case studies, we aim to formulate specific recommendations in the concluding two chapters. We seek to develop a more unified framework for research into Internet regulation, designed to work with these hard cases, and use the best of both software and legal code to create principles for regulatory intervention based on due process, effectiveness and efficiency, and respect for human rights. We describe this type of regulation as *prosumer law*.

2 Code Constraints on Regulation and Competition

Before beginning our case study examination, we examine some fundamental factors in how code can interact with regulation, enabling those from a nontechnical background to better understand the Internet's unique constraints on traditional regulatory tools. Understanding code and legal regulation leads to a better understanding of how regulation can work toward better code rather than simply avoiding the worst of code. That conjunction of code and regulation will lead to better outcomes than a Chinese wall designed to keep out code. We therefore explain in this chapter how mass Internet adoption and the proportionate increase in unskilled Internet users (in software literacy) have changed the nature of innovation on the Internet, before exploring how innovative regulatory and policy responses to the increasingly controlled Internet user experience can harness the power of code to create opportunities for innovation rather than erect entry barriers to new applications.

We first describe the successful attempts by encryption coders to outflank regulators during the 1990s and then bring the debate to the contemporary topics of control over information monopolies that we referred to in the Introduction. That leads to consideration of the code remedies imposed on Microsoft in the European Commission (EC) final settlement of its antitrust case in 2009 and Intel in its Federal Trade Commission (FTC) antitrust settlement of 2010. We will see that interoperability is the key to regulating dominant actors' uses of code.

Such checks to encourage competition do not in themselves ensure fundamental rights that must be respected in communications industries, and we argue in the final chapter that improved competition law enforcement to shape more interoperable code must be accompanied by human rights audits to create greater commercial and state respect for fundamental rights.

The outcome of the two decades of Microsoft competition litigation, beginning with U.S. antitrust investigation in 1991 prior to the dawn of mass Internet adoption, was to enforce interoperability and application programming interface disclosure (EC 2010c), with Intel settling a similar long-standing investigation into interoperability and anticompetitive practices. The interoperable code solution was extended and adapted by the complainants in both Google and Facebook investigations by the EC opened in 2010 (IP/10/1624). Apple's iTunes faced similar calls in its price discrimination settlement by the EC in 2007–2008 (IP/08/22) and its preliminary antitrust investigation into Apple's iPhone AppStore policies (IP/10/1175).

There are regulatory opportunities to shape the market in favor of interoperability if regulators choose such options. The open Internet policy coordination challenge is acknowledged by the Group of 8 (2011) nations: "As we adopt more innovative Internet-based services, we face challenges in promoting interoperability and convergence among our public policies on issues such as the protection of personal data, net neutrality, transborder data flow, ICT security, and intellectual property" (para. 14). These policy conclusions can be applied by the countries and regions that are both most engaged in and most able to influence the future of the fundamental policy objectives of Internet policy.

It has been suggested that open participatory standards are themselves better for the development of fundamental rights in terms of participation (Drahos and Braithwaite 2002) and more equal access to information (La Rue 2011). This raises normative questions such as:

• Is an open source operating system such as Linux ultimately a better foundation for the information society (Van Oranje et al. 2005) than a proprietary operating system such as Windows? Is Android better for wireless innovation than Apple's iOS? Is Firefox a better Web browser for developing countries than Microsoft's Internet Explorer?

• Is the nonhierarchical Internet Engineering Task Force better for participation and designing standards for human rights than the nation-state-dominated International Telecommunications Union?

In examining our hard cases, we test a profound claim of those who favor open standards: information standards that are more open and participatory are more just in terms of both competition and human rights

(Clinton 2011). That has been sloganized in terms of a basic norm as "information wants to be free" (Brand 1985), "information communism" (Benkler 1998, 2011; Lessig 2008), and even "dot communism" (Moglen 2003). These claims have been variously adopted by such entities as the Free Software Foundation, the Pirate Party, the Creative Commons movement, and the Access to Knowledge movement. There is no objective right answer to such normative claims, simply assertions of short- versus long-term efficiency or social welfare maximization. However, a solution that closes off the choice for innovators in how to develop their own products in such a contingent environment is gambling with the future.

Support for an open environment to stimulate innovation does suggest less corporate control of the value chain and possibilities for state censorship (Zittrain 2003) but does not in itself guarantee fundamental rights. The wider the choice of code available to users, the higher their ability is to choose code that respects their speech freedoms and personal data, but that is by no means a given.

Creating conditions for interoperability does not enable governments or corporations (or civil society) to shirk their responsibility to ensure Internet architectures respect fundamental rights. For example, communications equipment that can help repressive states monitor users and ultimately punish dissidents creates an obligation on manufacturers and democratic governments to prevent export of such technology to such states (see chapters 6 and 7). While that is not yet a regulatory aim that has been enforced, a fundamental rights argument (and Google's mission statement, "Don't Be Evil") argues that such a regulation would need to be placed on top of any innovation or competition arguments in such a specialized sector (Brown and Korff 2012).

Encryption as a User-Led Regulator

The widespread availability of encryption software is a fundamental constraint on state regulatory power, which enforces the end-to-end principle by limiting the ability of ISPs to monitor data passing between their users. The encryption algorithms commonly in use are effectively unbreakable by the best-resourced government agencies, so long as they are implemented and used correctly. At the same time, encryption software is often misconfigured and used on insecure computing devices that can trivially be hacked, while security agencies have become more adept at intercepting encrypted communications using techniques such as faked security certificates (Soghoian and Stamm 2010).

The adoption of encryption by Internet users in the early 1990s followed the invention of public key cryptography by Whit Diffie and others in the 1970s. Combined with the end-to-end architecture of the Internet, it resulted in a reduction of control over information flows by states despite their lengthy struggle to maintain the ability to surveil encrypted content (Froomkin 1995), a loss that many information regulation specialists expected to be permanent.

While states tried vigorously but unsuccessfully to restrict the spread of encryption software, it is used only sparingly as a conscious choice by most Internet users. Rather, encryption is a default set by some applications providers. The most frequently used encryption tools by most users came from the decision to adopt secure socket layer encryption for Twitter, e-commerce sites, or Google search pages (using https:// instead of http://).

Viruses, worms, and spam e-mail were an early reminder that a fully encrypted end-to-end architecture can remove some in-network security options. The vast quantities of unsolicited e-mail sent have required ISP spam filters to become progressively more sophisticated over the past decade, analyzing subject lines, relay addresses, message attachments, and sender addresses. These options would be lost if the entire message header and body were encrypted.

Not all users have learned not to open suspect e-mail and therefore potentially run a program that can infect their computer. Many lost their innocence in a dramatically unromantic fashion in May 2000 when the "I love you" virus was distributed by e-mail, the name relating to the subject line of the address. Less innocent users may have been infected by the knowingly entitled "Anna Kournikova" virus, distributed by e-mail just before Valentine's Day a year later, or the Happy99 worm in 1999, which infected the computer while wishing users a happy new millennium. Worms also enable remote logging of key strokes to uncover users' computer and Web site passwords, enabling later unauthorized intrusion into user accounts. A particularly sophisticated virus was the Conficker worm of 2008–2009, which compromised 15 million machines, including those of the French and British navies (Sommer and Brown 2011).

Government and major software corporations have made common cause against security threats as locust attacks on their systems. Microsoft's large installed base of Windows users makes it a locus for security vulnerabilities. Its attackers, the malware providers, can bait and switch from one type of Microsoft program to another, from Explorer to Office programs to Media Player. Like locusts, they feast, strip the ground, and move on. That creates a complex interdependence of governments, code providers, and users in finding security solutions.

In this respect, government and information giants such as Microsoft share a common fate, particularly as most developed nations' governments run on major multinational corporations' software and, with cloud computing, even their servers. Governments, facing serious security threats to citizens' computers and the entire broadband network, permit Microsoft to develop incremental security fixes for its systems (typically monthly) or fear the starvation (infection, infestation) of its bureaucracies, social systems, and citizens' access to medical, financial, e-commerce, and other services over their PCs. Building and rebuilding Windows NT for two decades (Windows 8 was ultimately a refined version of the original) is a short-term solution but a devil's gamble by Microsoft, other code developers for the Windows platform, and government, with so many PCs and users dependent on Windows and the Office productivity suite. Users are minimally inconvenienced, and legacy systems continue to operate with these patched systems (Moody 2010), whereas a complete clean-slate redesign could reduce many security problems but is impractical for most users.

The growth of peer-to-peer (P2P) distribution in the late 1990s, popularized by the Napster file-sharing software, led to greater debate about the uses of software to evade law in the absence of encryption. Copyright industries since the late 1990s have used litigation to try to prevent the Internet sharing of music files, described in chapter 4. The progressively more decentralized successors to Napster (KaZaA/Grokster, Gnutella, eMule) were progressively litigated. BitTorrent clients provided stronger encryption and a more distributed system such that no central node could be found against which to pursue litigation (Wu 2010). Even in 2012, more litigation was resulting in more encryption, with the prosecution of Megaupload site owners in New Zealand leading to more advanced cyberlockers and other obfuscation and encryption techniques.

Individual users can be pursued if they have not encrypted their communications (which remains trivial technically and free at point of use through such open source encryption tools as the Tor software) or run anonymous or encrypted P2P. As a result, it is the technically ignorant or naive user without encryption who can be pursued for potential copyright infringement rather than sophisticated file sharers.

The recent spate of graduated-response regimes intended to dissuade users from sharing files online (Yu 2010), discussed in our copyright case study in chapter 4, can by design prove effective only against naive users. By 2009 the sharing of copyrighted files had even become an electoral issue in Europe, with two Pirate party candidates elected to the European Parliament in the midst of the Pirate Bay Swedish trial, and therefore sitting as legislators over such issues as the review of European copyright law in the Parliament. (Pirate Bay was a file-sharing reference site subject to vigorous copyright enforcement in 2007 and 2008; the site's founders and supporters inspired the Pirate party political movement.)

Encryption also proved a significant issue for filtering, as we explore in the censors case study in chapter 5. The 1990s had seen the adoption of notice and takedown (NTD) regimes for offensive content in such legislation as the E-Commerce Directive of 2000 (Articles 12–15), accompanied by end user filters designed under the labeling system designed by the W3C working group on the Platform for Internet Content Selection. The NTD system, which was adopted for copyrighted material using the Digital Millennium Copyright Act of 1998 (s.512), was in practice reliant on individual Web hosts cooperating with users and police to remove illegal content. The voluntary nature of the filtering system had limits (Ahlert, Marsden, and Yung 2004), especially where content was hosted by a nonmember ISP or a foreign-based ISP, and in countries where child pornography was not actively prosecuted (notably Russia).

As a result, governments cooperated internationally to a limited extent to enforce the taking down of illegal content. The Council of Europe's Cybercrime Convention was created in 2001 (CETS No.185) to serve as a legal mechanism for increased cooperation. Widespread national harmonization of child pornography and other cybersecurity legislation followed in the years after the negotiation of the convention.

Governments ran out of patience with the evident flaws in voluntary systems in the years after the cybercrime treaty was ratified in 2003, and began to mandate ISP-level filtering. However, as mandated or industry-adopted filtering became widespread in the following years, child-abuse images had already become largely an encrypted peer-distributed crime, and it was acknowledged in European debate in 2011 that even a mandatory filter for unencrypted Web sites could only prevent involuntary viewing of such sites (Directive 2011/92/EU).

While encryption means that both copyright infringement and evasion of ISP filters remain technically trivial, it also allows users to maintain their privacy from surveillance. However, both privacy and data security more generally rely on robust software systems, and it is here that encryption has faced significant challenges. With most users deploying a single operating system, Microsoft Windows, and its associated productivity suite, Office, malware and viruses proliferated from 2001 on this software. Acknowledging the lack of technical competence and care of most domestic (and many business) customers, Microsoft in October 2003 adopted an automated updating system, the single largest software distribution event on the Internet each month on "Patch Tuesday," reaching over half a billion vulnerable and potentially infected machines.

Despite these monthly updates, many millions of broadband-connected machines are compromised daily, infected and remotely controlled by criminals, and used to launch distributed denial of service attacks. Banks, gambling businesses, governments, and other mission-critical electronic commerce Web sites have adopted more sophisticated controls, but this remains a significant problem (Brown, Edwards, and Marsden 2009). It has been accompanied by phishing attacks on individual users, as well as by massive data theft from unsecured and unencrypted databases of user credit details—notably the theft of 102 million Sony PlayStation users' details in 2011.

It is something of an irony that the encryption used in such attacks is employed by the infecting program itself to ensure its operations are protected from the average nontechnical user. Therefore, as affected users continue to believe their computer is operating only more slowly than usual, it is actually a "zombie" machine using its processing power and broadband connectivity to join in the distributed denial of service attacks with the thousands or even millions of other machines around the globe engaged in the criminal activity.

States have attempted more interventionist mechanisms to prevent insecure systems being compromised. The U.S. Congress included an "anti-circumvention" clause in Section 1201 DMCA, described further in chapter 4, which made it an offense for users to circumvent digital locks on copyrighted works, but threatened to stop academic exploration of the inherent security flaws in badly written copyright protection code. This led to a 2001 court case for declaratory relief by one of the most respected academics in the field, Princeton professor Ed Felten, supporting his students' routine security work. He had received a legal threat from the Recording Industry Association of America attempting to prevent his presenting an academic paper on the security flaws in the so-called secure digital music initiative. The court refused to grant relief, though the U.S. Copyright Office in 2003 and subsequently decided on a series of minor, relatively inconsequential exemptions to Section 1201 (Felten 2002).

More radically, in 2011 the Iranian government decided to form a closed national intranet— what it called a "halal" Internet—designed to prevent threats in both code and sociopolitical terms from entering the Iranian intranet space by imposing a firewall on all Iranian access to the global Internet (described further in chapter 5). It does not promise to be more secure than China's infamous "Great Firewall" security project (Clayton 2005), which attempted to create a regulated Chinese space within the Internet. However, such relatively crude censorship can be overcome by those skilled with encryption sufficiently to hide their identity while evading the surveillance of the authorities.

In such totalitarian police states, both data and physical surveillance occur on a regular and extended basis—including, for instance, seizure of private computers and random arrests in Internet cafés (Deibert et al. 2010; Keller 2000). As with privacy, copyright, and filtering, while encryption permits political dissidents and those exercising free speech to do so successfully, the vast majority operates under very different and closely monitored conditions.

Encryption is one of the most significant variables in the architecture of networked computing and shapes key regulatory options on a range of policy issues. But despite its potential advantages to users, it has seen widespread use only when deployed as a default by Web sites and software creators. This is an important lesson for the regulation of privacy, security, and copyright, which rely on the interplay of code, the law, and the norms of users and software producers (Lessig 1999). The socioeconomic factors that lead to the adoption of particular laws and code, influencing the choices of policymakers, regulators, software producers, and users, are critical.

Code and Regulation: Adaptability and Regulability

The easy adaptability of software enables rapid subtle dynamic (even emergent) changes and limits the effectiveness of regulating user behavior by regulating "toolmakers." The Internet has enabled a new mode of software creation, peer production (Benkler 2006), which enables noncommercial, highly distributed, loosely coordinated teams to build large complex software (e.g., Linux, OpenOffice), software libraries (e.g., OpenSSL) and distributed services (e.g., BitTorrent).

For regulatory purposes, these teams are hydra-headed and largely out of any one jurisdiction. They can quickly design software to work around new legal and regulatory restrictions—hence, the rapid evolution of the Pretty Good Privacy encryption software following U.S. government legal action during the 1990s, and P2P file sharing systems after Napster's indexing servers were constrained by California courts (Wu 2003a).

It would be very difficult to stop programmers from participating in these communities, and few jurisdictions have tried this approach. U.S. courts have given tentative First Amendment protection to software source code as free speech. That is a major underlying reason for the failure of efforts to ban strong encryption and DRM-circumvention tools.

This section develops our analysis of the dynamism of code and its ability to outrun the law in some cases and grow to fruitful mutual interaction in others. We identify two classic regulatory tussles: code overcoming law and law overcoming code. Code does "overcome" law in the case of "generativity" (Zittrain 2006). The generative power of the Internet derived from the openness embedded in the architectural end-to-end principle (Clark 1988). This reflected the initial situation in which intelligence and trust could safely be left to the users of the Internet and to the edge devices through which they gained access.

To facilitate their collective ability to pursue improvements, the network itself was meant to be as flat, as simple, and as open as possible—not least because more complex forms of facilitation within the Internet itself were technologically challenging. However, the situation has since become more complex. End users are no longer fully cognizant, let alone in control of, their devices, but the network itself can play a much more active role in managing collective problems.

Tussles in Code and Law

Clark et al. (2005) recognize that struggle or "tussle" between different interests is as important in technology evolution as in economic and political systems, suggesting that "we, as technical designers, should not try to deny the reality of the tussle, but instead recognize our power to shape it" (10). As Greenstein (2011) advises standards bodies, "doing the tussle" can create more robust and widely adopted industry standards.

Although this is a mandate for the technical community, it can be easily extended to the legal regulatory communities that directly shape the various aspects of Internet development, many of which already recognize that their shaping decisions are moves in a game rather than acts of sovereign design. Design choices in code can be as normative as law—decisions have to be made on the values that code embeds (Brown, Clark, and Trossen 2011).

Code has continued to morph rapidly even as legislation has tried to adapt. Investor certainty and democratic participation in legislative processes are arguably enhanced by the leisurely speed of legislation, contrasted with the rapid—but slowing—progress of Internet standards in which only technical experts can realistically participate.

Most progress has happened with technical protocol development within companies (and, arguably, open source communities), where coordination ("tussle") problems are less complex than in legislatures. IPv6 has been slowly, even glacially, deployed, but a big switch in Facebook design to facilitate the use of Secure Socket Layer connections was possible in a few days, and Windows security updates can be automatically distributed to hundreds of millions of users overnight. Consider single-company developments as a reminder of user empowerment through code:

• Facebook achieved 1 billion user accounts in under a decade.

• Skype achieved 650 million user accounts in less than a decade.

• Google has billions of users—multilingual and with functionality largely unaffected by culture, though China and Russia have their alternatives.

• Many millions of infected PCs have been infected and gathered into botnets—networks of computers hijacked and controlled by a single bad actor—since consumer broadband emerged (Brown, Edwards, and Marsden 2009) as a result of the actions of individuals and small groups of criminal entrepreneurs.

A more dynamic social networking tool than blogs and e-mail, a better P2P voice over Internet protocol client that could evade ISP control, and a new search algorithm and method of targeting advertising were all eagerly taken up by consumers. The development of Facebook, Skype, and Google is testimony to the ability of emergent code to respond to and keep pace with market demands.

Architecture, law, norms, and markets interplay (Lessig 1999). Regulators have only slowly woken up to regulation using technology. If regulators fail to address regulatory objects at first, then the regulatory object can grow until its technique overwhelms the regulator.

Napster as a "child" could have been shaped by regulation. Once it had exerted its network effects and grown, any blunt regulatory tool simply reshaped P2P—to more powerful tools of file sharing, overwhelming regulatory defenses by their architectural ingenuity, morphing to jurisdiction-hopping P2P "on steroids" (Wu 2003a). Digitally locked music formats were outpaced by the overwhelming Metcalfe's law effect of MP3 as a legitimate but untethered technology. Major rights holders were highly successful in coordinating demands for DRM from technology companies, but ultimately they were defeated when their own cartel was attacked by the dominant monster they created: iTunes. Apple used its pricing policy as a bargaining tool to push rights holders to abandon DRM (Williams and Gunn 2007). A horizon limit of Zittrain (2008) is a failure to fully incorporate the market structure limits to generativity versus stability and move beyond nudges into regulation (House of Lords 2011).

Reidenberg (2005) argues that law can use code to overcome code, as a court ordered Yahoo! to filter French users to prevent access to Nazi memorabilia auctions. Another example is China using Cisco routers and code to create its "Golden Shield" filter (Deibert et al. 2010). A combination of points of control (Zittrain 2008) and scale economies (Lemley and McGowan 1998) gives levers for law and markets to act on architecture. Traction results from the physical presence of the Internet company on the sovereign territory of the host government.

The forces of regulation can be shaped more subtly: forbearance in one dimension enables expansion in others. Where code is slow to evolve, law can assist by removing bottlenecks to innovation. Where law is designed expressly to stymie code innovation, code is likely to spill over any logjam by creating new paths to achieve user goals, as, for instance, in the P2P solution to friends sharing music files. Accusations of illegality did not serve as a veto on user adoption of P2P.

Sledgehammer Regulation and Its Flaws

Binary regulatory decisions can be ineffective and perilous if they attempt to force software developments into new forms, like flipping a set of railroad points. For example, DPI could be outlawed or permitted to develop without specific regulation—but the former is like banning cars, and the latter ignores the public goods affected by DPI. For instance, enforcing minimally invasive techniques can prevent full-spectrum DPI in traffic management. This avoids many privacy and filtering pitfalls and regulatory black holes caused by the power of DPI to expose its owners to the full liability of customer and third-party traffic (Marsden 2011).

Both permissive unregulation and prohibition create pitfalls in public understanding of the effect of regulation on technologies. In simple terms, these regulatory clichés of the Internet routing around censorship as damage, or the heavy hand of the law falling on all users (Thierer and Crews 2003), do not assist public and policymaker understanding of the wider challenges of Internet regulation any more than death penalty debates assist in understanding the scope of criminology.

Regulation that succeeds or fails based on the presence or absence of specific software tools is doomed to eventual failure, while most users own open computing platforms and can download and run the software of their choice. Despite Zittrain's (2008) concerns over the rise of "tethered" devices, the success of the iPhone and Android software platforms (with limited oversight from Apple, and even less from Google) demonstrates that the benefits to innovation of openness will continue to give manufacturers a strong incentive to provide such a capability (Ohm and Grimmelman 2010), though we note that mandated interoperability is neither necessary in all cases nor necessarily desirable (Gasser and Palfrey 2012). Moves to regulate all computing devices in an attempt to enforce copyright restrictions (in early World Intellectual Property Organization model copyright law discussions and the U.S. Senate Judiciary Committee) have faded away in the face of resistance from manufacturers and consumers, both by lobbying and in the marketplace.

Business models based around trusted computing hardware (discussed further in chapter 4) try to avoid this problem by releasing only protected new audiovisual content to devices certified to provide much stronger protection to data. The content industry in this model would give up on protecting its back catalogue but protect future revenue streams from new content. However, this still suffers the fatal weakness that controls need be broken only once for a piece of content to be stripped of its protection and then shared freely through P2P services. This may be good enough for business models depending on short-term revenues from live or new content, but not for those hoping to monetize the back catalogue (Ohm and Grimmelman 2010). It also cannot stop analog recordings being made and shared online, which seems to be an adequate experience for many users.

Trusted hardware can successfully control ongoing access to online services, since access can be revoked from compromised systems once detected. This is why conditional-access satellite TV systems have been successful, albeit imperfect (fraud happens, but at a manageable level).

Trusted software has so far proven to be an oxymoron, which is why software copy protection schemes failed so badly that most companies gave them up by the early 1990s. There have been limited attempts since then to use online registration to verify software (e.g., by Microsoft with Windows and Office), but hacked copies are widely available, and network effects mean it is also often in the interest of software companies to tolerate widespread infringement in developing markets. Limiting access to software provided online as a service may be more feasible.

Competition Law and the Internet

Are there solutions that may be effective ex ante to ensure the development of technologies that do not act against the public interest, without stifling innovation and introducing bureaucratic interventionist regulation to an area that has blossomed without it? Such a solution would avoid the economic determinism of belief in the invisible hand of the market, and the technological determinism of some (typically superprofitable multinational) technology companies that claim that progress all but inevitably results in wider choice and more desirable features, despite public policy concerns.

Two examples present themselves: one a remedy of necessity in competition law, the second a deliberate design feature increasingly being deployed by OECD governments. The first is the use of competition law to engage in predicting and designing prospective markets, and the second is the widespread adoption of interoperability policies across the European Union.

Institutions that apply the consumer interest in the case of mergers and other market concentrations differ markedly by country (Weiser 2010; Coates 2011). Agencies follow enabling legislation, and therefore the breadth of definition of merger problems should reflect and adapt from that original legislative intent, despite much of its age. For instance the United States applies the Sherman Act (1890) and Clayton Act (1914), and the EC applies the Treaty of Rome (1950, articles 101–102).

In some nations, there is only a general consumer and competition agency, which has oversight of communications market mergers. In others, such as the United States, there is cooperation between two competition and one communications agency: the Department of Justice, FTC, and Federal Communications Commision. In yet others, there is a single competition agency assisted by a communications regulator with some competition powers (in the United Kingdom, incorporating two appeals bodies that oversee regulator decisions). A growing European trend is toward the communications regulator forming part of a larger network utilities regulator, as with BNetZ in Germany and the Dutch networks regulator OPTA.

These institutional differences are obviously vital for our consideration of the regulation of code, as the proficiency of regulators will differ enormously based on institutional preferences as well as the vagaries and happenstance of personal skills. Thus one expects communications regulators to have greater code expertise than general competition agencies, though this may not always be the case, particularly where the communications regulator is poorly adapted to digital networks and relies on telecoms and broadcasting analysts with a paucity of software skills. The recognition of particular code problems and application of specialist staff and advisers is greatly to be desired in such cases. A particular example is the FTC creation of a post of chief technologist, filled by an academic visitor (Ed Felten), and a special advisor also taken from academia (Tim Wu), in 2010–2011 as the agency actively pursued solutions to code issues.

The recent literature on competition policy has tended toward substituting economic judgments of consumer harm for political judgments and the apparent triumph of the Chicago school of microeconomics and associated economic doctrines regarding the perfectability of competition (Lessig

1998). The notion of creative destruction, whereby a lazy monopolist is overwhelmed by an innovative flexible competitor, has gained much ground, following the work of Joseph Schumpeter and the Austrian school (Mehra 2011).

The Internet had appeared secure ground for Schumpeter's hypothesis, and social networks even more so, given News Corporation–owned MySpace's dominance that was replaced rapidly by that of start-up Facebook between 2007 and 2009. Against this must be placed two rival readings of this case study. The first is that social networks were an immature medium, and the growth of the market floated all ships in enabling all rivals to grow while consumers experimented. Consumer preference led to a maturing of the market, which itself tipped toward the eventual winner, Facebook, whose monopoly is now arguably durable. The second reading is more structural: that social networking had relatively low entry barriers in the past, as did, for instance, search engines, but that the advertising-dominated mass market model that currently applies is inimical to the successful overturning of Facebook's dominance. Internet markets are not in continuous "Schumpeterian emergency" (Bresnahan, Greenstein, and Hendersen 2011).

The fertile testing ground of social networks can be once more employed as Google+ challenges Facebook, just as Microsoft's Bing search engine challenges Google's main search engine business. Chapter 7 deals with a century-old monopoly over copper telephone wiring into the home that has been leveraged by state-sanctioned monopolies as it became possible to attach modems and other appliances to the copper telephone network. Schumpeterian creative destruction theory in such a durable and high-entry-cost environment is arguably a misapplication. One could date concern over closed walled garden social networks—closed areas of moderated content and services intended to encourage users to stay within affiliated Web pages and thus attract advertising—further back to the time of the MCI investment in News Corporation, leveraging its ISP access into content (Noam 1994).

A warning against overenthusiasm for rights discourse as a partner to competition policy is that in the Google purchase of Doubleclick, the Department of Justice and EC Directorate-General for Competition both refused to take privacy concerns into account in scrutiny (Coates 2011). Future cases or legislation would need to overturn this precedent if competition regulation were to be an effective mechanism for protecting fundamental rights as well as economic efficiency.

Interoperable Code and Communications Policy

An extensive legislative and regulatory history of public communications occupies a special place in regulatory policy far predating modern competition law. This has always justified an ex ante regulatory policy.

The loss of the ability to license does not of itself entirely negate ex ante regulation—standards define the architecture of code, and standards are heavily government influenced even when not government funded. The government imprimatur on standards enables significant adoption, which is arguably as true in the twenty-first century as it was for Marconi.

The notion that communications policy introduces certain rights and duties is as old as electrical and electronic communications media, with the 1844 Railways Act in the United Kingdom introducing the right for government to take control of the telegraph for the national interest—this only seven years after electric telegraph technology was standardized.

Cannon (2003) suggests that the fundamental regulatory constraint imposed on U.S. telecoms firms in the 1980s was open network architecture (ONA) under the 1985 Computer III inquiry by the U.S. Federal Communications Commission (FCC). (The Computer II and III inquiries refer to investigations by the FCC into the regulation of data transfer and the conditions necessary to achieve an increasingly competitive market for that data.) This constraint had its European equivalent and amounted to interoperability plus physical interconnection between networks (Coates 2011). This was a rare early example of full technical harmonization, which allowed the Internet to flourish across borders without being stymied by preexisting telephony regulation.

ONA had its legacy in the FCC championing regulatory forbearance (Oxman 1999) in the late 1990s, notably in the "Digital Tornado" working paper (Werbach 1997), which further institutionalized the policy of preventing telecoms companies from foreclosing Internet access and was widely admired and copied by European and other regulators racing to catch up with the phenomenal growth of the Internet. U.S. readers should note that mass consumer adoption of the Internet in Europe dates to 1998, as earlier per-minute charging for local telephone calls had chilled the market. In fact, the subtle interoperability pressures of Computer III were much criticized by innovators in the 1980s as they removed the structural remedies against incumbent telephony players (which Computer II had instituted in 1975, finalized in 1980), replacing them with a behavioral solution.

As it emerged, this type of control may have had its legacy in the failure to fully ensure unbundling in telecoms in the early 2000s (Frieden 2010a), but for our purposes, it more pertinently leaves a legacy in the interoperability imposed on AOL's Instant Messenger in the merger conditions for its takeover of Time Warner in 2000 (Faulhaber 2002). ONA and its forerunner, comparatively efficient interconnection, were still used in orders against U.S. incumbent telephony operators (the "Baby Bells") until 1999. More recent examples of using interoperability, the ONA legacy, include the conditions imposed on Microsoft by the EC in settling its competition lawsuit (EC 2010c).

The AOL/TimeWarner merger of 2000 introduced the notion of regulation for interoperability in the case of vertically integrated ISP social networks, even though interoperability was not eventually enforced. It also reflected a trend toward using merger proceedings to raise public policy concerns including privacy and interoperability, if not always to address them successfully. Thus, as detailed in chapter 7, the beginnings of the modern network neutrality debate date to cable TV mergers with ISPs in the late 1990s and the concern surrounding ISP control over access to information, recognized as an international human right since the Universal Declaration of 1948.

The use of competition proceedings to introduce human rights concerns in communications raises two threshold issues, the second of which (the special case of communications) we consider in the next section. The first is whether human rights concerns are ultra vires as not relevant to the consumer interest in mergers.

Note that this can depend on the width of the definition of consumer interest. That in itself can be unpacked to consider two issues: how much the consumer interest is subsumed into its proxy, competition policy, and whether the institutional governance of consumer welfare permits human rights considerations, dependent on whether the specialized agency (or agencies) has any such competence and expertise. In permitting the consumer interest to prevail over the private property rights of a corporation, we are of course balancing rights in the U.S. context, where corporations are granted more substantial legal personality, though fewer such considerations appear to apply in the European human rights context.

It has taken much longer for Internet access to become recognized as a right (Murray and Klang 2005). In 2010, Finland was the first of several countries introduced a universal right of access to the broadband Internet. This continues a universal service obligation on communications that dates to radio broadcasts, telephone service (the Kingsbury Commitment, made by the chairman of AT&T to the FCC, dates to 1913), and common carriage, which predates all these, as a common law duty and privilege imposed on certain activities, typically in transport (ferries, haulage, and stagecoaches; Cherry 2006).

Interoperability, Standards, and Code

There is an extensive history of competition policy in favor of open technology standards that long predates the Internet (Kahin and Abbate 1995), but the evidence of extensive network effects and innovation that can rapidly tip markets has helped focus policymakers' attention on the potential for using interoperability as a solution to the online competition and innovation problems that have emerged.

As competition policy provides for interoperable remedies, governments have set great store by the success of open standards as solutions for the well-known entrenchment of dominant Internet commercial actors using network effects (Pitofsky 1998; Lemley and McGowan 1998). Bar et al. (1995) observed that "interconnection is binary—you are either connected or not—but interoperability comes in degrees [and] presupposes a higher level of logical compatibility": the higher the compatibility, the greater the interoperability.

Dolmans (2010) suggests that an established common standard that is truly open allows the best-of-breed components from different manufacturers to be combined, with maximum efficiency. To qualify as "open," he argues that a standard must meet a number of open conditions:

- Access to the decision-making process
- Transparent and undistorted procedures
- Published, pro-competitive goals

- Published, objective, relevant criteria for technology selection
- No overstandardization

Most critical is access to the standard, which he argues includes open information on blocking patents (the cause of much patent thicket litigation in smart phones and tablet computing), no unjustified refusal to license, and fair reasonable and nondiscriminatory (FRAND) pricing (Coates 2011; EC 2011a).

Dolmans suggests that royalty-free licensing is advisable in the software arena, allowing both open source and proprietary software to compete on quality and functionality. However, the telecommunications sector should use FRAND licensing, given the price and complexity of standard-setting efforts. He states: "Mandating royalty-free licensing would likely recreate a tragedy of commons and discourage innovation, while allowing IPR owners to charge at will could create a tragedy of anticommons. To strike the right balance, therefore, a contract of mutual restraint is necessary" (2010, 126). This argues for a mixed market and against uniform royalty-free pricing (Lemley and McGowan 1998).

Unfortunately, open interoperable solutions have not entirely solved the market entry problem. The flexibility, or fungibility, of code and the degree to which default settings can adjust user behavior give rise to one of the more interesting experiments we can conduct using Internet policy. Given the claim by behavioral economists and their supporters (Thaler and Sunstein 2009) that signaling and "nudging" by government can adjust consumer and market behaviors, we also examine in our case studies to what extent government actions can be characterized not as a nudge but as a much more complicit association with private actors (Yeung 2012).

We could characterize that as two types: "nudge, nudge," where neither corporate nor government actions are carried out without mutual reinforcement, or at least joint dialogue, or "wink, wink," where nonlegislative solutions are adopted by corporate developers, but users decide whether to follow these nudge signals (e.g., including abandoning copyright enforcement by digital locks altogether using P2P software). Internet regulation appears to be a particularly promising arena in which to explore the types of weak signaling and their effect, if any.

The EC's thinking on interoperability and code has developed through the course of the Microsoft, Intel, and Rambus cases (Coates 2011). Neelie Kroes was competition commissioner from 2005 to 2009 and signaled more intervention on interoperability: "I will seriously explore all options to ensure that significant market players cannot just choose to deny interoperability with their product" (Kroes 2010). She argues that the lengthy Microsoft case has lessons for action: "Complex anti-trust investigations followed by court proceedings are perhaps not the only way to increase interoperability. The Commission should not need to run an epic antitrust case every time software lacks interoperability." Eighteen years of transatlantic competition proceedings against Microsoft resulted only in a choice of browsers, a very large but proportional fine, and some old code being released.

Kroes's solution to the Microsoft dilemma—solving the antitrust problem long after the competitors have died—is to require ex ante interoperability evidence, which had not previously been available except through antitrust suits: "Whereas in ex-post investigations we have all sorts of case-specific evidence and economic analysis on which to base our decisions, we are forced to look at more general data and arguments when assessing the impact of ex-ante legislation." She argues for a potential future legislative proposal, which would impose an ex ante requirement to publish interoperability information.

Microsoft and Intel's settlements illustrate a general point about smart structural remedies under competition policy: network effects demand very effective transatlantic cooperation plus policy formed from research into global information technology. This applies the Lessig "code is law" analysis but with Braithwaite and Drahos'a international coordination regulatory approach applied to the overall information environment (Braithwaite and Drahos 2000; Drahos and Braithwaite 2002). Note that the forerunners of the suggested policy direction are 1980s data protection and 1990s cryptography cooperation.

Where free and open source software has not proved a significant competitive check on information monopolists, that raises a significant regulatory challenge that governments must meet to create interoperability in dominant actors' own software. Kroes (2010) set out a radical agenda to ensure interoperability in European ICT procurement and regulation, drawing on procedural frustrations in the Microsoft case. It is in five parts:

• A new standard-setting framework

• New horizontal agreement guidelines to establish more transparency in licensing standards (EC 2011a: chapter 7)

- A common framework for ICT procurement
- A new European interoperability framework (EIF)
- Intervention in competition cases to establish a principle of interoperability, including through ex ante requirements

The EIF is a second version of a much less ambitious 2003–2004 first version of the framework. EIF Version 2.0 was adopted by the College of Commissioners "as of a higher status and importance than EIF version 1," which was more guidance than instruction. EIF 2.0 has still been severely criticized by open source advocates, with the EC accused of regulatory capture by large software companies and the interoperability requirements substantially watered down (Moody 2010).

The new standard-setting framework was established before the end of 2010, intended to result in a widening of participation from the European telecoms standards body, European Telecommunications Standards Institute (ETSI), to more Internet-based standards bodies, the W3C and Internet Engineering Task Force in particular, arguably about twenty years too late (International Telecommunications Union 2010).

Kroes explains that her proposal benefits these "truly open" standards with two paths to approval: "via a fast-track approval of their standards through a process hosted by a traditional European standards body such as ETSI, or through the assessment of these bodies' compliance with certain criteria regarding notably openness, consensus, balance and transparency." On licensing standards, she notes the commission drafted horizontal agreements guidelines in 2009, which came into force in January 2011, and aid in allocating FRAND pricing for accessing essential technologies (EC 2011a).

Kroes does not argue for uniformity: "Standard-setting for software interoperability is not the same as setting a new standard for, say, digital television or mobile telephony." She continues to suggest strategic action to encourage open standards. This suggests an additional legislative requirement that government support for standards must rely on best practice in licensing including royalty terms.

Kroes's agenda embraces research funding and government information technology procurement. European law requires governments to ensure they open public procurement contracts above a minimum size to all European firms to encourage the development of the single European market (Directive 2004/18/EC). As government spending is about half of European GDP, this opens the largest single information technology market to interoperability. Member states that fail to register procurement contracts with the EC are subject to infringement actions and ultimately court proceedings, though implementation has not been as rigorous as it might be. Market-setting procurement EC policy can be used to pursue EIF 2.0.

On IT procurement by European governments, Kroes (2010) suggests "detailed guidance on how to analyse a technology buyer's requirements in order to make best use of ICT standards in tender specifications." Governments became unintentionally locked into proprietary technology for decades. An IT vendor "cartel" was alleged by government buyers on both sides of the Atlantic in 2011, publicly voicing their frustration at the limited choices available. EIF 2.0 contains a "comply or explain" requirement if government buyers do not adopt an available open standard, which follows the practice in the Netherlands, Kroes's own country.

In the first phase, the EC (2010a) adopted the communication to "establish a common approach for Member States public administrations, to help citizens and businesses to profit fully from the EU's Single Market." The EC has a four-prong strategy: common frameworks in support of interoperability, "reusable generic tools," "common services" (operational applications and infrastructures of a generic nature to meet user requirements across policy areas), and "analysis of the ICT side in the implementation of new EU legislation." As Ganslandt (2010) argues, the four prongs are not likely to be sufficient without a more effective enforcement strategy.

The European Parliament (COD/2011/0150) responded to the standards strategy by proposing direct funding for small and medium-sized enterprises and civil society to participate in the standards that underpin the entire strategy, confirming a multistakeholder approach to be adopted, though substantial disagreement ensured in committee over whether "'balanced," "relevant," or "appropriate" representation should be established and financially supported. These proposals are promising, but no conclusions can be drawn, as they are both ambitious and yet to be implemented in practice.

We focus in the concluding chapter on the creation of legislation with an approach directed toward interoperability and suggest that the EC and United States should include interoperability requirements in legislation in all cases where there is not an overriding public interest in favor of a proprietary ICT solution. In particular, given that interoperability can allay the types of abusive vertical integration found in the Microsoft case, we argue that financial models intended to create best current value for taxpayers may both tend to limit future competition by creating lock-in as well as lead to an "ICT vendor cartel." Such an outcome could have been foreseen and would have been avoided with greater dedication to choosing interoperable solutions.

Driving Interoperable Code

This chapter has given several examples of the manner in which code can outflank regulation in the cases of encryption of communications and of P2P software. We explained that despite the security advantages of encryption software, it has not been a magic bullet making government regulation untenable because so few users have consciously adopted the technologies. This is despite the ready availability of free open source implementations.

In response to the dominance of commercial code sellers, notably Microsoft but also other infractors of competition rules, antitrust and regulatory authorities have adopted comprehensive interoperability strategies including EIF 2.0. Among them are standardization strategies that extend to the entire organization of standards bodies themselves and establish class monitoring of standards. They also include procurement requirements for interoperability on government contracts of more than about $200,000 (Regulations 1177/2009 and EU/1251/2011). This strategy is intended to ensure a fundamentally open approach to information technology standards.

In terms of code outcomes, we also need to ask whether there are alternate ways to consider solutions rather than those adopted: forks in the path or alternate dependencies? An example might be using legislation rather than code (or vice versa) or industry or consumer-led solutions where the opposite actually occurred (Bresnahan, Greenstein, and Hendersen 2011). Institutional examination needs to account for alternative histories, as previous Internet policy studies have concluded following North (1990; Mueller 2010; Benkler 2006).

Toward Case Study Exploration

We now continue to the examination of our five case studies, bearing in mind the lessons in this chapter about code, its market and user deployment challenges, and the policy choices that private actors, governments, and civil society have in deciding on the manner in which they shape code.

The initial part of each case study chapter sets out the policy environment and its drivers: the social impact of technology and its adoption. We then consider the enablers of a competitive technology marketplace: entry barriers; the network and scale effects that successful technologies deploy, and the potential for interoperability in that market. We go on to consider fundamental rights in policy design for that technology and lessons from the initial consideration of developments. This brings the nonexpert reader to the point at which we can consider both technological and institutional policy developments in turn.

The next section of each case study considers types of software code and regulation of that code. It considers the layer at which the code is deployed according to the open systems interconnect layers model we considered in chapter 1, the location at which the code is deployed, whether by manufacturers of routers and other control devices (e.g., Cisco or Alcatel-Lucent), ISPs as access bottlenecks (e.g., British Telecom or Verizon), servers located with application developers and in content delivery networks (e.g., with Google and Facebook), or software clients that operate on users' computers (e.g., Web browsers). This leads to analysis of the enforcement of code by its developers and the role of governments in attempting to regulate code in the public interest.

We then consider the actors who are engaged in policy debate in each of our case studies—the institutional political economy of code, as explored in chapter 1. We first explore and identify the key actors: national, regional, and global. We examine how legitimate and accountable they are and particularly explore the role of multistakeholderism. Given our hypothesis that good regulation works with efficient code wherever possible, we assess key technical actor buy-in to regulatory goals and aims. Finally, we draw lessons from the political economy of each case study.

A final section focuses on outcomes, assessed according to transparency of outcome, enforcement of regulatory goals, interoperability as a solution, and efficiency. This final challenge addresses the central concerns of lawyers and computer scientists: Does the regulation work? Whether the central concern is economic efficiency or human rights, a regulatory goal that is patently unachievable in political, technical, or market terms is of purely academic interest.

In each case study, we examine whether governments have moved from sledgehammer prohibition-based, enforcement-oriented regulation to smarter regulation that works technically, with some degree of outcome legitimacy in terms of goals. These might be supporting the creation of public goods and disruptive innovation in markets rather than a purely political goal such as "outlawing social evils." A smart solution in terms of code and regulation would provide effectiveness, efficiency, and legitimacy. Unsurprisingly, the outcomes are likely to be trade-offs among these three goals.

3 Privacy and Data Protection

Long before the arrival of Google and Facebook, the impact of computing and communication technologies on privacy presented one of the most significant regulatory challenges of the information age. From the middle of the twentieth century, the use of mainframe computers to process government and company data started to have an impact on individual privacy. This process accelerated in the 1970s as minicomputers and then personal computers became a pervasive part of organizations in advanced economies.

Now, Internet users' browsing, searching, and even e-mailing behavior is routinely profiled by advertising networks and of great interest to law enforcement and intelligence agencies. The nascent "Internet of things" (allowing remote virtual interaction with physical objects) will add billions of sensors to the network, potentially allowing individual behavior in the physical world to be as closely tracked as online activity. Many governments have responded with national laws and international treaties implementing fair information practices to improve the transparency and safeguards associated with the processing of personal data.

Privacy and data protection is a well-studied field—not least because it has proven difficult for legislators and regulators to keep up with the rapid pace of change in Internet technologies that gather, process, and share data related to individuals. In this chapter, we assess more recent attempts to shape the development of Internet technologies in an effort to improve the efficacy of regulation by embedding privacy by design into new systems. These efforts have been led by the EU, while the U.S. government has largely left privacy concerns about business behavior to be met through self-regulation, with limited policing of deceptive practices by the Federal Trade Commission (FTC). Regulation has therefore been driven to some extent by the interaction between large U.S. Internet companies and EU legislators and national data protection authorities.

Public Policy Objectives

Social Impact of Technology

The impact of new information technologies on privacy has been the subject of intense debate since the development of the portable camera in the nineteenth century. Combined with the relatively new newspaper industry, this created the forerunner of paparazzi photographers and scandal sheets.

In response, Samuel Warren and Louis Brandeis famously described privacy as the "right to be let alone" (1890), emphasized in a later dissenting U.S. Supreme Court opinion by then-Justice Brandeis as "the most comprehensive of rights, and the right most valued by civilized man" (*Olmstead* v. *United States* 1928). But it took decades of widespread telephone use for that Court to decide that constitutional protections against unreasonable searches also applied to telephone conversations (*Katz* v. *United States* 1967).

During the 1970s, governments in North America and Europe developed fair information processing principles designed to protect privacy, as mainframes and minicomputers became widespread in the public and private sectors. The principles were first expressed in the laws of several European nations such as Sweden and France, and in rudimentary form in the U.S. Fair Credit Reporting Act in 1970. They were then agreed at the international level, leading to the OECD Guidelines (1980) and the Council of Europe Convention (CETS No.108 1981). The principles have seen their strongest and most influential expression in the EU (Directive EC/95/46).

However, the Internet and modern computers have presented a significant challenge to data protection regulation. Underlying computing power has been doubling every eighteen to twenty-four months since Intel cofounder Gordon Moore famously observed this relationship in 1965. Bandwidth and storage capacity have been increasing even more quickly. All of this has made it easier than ever before for governments and companies to store, share, and process ever greater quantities of personal data.

Law enforcement and intelligence agencies have, at varying speeds, woken up to the surveillance potential of the digital tsunami of personal data now being generated by individuals' day-to-day interactions with information systems. Data retention laws passed in Europe (and proposed in the United States) require telephone companies and ISPs to store information about their customers, including details of telephone conversations and e-mail correspondents. Mobile phone companies have detailed data on their customers' location and can carry out real-time tracking of specific individuals. Web sites usually store detailed logs of their users' activities, which can be accessed with varying degrees of judicial oversight in the United States and Europe (Brown 2009). Even offline activities such as buying travel tickets now commonly generate a digital trail, which under bilateral agreements (such as between the EU and Australia, the United States, and other nations) can be automatically shared and stored for a decade or more.

Other government agencies are eager to move services online, both for customer service improvements (such as personalization and immediate delivery) and cost savings. E-government initiatives commonly link up and centralize previously separate databases of personal data across government departments, creating the potential for much more detailed profiling of individual citizens (Anderson et al. 2009).

The United Kingdom has been a leading example of this trend. While prime minister, Tony Blair committed the government to make all services available online by 2005. Initiatives such as national health, identity, and social security databases caused fears of a "database state," with the information commissioner warning that the country was "sleepwalking into a surveillance society" (Ford 2004). This became a significant election issue in 2010, with the winning Conservative and Liberal Democrat parties abolishing Blair's national identity scheme and children's database.

At the same time, an advertising economy has developed on the Internet, whereby most Web sites' business models are based around selling advertising space and clicks. Users remain extremely reluctant to pay for content beyond specialized areas such as financial journalism. Publishers and providers of services such as Web mail, online document editors, and social media (covered in more detail in chapter 6) are eager to deploy technology that increases the effectiveness, and hence revenues, of advertisements. "Behavioral advertising," tailored to profiles built around users' previous browsing behavior, promises to do so—although few data in the public domain show its specific effects.

A second major technological shift underway is the gradual introduction of an Internet of things, where physical sensors such as radio frequency identifier (RFID) tags generate data about real-world objects that are then linked to online databases. RFID has already seen significant deployment, with multinational organizations such as Walmart and the U.S. Department of Defense requiring tags on all supplies to help manage logistics.

RFID and more sophisticated tags are now used in transport payment cards (such as London's Oyster and Hong Kong's Octopus cards) and for low-value payments using credit cards (Visa's PayWave and Mastercard's PayPass standards). These tags could ultimately lead to individuals' behavior in the physical world being tracked and integrated into profiles of their online activity.

Market Failures
Modern privacy and data protection regulation has two main economic objectives. The first is to ensure that national rules to protect individual privacy do not become a barrier to international trade by blocking the flow of personal data necessary for transactions and the provision of goods and services. The 1980 OECD guidelines were adopted at a point when half of its member countries had passed privacy laws. These guidelines are not binding on OECD members but have been significant in shaping privacy laws.

The OECD's expert group cooperated closely with the Council of Europe, which during the same period was producing a convention (CETS No. 108). The 1981 convention similarly includes an article that limits restrictions on personal data flows among signatories. It is open to nonmembers of the Council of Europe for ratification, and since 2008 a consultative committee has assessed accession requests from non-European states. Uruguay was the first to go through this procedure, and was invited to accede in 2011. In the medium term, the convention is the only realistic prospect for a global privacy instrument (Greenleaf 2013).

The most significant regional privacy agreement is the EU's Data Protection Directive (95/46/EC), which was developed under single-market procedures. The dual objective of the directive is to protect individual privacy while preventing the restriction of the free flow of personal data among member states. It implements the OECD Guidelines and Council of Europe

Convention, with additional protections including limits on data exports outside the EU and enforcement mechanisms—with a requirement for independent data protection authorities and individual rights of appeal to the courts (Greenleaf 2013). These additions were themselves introduced by the Council of Europe to strengthen the convention by its 2001 Additional Protocol (CETS No.181). In 2012 the EU began a revision of the directive and proposed a new directive to cover criminal justice agencies' processing of personal data.

The second economic objective of recent data protection rules is to protect consumer confidence in e-commerce, given the large quantities of personal data often gathered by online service providers. Numerous surveys have found significant individual resistance to online transactions due to concerns about giving away personal data and potential identity fraud.

Effective data protection has therefore been a key part of the European Commission's programs to encourage online consumer transactions, such as the Safer Internet Action Plan (Edwards 2004). This includes providing clear information to customers about how personal data are gathered and used, and more recently in some U.S. states and the EU, notification of breaches of data security to regulators and affected individuals (through the updated Privacy Directive 2002/58/EC as amended in Directive 2009/140/EC).

Both of these elements are stressed in the European Commission's plans for updating the data protection framework (2010). The commission vice president for the digital agenda, Neelie Kroes, told an industry roundtable that "users should feel they have the effective possibility to choose whether they want to be tracked and profiled or not. Irrespective of their legality, any such practices are damaging—they damage the already fragile confidence in the online digital economy. Today only 12% of Europeans fully trust online transactions, so this sort of behaviour is a case of the industry "shooting itself in the foot" (Kroes, 2010).

Fundamental Rights

The idea of protection of an individual's private sphere from government activity goes back to Aristotle (Westin 1967). It has been read into the U.S. Constitution by the Supreme Court and explicitly included in constitutions and treaties around the world. Privacy protection is a key part of the Universal Declaration of Human Rights, the International Convention on

Civil and Political Rights, and, more recently, the EU Charter of Fundamental Rights.

The U.N. Human Rights Committee has stated that the International Convention on Civil and Political Rights requires protection against interference in privacy by both state and private bodies, and regulation of "the gathering and holding of personal information on computers, databanks and other devices" (U.N. Human Rights Committee, 1988). The Council of Europe's Convention is the main international instrument implementing this more technology-specific focus on privacy, often referred to as "data protection." Alongside a general right to privacy, the EU Charter gives a specific right to data protection, which includes rights such as individual access to personal data.

Privacy is viewed as both a key individual, liberal right (especially in the United States) and a wider social good. It is seen to help secure individuality, autonomy, dignity, emotional release, self-evaluation, and positive emotional relationships. In Germany and some other countries, it is further seen to protect democratic rights to participation in public life (Bygrave 2010). Australian civil society groups captured these ideas in their Australian Privacy Charter (Australian Privacy Charter Council 1994), which states:

A free and democratic society requires respect for the autonomy of individuals, and limits on the power of both state and private organisations to intrude on that autonomy.

Privacy is a value which underpins human dignity and other key values such as freedom of association and freedom of speech.

The protection of young people's privacy has particularly widespread support. This is because children are seen to be less able to make their own informed decisions about disclosing personal information than adults, and are at greater risk of harm from activities such as deceptive marketing or physical attack.

Article 16 of the 1989 U.N. Convention on the Rights of the Child protects against "arbitrary or unlawful interference" with children's "privacy, family, home or correspondence." Even the U.S. Congress, which generally takes a self-regulatory approach to private sector data protection, passed in 1998 the Children's Online Privacy Protection Act (15 U.S.C. sec. 6501–6506) with fair information practice requirements for Web sites targeted at children under thirteen years old.

Table 3.1
Public policy and market failure

Social impact of technology	Bandwidth, storage, processing capacity all doubling every 12 to 24 months, making it much easier for organizations to process and share personal data. E-government drives for personalization and savings; law enforcement and intelligence agency surveillance a further impetus.
Policy drivers—barriers to entry, network and scale effects, competition	EU promotion of a single market in data flows, personal data hoarding by information giants.
Fundamental rights in policy design	European Convention on Human Rights and EU Charter of Fundamental Rights key policy drivers.
Lesson	Privacy is a key human right that may need significant government intervention to protect.

Table 3.1 summarizes the public policy concerns and drivers relating to online privacy. This case study represents the clearest case of a fundamental rights concern leading to significant regulatory intervention in digital markets, led by European legislators and data protection regulators.

Types of Code Regulation

Online privacy protection in most jurisdictions has depended so far mainly on a notice-and-consent model, where users are informed of Web site practices related to the collection and processing of their data. Users are taken to consent to complex, legalistic privacy policies that are often dozens of pages long. In the United States, there is minimal oversight of this system by the FTC, which has complained that "current privacy policies force consumers to bear too much burden in protecting their privacy" (FTC 2010b).

Browser vendors tried to reduce this burden through the development of a platform for privacy preferences (P3P) standard. It allows Web sites to describe their data collection and processing practices in machine-readable format. In theory, it allows users to configure their Web browsers to only provide personal data to sites with privacy policies acceptable to that user. In practice, it had little impact. This was partly due to the complexity for small businesses of converting their day-to-day privacy practices into P3P terms and the difficulty in designing a usable browser interface that allows users to easily understand P3P settings. There have also been significant concerns from privacy advocates that P3P would be unenforceable and pushed by industry as a replacement for rather than complement to data protection laws (Electronic Privacy Information Center 2000).

Aside from Microsoft Internet Explorer, P3P has only limited support in other browser software. The World Wide Web Consortium members could not reach consensus on a second version of the standard, and its development was suspended in 2007.

Further legal constraints apply in the EU under the Data Protection Directive and e-Privacy Directive. Personal data can be collected only for particular, specified purposes; not be excessive for those purposes; and must be deleted after use. Individuals have the right to access and correct personal data held by organizations.

EU states (and other jurisdictions with similar laws, such as Canada, Australia and Hong Kong) have independent national data protection regulators to oversee enforcement of these rights. The EU model has been extremely influential, seemingly initiating a race to the top in privacy regulatory standards, because it limits exports of personal data to countries without adequate standards of protection (Greenleaf 2013).

There is increasing evidence from behavioral economics that a "consent" model has significant failings. Very few users have the time or legal training to fully read and understand privacy policies, let alone enforce them. Privacy-related decisions are heavily context specific, dependent, for example, on how much a user is thinking about privacy at the time, along with his or her trust in the other party and often-inaccurate assumptions about how data will be used. It is extremely difficult to calculate the probability of harm that results from a single disclosure, let alone the cumulative impact, and what data could reveal when combined with a large number of other possible data sources.

This is illustrated by the U.S. situation, which in the private sector largely relies on individual action to recover damages suffered through a limited number of statutory rights. Courts are reluctant to award damages for data privacy offenses in the absence of monetary harm, and the cost of litigation is then disproportionate (Reidenberg 2006). Alternatively, the FTC has discretion regarding the pursuit of an action against a private enterprise. The FTC pursues only a small fraction of violations each year (Marcus et al. 2007). From 2002 to 2007, it brought only eleven actions for impermissible collection of personal information on the Internet from children (FTC 2007). The action against the social networking site Xanga.com for illegally collecting information from 1.7 million children resulted in a fine of $1 million (less than $0.60 per child victim).

Organizations will adequately invest in protection of personal data only if they suffer the full costs to individuals of breaches of that protection. Limited enforcement to date of penalties for breaches is one reason for continuing successful attacks of the scale of that on Sony's PlayStation and Online Entertainment networks in 2011, where details were stolen from 102 million user accounts (Arthur 2011b).

Policymakers have therefore become concerned with increasing effective privacy protection for citizens, to protect individual autonomy and consumer interests, along with the wider democratic interest in a confident and powerful citizenry willing to engage in the public sphere (Bygrave 2010). Both the EU and the FTC are now looking to code solutions that will strengthen user choice over online tracking and embed privacy by design much more strongly into information systems within companies and government agencies that are processing large quantities of personal data.

Basic requirements for organizations to take technical steps to protect personal data were present in the 1974 U.S. Privacy Act and included as Principle 11 of the 1980 OECD guidelines: "Personal data should be protected by reasonable security safeguards against such risks as loss or unauthorised access, destruction, use, modification or disclosure of data." Article 17 of the EU's Data Protection Directive similarly includes an obligation for data controllers to "implement appropriate technical and organizational measures to protect personal data." South Korean and Hong Kong law both provide more detailed security standards (Greenleaf 2011).

In practice, these provisions have had limited impact. Even European data protection authorities, who are much more interventionist than the FTC, rarely take steps to enforce this obligation. The only standards with significant deployment are the Payment Card Industry Data Security Standard, a self-regulatory framework covering companies that accept and process card payments. In some countries (including the United Kingdom), financial regulators have taken much stronger enforcement action than is available to data protection authorities against banks that have lost sensitive customer information.

The European Network and Information Security Agency (ENISA) has suggested regulators require the use of best available techniques, a process already in use in European environmental regulation. For different application areas, regulators identify a "particular combination of technologies, protocols, standards, [and] practices" that should be used by data controllers (ENISA 2008, 35–36). An example of such standards is the series produced by Germany's Federal Office for Information Security, which covers the use of RFID tags in public transport e-ticketing, event ticketing, trade logistics, and employee electronic ID cards (Bundesamt für Sicherheit in der Informationstechnik 2010).

Behavioral Advertising

In the online world, behavioral advertising, with its widespread profiling of user browsing, has become an increasingly common practice. In 2011 advertising company WPP announced it had built profiles on over 500 million users in North America, Europe, and Australia. Policymakers in the United States and EU have responded with more specific regulation targeted at the browser software functionality that enables this profiling.

The EU's e-privacy directive, updated in 2009, requires consent from users before the "storing or accessing of information stored in the user's terminal," mainly targeted at the "cookies" that Web sites commonly use to track user activity. Users must be given "clear and comprehensive" information about how their data will be used and can give consent using browser options as long as that is "technically possible and effective."

Browsers that accept cookies by default do not meet this test, according to the European Data Protection Supervisor (EDPS), since most users lack the skills to change these settings. The EDPS suggests instead that browser software provide a more user-friendly "privacy wizard" or other user interface to help users decide whether they wish to be tracked and receive targeted advertising, with the default setting that they do not (Hustinx 2011).

The FTC has focused on a related mechanism: a "persistent browser setting" that can be used to signal that a user does not wish to be tracked by third parties or served targeted advertisements (FTC 2011). This "do-not-track" option has quickly been added to browsers such as Firefox and praised by U.S. and EU politicians—with U.S. president Barack Obama launching a "consumer privacy bill of rights" that encourages companies to implement such measures and asking Congress to give them statutory backing (U.S. Government 2012). The EDPS has added that a do-not-track standard would be one way for advertisers to comply with the e-privacy directive, so long as the default setting was privacy protective (EDPS 2011b).

Although industry associations have promoted self-regulation for behavioral advertising, examples such as Google's circumvention of privacy controls in Apple's Safari browser (Mayer 2012) have increased pressure for regulatory intervention.

Privacy by Design

The EU and FTC have broadened these regulatory proposals to other technical systems that process personal data. By focusing on privacy protection right through the technology life cycle, regulators have called for privacy to be embedded by design into new systems (U.K. Data Protection Registrar 1999; Cavoukian 2009). Requiring this principle to be followed is a key aim of the revision of the EU Data Protection Directive (European Commission COM(2010) 609), with Commissioner Viviane Reding telling the European Parliament that "Privacy by Design will lead to better protection for individuals, as well as to trust and confidence in new services and products that will in turn have a positive impact on the economy" (Reding 2010). The FTC has similarly proposed that "companies should adopt a 'privacy by design' approach by building privacy protections into their everyday business practices" (FTC, 2010b, v).

One mechanism that companies can use to signal such an approach is to gain certification from independent auditors. The most in-depth assessment tool is the EuroPRISE seal developed by the data protection agency of the northern German state Schleswig-Holstein. Approved assessors examine the software and development processes behind information technology products and services, ensuring that they include privacy-protective functionality throughout. German public procurement rules allow government agencies to give preference to such certified products (Korff and Brown 2010).

Internet of Things

The Internet of things is the second area where privacy regulators have taken specific steps to shape the development of technology to better protect personal data, beginning with RFID tags. The industry association GS1 estimated that around 87 billion tags would be deployed in Europe between 2010 and 2020 (GS1 and Logica 2007), and there has been understandable public interest in a technology that some privacy campaigners have characterized as "spy chips."

In response, the European Commission has recommended that industry should develop a framework for privacy assessments of RFID applications, "in collaboration with relevant civil society" and subject to approval by the data protection authorities of the EU member states (C (2009) 3200). The second proposed version of the framework was approved in 2011. It is designed to help operators of RFID systems to "uncover the privacy risks associated with an RFID Application, assess their likelihood, and document the steps taken to address those risks" (Article 29 Working Party 2011a, Annex A3). It covers the tags themselves, as well as "back-end systems and networked communication infrastructures" used to process tag data.

The framework encourages the creation of industry and application-specific templates. It includes an initial analysis step, followed by a small-scale or full-scale risk assessment phase. The application operator then describes the technical and organizational steps taken to mitigate these risks in a Privacy Impact Assessment Report, which should be available on request to national regulators. The report must also include a detailed inventory of data items stored and processed and a list of internal and external data recipients.

While the risk assessment process is focused on the Data Protection Directive principles, the framework can be easily adapted for use in other jurisdictions and had significant input from non-European companies. This format means that a PIA can also be used to carry out a legal compliance check for a system; companies are unsurprisingly reluctant to carry out a separate PIA and compliance check (Spiekerman 2011).

Table 3.2 summarizes the features of code regulation now being explored by regulators, particularly within the EU, in an effort to improve the

Table 3.2
Types of code and code regulation

Layer	New focus on RFIDs, browser code (do not track, cookies) and privacy by design.
Location (manufacturers, ISPs, servers, clients)	Software and system architects.
Enforcement of code	Threat of Data Protection Directive enforcement; revision of Data Protection Directive to include more specific requirements for privacy by design.

efficacy of privacy protection—initially in the Internet of things and with behavioral targeting for adverts.

Institutional Political Economy

In Europe, where privacy has long been seen as a core requirement for democratic government, legislators and statutory regulators have played key roles in promoting and enforcing privacy regulations. They have been strongly supported by national constitutional courts and the European Court of Human Rights, which has made technology-specific decisions such as requiring better security protection for large databases of personal information (*I* v. *Finland*, 2008) and stopping states from building large databases of sensitive forensic information from unconvicted individuals (*S and Marper* v. *UK*, 2008).

The European Parliament has played an increasingly significant role: a leaked U.S. State Department cable noted that "the media-savvy EP has cultivated a high profile role on data protection policy through public hearings, resolutions, non-binding statements, opinions, and lobbying the Council and Commission for action" (U.S. Mission to the EU 2009).

States with a particularly strong constitutional tradition of privacy protection, such as Germany and Austria, have played a significant role in the development of EU data protection law. The German Constitutional Court's notion of informational self-determination, developed in its 1983 decision on the national census, has influenced later legislation and judicial decisions across the continent, and led to the inclusion of specific rights to privacy and data protection in articles 7 and 8 of the EU Charter of Fundamental Rights. These will play a key role in decisions of the European Court of Justice on issues such as the mandatory retention of personal data by ISPs and telephone companies under the Data Retention Directive (Directive 2006/24/EC).

The EU has successfully influenced other regional privacy laws by restricting the transfer of personal data from member states to countries without adequate privacy protection. This determination of "adequacy," overseen by the European Commission, in practice requires other states to introduce most of the key protections from the Data Protection Directive into their own national laws.

The commission has now assessed Argentina, Canada, Israel, New Zealand, Switzerland, Uruguay, and five smaller European territories to meet this test. Greenleaf (2013) argues that Colombia, Mexico, Peru, South Korea, India, Taiwan, Hong Kong, and Australia could all put up a case that they could meet the adequacy test, as could some western African states.

Against these European governmental and judicial advocates for stronger privacy protection, resistance has come particularly from the U.S. government, where politicians have been strongly lobbied by technology and services companies and national security agencies that want greater access to personal data. U.S. policy goals were succinctly summarized by the mission to the EU: "to ensure that data privacy rules will not hinder economic growth, endanger economic recovery, or discourage greater [law enforcement] cooperation" (2009). The U.S. Supreme Court has at times protected privacy against the state under the Fourth Amendment to the Constitution (*Katz* v. *United States,* 1967), but has also found some privacy rules to conflict with the free speech guarantee in the First Amendment (*Sorrell* v. *IMS Health,* 2011).

The United States has tried to influence international privacy regulations by leading a policy development process in the Asia-Pacific Economic Cooperation group, intended to supplant stronger European standards. This process has focused on accountability for harms caused by privacy breaches rather than detailed rules on data handling. It has so far had limited success. Many members of the Asia-Pacific group have since found it in their own interests to base new laws on the EU Data Protection Directive. Analyzing these efforts, Greenleaf (forthcoming) concluded that "attempts by US companies and the US government to use their combined economic and political influence to limit development of data privacy laws in other countries will continue to be important, but are probably now on the wrong side of history."

Significant opposition to privacy rules has also come from a wide range of law enforcement and intelligence agencies. The terrorist attacks on the United States in September 2001, on Madrid in 2004, and on London in 2005 all gave significant impetus to counterterrorism agency demands for access to more personal data. While many countries' privacy regulations do not apply to data processing for these purposes, security agencies increasingly trawl through commercial databases that are subject to data protection rules.

Former U.K. security and intelligence coordinator Sir David Omand (2009) wrote that intelligence agencies would need blanket access to "personal information about individual [sic] that resides in databases. . . . Access to such information, and in some cases the ability to apply data mining and pattern recognition software to databases, might well be the key to effective pre-emption in future terrorist cases" (9).

In the EU, the blanket exemption of Justice and Home Affairs policy from the directive ended when the Lisbon Treaty came into force in 2010, with this policy area becoming the joint responsibility of member states and the European Parliament. The U.S. administration faced significant opposition from the parliament during the drafting of U.S.-EU treaties that would provide U.S. access to European passenger name records (related to air travel) and Society for Worldwide Interbank Financial Telecommunication payment records (de Hert and Papakonstaninou 2010). The U.S. Mission to the EU strongly criticized the European Commission for a failure of policy leadership, allowing the EDPS and national data protection authorities to "regularly make high-profile public statements on areas outside of their formal competence . . . [which] tend to give primacy to civil liberties-based approaches for the EU's Single Market, consumers, or law enforcement" (U.S. Mission to the EU 2009).

Advocacy groups have played an important role in campaigning for stronger privacy laws, highlighting actual and potential abuses by governments and companies and bringing test cases before courts and regulators. Their strategies have included influencing media and political discourse; conducting research and providing information to the public and politicians about the privacy consequences of policy proposals (often making heavy use of freedom of information laws); and "naming and shaming" organizations (Bennett 2008). This includes participating at the annual international conference of privacy regulators, open to anyone who can afford the (not insignificant) conference travel and registration costs, for which some funding has been provided by philanthropists such as George Soros' Open Society Foundations.

Privacy is of interest to many Internet users around the world, and privacy advocates have made extensive use of the Internet to share information and coordinate their campaigns. They have also built issue-specific coalitions around issues such as behavioral advertising and RFID tags. These activism networks are open and easily reconfigured, facilitating fast-paced campaigns against invasive new policies or products. This quality may, however, make it more difficult for campaigns to achieve longer-term goals and growth. As Bennett concluded, "There is clearly no worldwide privacy movement that has anything like the scale, resources, or public recognition of organizations in the environmental, feminist or human rights fields" (Bennett 2008, xv).

Regulators and civil society have had some success in persuading software companies to improve the privacy protection in their products. There has been occasional competition on privacy functionality between search engines (Bing, Google, and Yahoo!) and browser vendors (Mozilla, Microsoft, and Apple). Mozilla was praised by the FTC and European Commission after introducing a do-not-track option in its Firefox browser. However, these companies often face conflicts of interest, particularly where they derive revenue from advertising. For example, Microsoft made an improved "private browsing" mode harder to leave switched on in Internet Explorer after pressure from the advertising division of the company (Soghoian 2011).

Internet advertising companies have lobbied heavily against "unnecessary and ill-informed" EU rules on targeted advertising. Their industry association, the Internet Advertising Bureau Europe, lobbied unsuccessfully against the creation of sector-specific rules on data protection for electronic communication services in what became the 2002 e-Privacy Directive. The European Parliament amended the draft directive to include a specific ban on the use of cookies without explicit user consent, but these were modified during negotiation with the commission and council to allow an opt-out approach. This was the result of an industry Save the Cookies campaign that emphasized the costs and competitiveness impact on European companies. Privacy advocates had placed a higher priority on protecting the rules in the directive banning unsolicited e-mail (Kierkegaard 2005). However, privacy regulators and advocates reversed this opt-out provision at the next revision of the directive in 2009. The industry has continued to push a self-regulatory model, producing a Best Practice Recommendation on Online Behavioral Advertising (European Advertising Standards Alliance 2011).

RFID standards have developed more slowly, partly because computing hardware evolves less quickly than software. Little consideration was given to privacy in the original RFID standards. This changed when advocacy groups began campaigns against what they called "spy chips," something that resonated strongly with voters and led to pressure from policymakers and politicians (Bennett and Raab 2006).

The European Commission's approach was to set up an informal RFID working group of industry, academic, and civil society representatives to agree on a coregulatory framework code. The industry representatives were initially reluctant participants, producing a "barely structured pamphlet" lacking any risk identification process or link to European privacy laws. Civil society had little input into this document and felt their presence at working group meetings was being used to legitimate a document being written largely by the GS1 trade association (Spiekerman 2011).

Unsurprisingly, the Article 29 working party of data protection authorities, whose approval was required by the European Commission, rejected this proposal. An alternative industry consortium produced a much stronger second code with academic input and threatened to submit this code for approval. This pressure led to industry agreement within the working group with civil society on a compromise code, the third effort, which was finally approved by the Article 29 working party (2011c).

Table 3.3 summarizes the institutional policy economy of online privacy protection. It makes clear that national data protection agencies and, to a lesser extent, consumer protection agencies play a clear role, with some significant opposition from industry actors with a commercial interest in greater processing of personal data. The extremely effective alliance described in the next chapter between Internet users and industry over proposed copyright measures would be less likely to arise in a privacy context.

Outcomes

It can be difficult to assess the impact of privacy and data protection regulation. Strong laws and enforcement agencies can be less important in practice than the degree to which government attitudes, industry standards, and cultural factors are supportive of privacy. Data protection agencies often prefer to work through private negotiations with government and industry rather than through high-profile enforcement actions. Privacy rules aim to prevent abuses before they occur (Bygrave 2010). The privacy impact of public and private sector actions can vary across different sections of society (Bennett and Raab 2006).

Table 3.3
Institutional political economy

Key actors: national, regional, global	National data protection regulators; consumer protection agencies (e.g., FTC). Coordination in EU, Council of Europe, Asia-Pacific Economic Cooperation. Law, enforcement agencies, advertisers, and their technology partners.
How legitimate and accountable?	Regulators are mainly legislative creatures and hence democratically accountable, although self-regulatory policy outside the EU is less legitimate or accountable.
Multistakeholderism	Annual regulators' conference open to all stakeholders. RFID process explicitly multistakeholder, although industry tried hard to ignore civil society.
Key technical actor buy-in	Firefox (Do Not Track), Apple Safari blocks third-party cookies by default (no ad network, unlike Microsoft and Google). RFID industry wrote privacy framework with some other stakeholder input; code approved by Article 29 Working Party.
Lessons	Strong intervention from legislators and privacy regulators is sometimes needed to counteract the powerful voice of law enforcement agencies and technology companies that have shared interests in weaker restrictions on access to personal data.

That said, there is widespread recognition of the EU's detailed rules as a gold standard to which many other jurisdictions aspire (Greenleaf forthcoming). The European Commission is strengthening and broadening these rules during the revision of the data protection directive, especially regarding incentives for privacy by design.

At the other end of the scale, there is clearly less protection for individual privacy in the U.S. legal system than in most other advanced economies. Outside the federal government, regulation is patchy, sector specific, and state-by-state, with limited individual rights and enforcement only under very specific circumstances by the FTC (Hoofnagle 2010). Most responsibility is placed on consumers, regardless of their capability to understand legalistic privacy notices or the availability of other options in often concentrated markets.

This is problematic, given the geographic (and cultural) location of most major Internet companies' headquarters. Many U.S. companies emphasize the need for consumer "empowerment" and dismiss European-style rules as bureaucratic, ineffective, and obstructive of innovation.

Consumer education and action are important parts of any data protection regime, and one study found that U.S. consumer Web sites had privacy policies at least equivalent to, and in some cases better than, EU sites (Scribbins 2001). But notice-and-consent and self-regulatory regimes have not in general proved effective in the face of government and industry interest in access to ever-greater quantities of personal data. They work best as elements of a broader, statutory regime (Greenleaf 2013).

This is not to say the EU has reached privacy nirvana. Several studies have found that data protection authorities are underresourced; that companies generally support privacy rules, but have a mixed record in following them; and that individuals have a limited awareness of their rights (Bygrave 2010). Greenleaf (2013) speculated that "many businesses and government agencies internalise the norms of data privacy principles once they are enacted and observe legislation to a significant extent even in the absence of effective enforcement activities."

The OECD guidelines requiring data controllers to take "reasonable security safeguards," echoed in the data protection directive's "appropriate technical and organizational measures to protect personal data," have not been enough to stop some spectacular breaches of large databases, such as Sony's loss of 102 million users' PlayStation and Online Entertainment account data (Arthur 2011b). Given the widespread availability of encryption tools to prevent unauthorized data access, it is extremely surprising that many of these breaches were technically trivial. The lack of enforcement of minimum standards is one reason for this.

As legal requirements have spread in U.S. states for organizations to notify customers of breaches (Hoofnagle 2010), there is a greater risk for careless organizations of reputational damage and claims for individual losses, although these can be difficult to quantify (Acquisti, Friedman, and Telang 2006). Studies have shown little long-term impact on the share price of companies affected by data breaches (Acquisti, Friedman, and Telang 2006). Privacy harms are frequently probabilistic and long term, making it difficult for courts to assess damages (Acquisti 2002). But outcomes in the United States have been persuasive enough for the European Commission to add breach notification during the revision of the electronic communications framework, and to other information society services in the revision of the data protection directive.

There has been significant research into privacy-enhancing technologies (PETs) that could provide much stronger technical protection of personal data, but very little mainstream deployment of these tools. One explanation, despite "relatively high levels of concern about privacy in online settings," is "widespread indifference on the part of individuals when it comes to actual buying decisions. . . . Market imperfections, which can include asymmetric information, externalities, lack of information sharing about privacy risks and coordination failures, mean that the individually rational decisions of data controllers do not necessarily lead to the optimal level of PETs deployment" (London Economics 2010, xi). Another is that adoption requires a certain critical mass of users that has not yet been reached and may require support from data protection authorities and public bodies. Many businesses do not yet fully understand the costs and benefits of PETs and so have delayed their deployment. But this leaves customers with little meaningful choice over whether to disclose personal information (London Economics 2010).

There can also be significant opportunity costs in adopting PETs. Many organizations use personal data to supply targeted advertising, offer personalized services, or adjust prices based on a customer's previous willingness to pay. They will accept the loss of some of these benefits by deploying PETS only if there are at least equivalent gains from attracting privacy-sensitive customers, avoiding potential reputational damage, or meeting regulatory requirements (Rubinstein 2012).

Regulators in the United States, Canada, and the EU have recently focused on code in browsers (for behavioral advertising and social networking) and RFID systems. While some regulators have been calling for the use of privacy-by-design principles since the 1990s, it has taken the threat of enforcement action to persuade some companies to take these principles seriously. Most notably, the federal Canadian privacy commissioner took action in 2009 against Facebook over its photo-sharing and "app" Web site features and persuaded the company to introduce more privacy-friendly default settings (Smith 2009).

Without such action, industry self-regulatory efforts have generally been weak and rejected as such by civil society. For example, the World Privacy Forum (2011) criticized the draft European Advertising Standards Alliance code on behavioral advertising as "dismiss[ing] consumer privacy concerns by not engaging with them in any significant way" (2011, 2).

The second version of the code more strongly emphasized its complementarity to consumers' legal rights under the e-privacy directive, but was still found by the Article 29 Working Party to be "not adequate to ensure compliance with the current applicable European data protection legal framework" (2011b). As Winn (2010) observed: "The institutional differences between European and US standards systems is due in part to the greater deference of US regulators to market-oriented private-sector standards bodies. . . . If EU regulators decide they want to integrate ICT standards into the existing framework of EU data protections laws, then they may have no choice but to find a way to out-maneuver US efforts to minimize government intervention in global information networks." That said, the FTC and Obama administration have gone further than expected in promoting privacy in technical standards.

It is too early to judge the impact of the privacy-by-design regimes being introduced by the European Commission and elsewhere. Detailed technology-specific rules can become outdated very quickly and risk constraining innovation without preventing invasions of privacy through different technologies. The online advertising industry has criticized the cookie provisions of the e-privacy directive in these terms, although regulators have responded that they are essential to give users control of behaviorally targeted advertisements.

Rubinstein (2012) suggests several measures that the FTC could adopt to support privacy by design were Congress to give them such powers in new privacy legislation. These include allowing organizations to experiment with new approaches to achieve privacy goals, such as standardized, easy-to-read privacy notices, in exchange for exemption from detailed regulatory requirements. Such approaches could be part of more general safe harbors that provide industry sectors with flexibility in their approach to meeting statutory requirements and were echoed in the Obama administration's plans for enforceable consumer privacy rights (U.S. Government 2012).

The EU RFID privacy framework could prove to be more widely influential in terms of privacy regulation. Rubinstein suggested the FTC use a similar process of negotiated rulemaking to bring together industry, civil society, and regulators to agree on behavioral advertising rules (2012, 32). Senior European Commission officials have stated that they hope the RFID framework will be a model for initiatives in other areas, such as

Table 3.4
Outcomes and divergences

Transparency	Limited impact of opaque privacy policies and user education, which are often unintelligible to users, who often are in a poor position to judge privacy risks.
Enforcement	Varied levels of enforcement by EU regulators suggest cultural factors also important.
	Data breach requirements and code solutions could increase privacy protection more uniformly.
Interoperability	Broad European standards are driving a global race-to-the-top, with export controls and "adequacy" assessments driving interoperability between national regimes.
Efficiency	Efficiency via internalized data controller self-enforcement? Norm enforced by law.

cloud computing and online advertising (Santucci 2011). They foresee several benefits over traditional data protection regulation. For example, action by RFID application operators can reduce the privacy compliance burden on small businesses that use turnkey systems with only minor customization.

The coregulatory process that led to the approval of the framework was fraught with obstacles (Spiekerman 2011) but ultimately succeeded in incorporating technical expertise from industry and academia while achieving privacy protection acceptable to the EU's data protection authorities. Time will tell whether the process has achieved sufficient industry buy-in to avoid the need for later enforcement action by regulators. In chapter 6 we assess the impact of similar coregulatory proposals on social networking sites.

Table 3.4 summarizes the outcomes of online privacy regulation, noting that the industry-preferred regulatory option of transparency and consumer choice has had limited success and that the greater market intervention of European regulators has had some impact even on the U.S.-dominated sector of behavioral advertising.

4 Copyrights

Copyright—authors' exclusive right to authorize reproduction of their creative works, and related rights—has been the subject of some of the most contentious regulatory debates of the information age. Before the Internet, it was largely an industrial policy issue affecting companies in the publishing, music, film, and consumer electronics industries. But as the Internet and digital duplication tools have lowered the marginal cost of reproduction and distribution of digital works toward zero, copyright law has increasingly come into conflict with decades-old consumer behavioral norms about the noncommercial reuse of copyrighted work.

Regulation based on blanket restrictions on reproduction now faces severe effectiveness and legitimacy challenges, with very large volumes of copyrighted work being shared without authorization every year over peer-to-peer (P2P) file-sharing networks.

Right holders, claiming that "the answer to the machine is in the machine" (Clark 1996), have persuaded governments to target new copyright regulation at personal computers, media devices, and ISPs. In particular, new legal protection has been given to digital locks that restrict access to protected work, and more recently some governments have placed graduated-response requirements on ISPs to police the behavior of their users. Potential sanctions range from warning letters, through restrictions on connection speed, to disconnection.

In this chapter, we assess the outcome and broader lessons of these attempts to regulate the technology underlying the control and distribution of digital creative works.

Public Policy Objectives

Market Failures

The fundamental economic justification for copyright is that without regulatory intervention, it is difficult for producers to restrict information goods to paying customers. A laissez-faire approach would likely suffer from free riding by information consumers, and hence theoretically from the underproduction of works in the market.

Since the eighteenth century, governments have granted exclusive rights of reproduction to authors in an attempt to incentivize the creation of printed books "for the Encouragement of Learning" (Statute of Anne 1710) and "to promote the Progress of Science and useful Arts" (U.S. Constitution 1787). The continental European approach to authors' rights emphasizes the natural right of individuals to control their work (Hugenholtz 2002, 241), which includes "moral rights" such as the right to be acknowledged as the author of a work, and the right to object to "distortion" or "mutilation" (Berne Convention 1886, sec. 6bis).

There are significant social costs to providing exclusive rights to authors. Information goods are nonrivalrous in consumption; as Thomas Jefferson wrote in 1813: "He who receives an idea from me, receives instruction himself without lessening mine; as he who lights his taper at mine, receives light without darkening me" (Jefferson 1854). Therefore a deadweight loss results from a marginal price above zero, since all those consumers who would have been willing to pay between that and the actual price of an information good miss out on its value.

Information goods are recognized as essential to democracy, education, research, and other public goods (Stiglitz 1999). Copyright also has the potential to stifle freedom of expression. Hence copyright policy must try to balance the rights of authors and their incentives to create against potential social losses resulting from overprotection.

In the United States this has led the courts to develop a fair use doctrine that allows certain uses of copyright works without prior authorization as long as this does not damage the commercial market for the work. In the EU, an exhaustive list of optional exceptions is included in the 2001 Copyright Directive (2001/29/EC), including parody, research, and news reporting. The member states of the EU have implemented widely different combinations of these exceptions in national law, creating an extremely fragmented market for copyrighted work in a supposed free trade area (Hugenholtz 2000).

Copyright is a limited monopoly rather than a market intervention to promote competition. Most information goods also have high fixed costs but low marginal costs of production. It is therefore unsurprising that many industries structured around copyright ownership are highly concentrated. The three major recording labels (Sony/BMG, Universal Music Group, and Warner Music Group) control around 65 percent of the world market, and there are only six major U.S. film studios (Patry 2009).

The limited interventions that have been made by competition regulators have been at the periphery, for example, with attempts by the European Commission to increase competition among the national collecting societies that collect royalties for music performances in each member state (Ungerer 2005).

Social Impact of Technology

Data on levels of unauthorized online sharing of copyright works are difficult to gather and are often modeled using proxies such as levels of P2P file-sharing traffic on large networks. Cisco Systems (2011) estimated such traffic would see a compound annual growth rate of 23 percent between 2010 and 2015. Market research companies conduct frequent surveys asking respondents about their downloading behavior. One of the largest surveys, covering 8,000 adults across thirteen countries, found that 29 percent had downloaded music without payment (Synovate 2010). Some unauthorized sharing traffic has shifted to "cyberlocker" sites such as Megaupload, which was shut down by coordinated international police action in 2012 (U.S. Department of Justice 2012).

It is difficult to use such statistics to produce accurate estimates of economic effects, especially on the wider economy. Different types of downloading activity are legal in different jurisdictions. Survey respondents may be afraid to report illegal activity or exaggerate it. The rate at which consumer access to infringing copyright works reduces expenditure on legitimate works is extremely hard to measure (Hargreaves 2011b). Infringement has a complex range of economic impacts, some positive, for different stakeholders (U.S. Government Accountability Office 2010).

An independent review for the U.K. government concluded that "sales and profitability levels in most creative business sectors appear to be holding up reasonably well . . . many creative businesses are experiencing turbulence from digital copyright infringement, but . . . at the level of the whole economy, measurable impacts are not as stark as is sometimes suggested" (Hargreaves 2011a, 6). The review noted that music industry revenues have continued to grow year-on-year, up 5 percent in 2009, as did book sales from 2004 to 2009.

Fundamental Rights

Article 15 of the International Covenant on Economic, Social and Cultural Rights emphasizes the social nature of copyright: to protect authors' rights, but also to enable everyone to participate in cultural life and benefit from scientific progress.

The EU Charter of Fundamental Rights specifies that "intellectual property shall be protected" (sec. 17(2)). This is most plausibly read as an explicit confirmation that copyright protection is included within the more general right to the protection of property—an important but qualified right to be balanced against conflicting public interests (Griffiths 2011).

These rights sit within the wider human rights framework and must be balanced with others, particularly freedom of expression and privacy. Copyright laws already to some extent internalize this balance with freedom of expression through limits such as the protection of expression, not ideas; term limits; and exceptions and limitations. The main tension between privacy and copyright comes with the introduction of enforcement mechanisms that involve covert surveillance by public or private bodies.

Under the European Convention on Human Rights, such measures require a clear justification and must be proportionate to their goals and include safeguards against abuse. The EU Court of Justice in its *Promusicae* case acknowledged this "fair balance," reiterated in *Scarlet* v. *SABAM* (2011) and *SABAM* v. *NetLog* (2012). It has been especially stressed by the European Data Protection Supervisor opinion on the Anti-Counterfeiting Trade Agreement, which emphasized that some proposed measures were "highly invasive," entailing "generalised monitoring of Internet users' activities" affecting "millions of law-abiding Internet users, including many children and adolescents" (2010, 3).

Intellectual property rights have also become a key part of global discussions on a "right to development." Many low-income countries have

Table 4.1
Public policy and market failure

Social impact of technology	Perfect digital reproduction at almost zero marginal cost on user equipment has rendered copyright ineffective. Massive infringement over P2P nets, cyberlocker sites.
Policy drivers—entry barriers, network and scale effects, competition	Incentivizing creativity. Grant of exclusive rights plus high returns to scale have created highly concentrated markets in music, film, software (the last with additional network effects).
Fundamental rights in policy design	Rights to remuneration in Universal Declaration of Human Rights, and moral rights in Berne Convention.
Lessons	Policy focus has largely been on protecting the rights of creators at the expense of freedom of expression and privacy.

complained about the high price of software and textbooks resulting from international intellectual property agreements. These types of copyright-protected goods are essential for development in a global knowledge economy. As the government of Pakistan told the U.N. Commission on Human Rights in 2001, "It is painfully evident that in the short and medium term, the costs being borne by the developing countries are higher than the gains, and that the balance between the rights holder (mostly from the developed countries) and the user of intellectual property has shifted dramatically in favour of the former."

We summarize the issues in public policy and market failure in table 4.1. The ability of end users to reproduce and distribute digital work on a large scale using the Internet has limited the effectiveness of regulation based on control of copying, although the overall economic impact on the music, film, and other copyright industries is highly disputed. There has been limited sensitivity to privacy and freedom of expression harms caused by code regulation efforts.

Types of Code Regulation

New copying technologies throughout the twentieth century were first seen as significant challenges to copyright regulation, but then successfully developed into new industries that ultimately benefited rights holders. Player piano rolls, phonograph records, jukeboxes, radio, and cable television all developed in the United States with the aid of copyright exemptions and compulsory licenses, while the video rental industry depended on the first-sale doctrine permitting a wide variety of uses for lawfully owned work (Litman 2001; Ginsburg 2001; Lesk 2003).

Home audiotape and video-recording equipment became mass-market items during the final third of the twentieth century, for the first time putting cheap, high-quality reproduction machinery into consumers' hands. Industry lobbyists complained that "home taping is killing music" and that "the VCR is to the American film producer and the American public as the Boston strangler is to the woman home alone" (Lesk 2003). The executive secretary of the American Federation of Television and Radio Artists told the U.S. Congress that the electronics revolution could "undermine, cripple, and eventually wash away the very industries on which it feeds and which provide employment for thousands of our citizens" (Litman 2001, 106–107). It was only a narrow decision by the U.S. Supreme Court (*Sony* v. *Universal Studios* 1984) that protected the manufacturers of technologies with "substantial non-infringing uses" from liability for copyright infringement by users.

Primitive attempts were made to limit the capabilities of these technologies, with restrictions on tape-to-tape recorders (*CBS Songs* v. *Amstrad Consumer Electronics* 1988; Australian Tape Manufacturers Association 1993). The Cartrivision system prevented consumers from rewinding rented videotapes for viewing a second time, requiring the payment of a fee to a rental store with specialist equipment (Patry 2009).

The first sophisticated attempt to regulate home copying through regulation of home copying technologies came with the introduction of the digital audio tape (DAT) standard. The Recording Industry Association of America opposed the U.S. sale of DAT recorders in the late 1980s, threatening legal action against anyone selling DAT machines (Patry 2009). The recording industry (particularly CBS Records) lobbied Congress for a legal requirement for DAT machines to implement a system called CopyCode, which would prevent the reproduction of prerecorded music. CBS's opposition weakened when it was bought by DAT manufacturer Sony.

Eventually rights holders settled for a requirement that DAT recorders implement a Serial Copy Management System (SCMS) that prevented the reproduction of first-generation copies. This became part of the U.S. Audio Home Recording Act of 1992, which also levied taxes on recorders and blank media (Ginsburg 2001). SCMS was also included in the later Mini-Disc and Digital Compact Cassette formats. At the same time, the United

States introduced a ban on the supply of devices that assisted with unauthorized decryption of satellite programs. This provision was later included in the North American Free Trade Agreement (sec. 1707(a)).

Technological Protection Measures and Rights Management Information
From the late 1980s, the World Intellectual Property Organization (WIPO) debated including in its model copyright law provisions that would require copy protection functionality in all devices used to access copyrighted work. However, because of concerns about the impact on competition and innovation, WIPO instead developed provisions that restricted the circumvention of copy control functionality (Ficsor 2002). Both of WIPO's "Internet treaties" (the Copyright Treaty and Performances and Phonograms Treaty), agreed in 1996, contain provisions that parties "shall provide adequate legal protection and effective legal remedies against the circumvention of effective technological measures that are used by authors in connection with the exercise of their rights."

The United States introduced with the Digital Millennium Copyright Act of 1998 a ban on the circumvention of "effective access controls," as well as of circumvention devices and services. The EU mirrored this restrictive language in article 6 of its Copyright Directive. However, some member states that joined the EU in 2004 gave users more flexibility in national laws, allowing them to circumvent access controls in order to make legitimate use of copyright works (Gasser and Ernst 2006; Kerr 2010).

Because all access to and use of digital work involves temporary reproduction within computing devices and communication networks, copyright has a much greater impact on the use of digital than analog works. It has moved from regulating duplication to regulating access. This has given rights holders much greater influence over the design of digital media technologies than they ever had over printing presses, radios, televisions, or videotape players. It has been backed up by anticircumvention laws that cover all access to protected work, the seeming consequence of ambiguous language adopted by WIPO (Cunard, Hill, and Barlas 2003).

Also included in the WIPO Internet treaties are protections for rights management information that identifies a copyrighted work, its author, or terms and conditions of use. This information can be used to protect the moral rights of authors, such as attribution. It can also facilitate lower transaction costs in acquiring rights to use specific content. These rights management provisions have been much less controversial than the equivalent anticircumvention provisions, mainly because they do not prevent users of such work from exercising their rights under copyright law.

Intermediary Liability

In addition to statutory protection for technological protection measures (TPMs) and rights management information, rights holders have attempted to co-opt Internet intermediaries in copyright enforcement action. This has included lawsuits against the operators of P2P systems such as Napster, Grokster, KaZaA, and Pirate Bay; attempts to gain injunctions requiring ISPs to block access to infringing sites; and legislation to introduce "notice and takedown" liability safe harbors.

The operators of the first mass adoption P2P file-sharing systems were obvious targets of legal action for rights holders. In the first major case, *A&M Records* v. *Napster* (2001), the U.S. Court of Appeals for the Ninth Circuit found that Napster was liable for contributory and vicarious copyright infringement. Napster claimed its system was "capable of substantial non-infringing use," a defense under the 1984 Betamax decision (*Sony* v. *Universal* 1984). But the court found that Napster, which indexed the files being shared by its users, could segregate and prevent infringing uses. By not doing so, it was guilty of contributory infringement, since it "had actual knowledge that specific infringing material is available using its system" (1022).

The trial court ordered Napster to prevent the trading of copyrighted works using its system. The company agreed to pay a $26 million settlement to rights holders and attempted to design a subscription service that would use audio fingerprinting software to block infringement. Because the company could not meet the "near-perfection" standard demanded by the trial judge, it shut down the network (Samuelson 2006). In the meantime, a judge blocked the sale of the company to Bertelsmann Music Group, which led to its bankruptcy (Evangelista 2002).

Later generations of P2P systems were designed so that operators could claim to be lacking such actual knowledge of infringement. Grokster, Streamcast, and Sharman Networks (running KaZaA systems) and Pirate Bay (running a search engine and tracker for the BitTorrent system) were still found by courts to be "inducing" (in the United States), "authorizing" (in Australia), or "assisting" (in Sweden) infringement.

In the United States, the Supreme Court found in *Metro-Goldwyn-Mayer Studios* v. *Grokster* (2005) that "one who distributes a device with the object of promoting its use to infringe copyright, as shown by clear expression or other affirmative steps taken to foster infringement, is liable for the resulting acts of infringement by third parties." Grokster distributed an e-newsletter promoting users' ability to access popular copyright music, did not use filtering tools, and profited from increased advertising revenue as infringement increased. The Court decided that the Sony Betamax defense was not relevant given this active inducement (Ginsburg and Ricketson 2006). Grokster then settled with the plaintiffs, stopping distribution of its software and support for the associated network. It agreed compensation of up to $50 million damages but lacked the resources to pay (Leeds 2005).

The Australian federal court reached its decision regarding KaZaA because it found that Sharman had given ineffective warnings to users about infringement and taken no technical measures to reduce it. Since Sharman's business model depended on maximizing sharing, it did "authorize" infringement. Sharman Networks ultimately agreed to pay $100 million to settle the case and became a legal download service (BBC 2006).

In Sweden, a district court found that Pirate Bay's monitoring of the location of tracker file components and search facility for torrents meant that the site operators were criminally liable for assisting users in making copyright work available (Carrier 2010). On appeal, each of the four defendants was sentenced to several months in prison and fines totaling 46 million kronor, confirmed by the Swedish Supreme Court (TorrentFreak 2012).

In all of these cases, the ongoing relationship between the P2P system operators and users was a key element in a finding of liability. Unlike the sale of tape-to-tape recorders, these organizations' relationships with their users continued after the sale, with upgrades and even help lines, as well as the provision of server capabilities (Ginsburg and Ricketson 2006).

More generally, there was widespread concern as the Internet industry developed in the 1990s that intermediaries such as ISPs could become liable for hosting or carrying infringing material from third parties. Many legal systems include principles such as vicarious and contributory liability (such as the United States) and authorization of distribution (the United

Kingdom and Australia), which could have led to serious damages being awarded by courts (OECD 2011c).

In response, many jurisdictions created safe harbors that protected intermediaries against liability as long as they took specific actions to reduce infringement, created in Title II of the U.S. DMCA and articles 12 to 15 of the EU's Electronic Commerce Directive (ECD). These notice and takedown regimes protect service providers from liability until they have "active knowledge" (usually supplied by notice from a rights holder) of infringing content. At this point providers must expeditiously remove or block access to such content. The DMCA further requires that providers identify infringing customers in response to a subpoena and terminate the accounts of repeat infringers. Both regimes specifically protect ISPs that merely transmit or temporarily cache data for their users; the DMCA also explicitly protects information location tools such as directories and search engines.

One question that has remained controversial is the extent of these safe harbors and particularly the scope of "actual knowledge" (Seltzer 2010). In reviewing U.S. cases, Ginsburg (2008) suggested that some courts had required an "immense crimson banner" rather than a red flag identifying infringement. In *Perfect 10* v. *CC Bill* (2007), the U.S. Ninth Circuit Court of Appeals found that the use of domain names such as "illegal.net" and "stolencelebritypics.com" did not in itself provide knowledge that the featured photographs were infringing, since it could simply be "an attempt to increase their salacious appeal." However, the use of specific movie, TV program, or recording titles might raise greater concern, especially if those titles had been repeatedly included in takedown notices or uploaded by a user who had previously posted infringing content.

A further question is how well these regimes will adapt to new Internet technologies and business models, in particular in the United States, where the DMCA safe harbor is limited to specific types of intermediaries (Lemley 2007). In addition, courts have so far refused to impose any obligation on intermediaries to use more sophisticated technology that might automatically identify infringing works, such as YouTube's ContentID system (Hassanabadi 2011).

ECD explicitly prevents a general monitoring requirement being placed on intermediaries or a requirement to "seek facts or circumstances indicating illegality" (ECD Art. 15). Samuelson (2006) suggested that *Grokster* was a pyrrhic victory for rights holders, since it leaves open the possibility that

P2P system operators may avoid liability for "inducement" by operating the same technology while avoiding making any statements encouraging its use for infringement.

That said, the DMCA and ECD both allow rights holders to take action for injunctive relief against intermediaries; this is explicitly required by Article 8 of the EU Copyright Directive (Directive 2001/29/EC). A test case in the United Kingdom saw movie studios obtain a High Court order against the country's largest ISP, British Telecom, requiring it to block customer access to Newzbin2, a site that allowed users to search for indexes of infringing Usenet files. The judge agreed with the applicants that the order would be justified "even if it only prevented access to Newzbin2 by a minority of users" (Marsden 2012). The judgment referred to a number of similar orders granted by courts in Denmark, Belgium, Italy, Sweden, and Austria (sec. 96). Further orders were quickly made against other ISPs and filesharing sites (*Dramatico Entertainment* v. *British Sky Broadcasting* 2012).

"Graduated Response"

A more recent rights holder strategy has been the introduction of "three strikes" or "graduated-response" schemes, by statute (Taiwan, France, South Korea) or following legal action (Ireland). Under these schemes, ISPs send warnings to customers alleged by rights holders to have been detected committing copyright infringements. After several such warnings to an individual customer, ISPs take further action such as reducing bandwidth, imposing download caps, blocking access to specific sites or P2P protocols, or terminating customer accounts (Yu 2010).

Irish ISP Eircom agreed to introduce such a scheme after legal action by four multinational record companies that wanted to require it to monitor all subscriber traffic for evidence of infringement. The Irish data protection commissioner investigated this scheme after 300 users claimed they had wrongly been accused of infringement (McIntyre 2011).

The first version of France's so-called HADOPI three-strikes law was found to be unconstitutional because it allowed users to be disconnected by an administrative agency. The revised law, approved by the Constitutional Council, allows judicial review of disconnection. The U.K. Digital Economy Act 2010 includes powers for the government to introduce "obligations to limit Internet access" and "injunctions preventing access to

Table 4.2
Types of code and code regulation

Layer	1990s focus on TPMs has largely failed. Now graduated response, ISP blocks.
Location (manufacturers, ISPs, servers, clients)	Previously software and hardware vendors. Now ISP Domain Name System blocking and so on.
Enforcement of code	WIPO Internet treaties require anticircumvention measures. The Digital Millennium Copyright Act 1996 and EU Copyright Directive ban devices and circumvention. HADOPI, DEA, and infringement actions used to impose on ISPs.

locations on the Internet," although for now, these are not to be introduced following the High Court's Newzbin2 injunction, which was issued under earlier legislation.

In its first nine months of operation, the Haute autorité pour la diffusion des oeuvres et la protection des droits sur internet (HADOPI) HADOPI (High Authority of Diffusion of the Artwords and Protection of agency received 18 million notifications from rights holders, identified around 900,000 alleged infringers, and sent 470,000 first warnings and 20,000 second warnings (Columbus 2011). As Patry (2009) observed of earlier takedown notices in the United States, they are sent by outsourced companies that "rely on automated processes, indirect evidence of infringement, but who have a direct financial incentive to send out as many notices as possible" (169).

Table 4.2 summarizes the types of code and code regulation that we have assessed. Code regulation of TPMs in end user systems largely failed to achieved its objectives in the 1990s and early 2000s, and attention has now shifted to blocking at the ISP.

Institutional Political Economy

In the nineteenth and early twentieth centuries, the main copyright actors were publishers and book exporting states. France, Germany, Spain, and the United Kingdom signed the 1886 Berne Convention for the Protection of Literary and Artistic Works on behalf of their colonies. Along with the Berne Union secretariat, they actively encouraged these states to remain signatories after independence. However, subsequent attempts by developing nations to revise the treaty to support their education systems failed, with a 1967 Stockholm Protocol ignored by developed countries and a compromise 1971 revision achieving little (Drahos and Braithwaite 2002).

Later in the twentieth century, the music, film, software, and semiconductor industries became important players. These industries successfully coordinated their lobbying to globalize U.S. intellectual property rules, beginning in 1983 with the Caribbean Basin Recovery Act. This was the first time the U.S. government linked trade and intellectual property policy, blocking U.S. market access to Caribbean nations where government-owned organizations were rebroadcasting copyrighted material without consent. In 1984 rights holder groups persuaded Congress to extend this regime to the U.S. Generalized System of Preferences, which applied to 140 developing countries and territories (Drahos and Braithwaite 2002).

With strong encouragement from rights holders, Congress also amended section 301 of the Trade Act to give the president authority to take action against trading partners that were not giving "adequate and effective" protection to intellectual property. Rights holder groups supplied extensive support to the U.S. trade representative to make use of these powers in bilateral negotiations, putting pressure on trading partners including Korea, Italy, Malaysia, Singapore, India, and Brazil. The European Community created a similar mechanism, the "new commercial policy instrument," which was used to take action against Indonesia, Thailand, and Korea (Drahos and Braithwaite 2002).

These mechanisms were used to persuade developing countries to support the development of the Agreement on Trade-Related Aspects of Intellectual Property Rights (TRIPS) within the General Agreement on Tariffs and Trade (GATT) trade negotiations. Previous international IP discussions had taken place at WIPO, where developing countries had a stronger voice. The other prong of this approach by rights holders, acting mainly through their joint Intellectual Property Committee, was to put pressure on the European Community and the government of Japan—the other main actors in the GATT process. This succeeded in creating a strong TRIPS agreement as part of the establishment of the World Trade Organization. The tight coordination of interests between copyright holders (mainly the publishing, film, recording, and computing industries) and other major rights holders (particularly the patent holders of the pharmaceutical industry) was vital in achieving this outcome (Drahos and Braithwaite 2002).

TRIPS contains a broad range of provisions concerning copyright term, scope, and enforcement. However, it came too early to include anticircumvention provisions protecting TPMs. These provisions were taken up enthusiastically in the United States during the 1990s. President Clinton's Intellectual Property Working Group proposed a new Copyright Act chapter to ban circumvention devices or services, acknowledging that this "provision will not eliminate the risk that protection systems will be defeated, but it will reduce it" (IP Working Group 1995, 177).

The chair of the working group, Bruce Lehman, was also the U.S. representative to WIPO and saw that body as a route to get international agreement on these provisions body as a way to bypass congressional objections (Samuelson 1997). At WIPO, the United States pushed detailed model provisions on circumvention devices or services. However, in the run-up to the finalization of the Internet treaties, the developing world, led by South Africa and with significant input from civil society groups, resisted this language. As a result, Articles 11 and 18 of the Copyright and Performances and Phonographs Treaties, respectively, contain much more generic language (Ficsor 2002).

Further development of protection for TPMs has taken place in bilateral negotiations of free trade agreements (FTAs) with less powerful nations in the developing world and in multilateral groupings of advanced economies. Broad anticircumvention provisions have subsequently appeared in U.S. FTAs with a wide range of countries (Brown 2006) and more recently in EU FTAs (such as Article 10.12 of the EU–South Korea FTA agreed in 2010). They are also included in Article 27(5) of the Anti-Counterfeiting Trade Agreement (ACTA) agreed in 2010 by the United States, the EU, Japan, Canada, Australia, Mexico, Morocco, New Zealand, Korea, Singapore, and Switzerland, but rejected in 2012 by the European Parliament.

While WIPO and its members were busy giving legal protection to content protection mechanisms, TPMs initially received little support from major technology companies and were easily hacked. The mechanisms tested in the 2000 Secure Digital Music Initiative challenge were immediately broken by just one academic research team (Craven et al. 2001). Widely deployed systems, such as the content scrambling system used in the DVD video format, were so easily circumvented they became ridiculed. Many came from small companies with a greater appetite for risk than large rights holders, eager to gain market share (and power) for their platform. This encouraged the deployment of poorly tested systems that could easily be broken and sometimes threatened the security and privacy of users (Halderman and Felten 2006).

Only later did rights holders get buy-in from the major companies producing computing hardware (e.g., Intel and Apple) and operating system software (Microsoft and Apple). These were the only companies that could introduce even vaguely effective digital locks. But while all of these technology giants now include TPMs in their core product lines, market developments, particularly the triumph of the unprotected MP3 music format, driven by ease of use and interoperability, have rendered them irrelevant in the music market. New high-definition protected video formats such as HD-DVD, designed with much greater care and industry input than earlier TPMs, are still being broken (Waters 2007).

Rights holders with hardware divisions such as Sony had a strong incentive to push the use of protected formats best suited to their own players and recorders (Halderman and Felten 2006). But ironically the market power that Apple gained with the success of the iTunes Music Store allowed the company to demand better access to unprotected content from the major recording labels. Very little music is now sold in TPM-protected formats, although Apple still applies it to TV programs, films, and applications in the iTunes store. Amazon is building a similar dominant position in the e-book market, partly based on the control it gains over users through its protected Kindle format.

ISPs were very successful in lobbying for notice and takedown regimes during the late 1990s, protecting them from broader liability for copyright infringement by their users. They have been less successful in resisting graduated-response regimes. The industry costs associated with these regimes can be significant. An Industry Canada study showed that sending a single notification of alleged infringement cost large ISPs C$11.73 and small ISPs C$32.73 (2006). The U.K. government estimated that the three-strikes regime in the Digital Economy Act would cost ISPs 290 million to 500 million pounds (Department for Business 2009).

This difference in political efficacy may reflect the fact that ISPs have more divided interests with three-strikes regimes than over secondary liability protection. P2P traffic is often the largest single category of data flowing over ISP networks, which can lead to significant congestion and bandwidth use charges. Many ISPs are trying to develop businesses as premium content providers, and some are part of larger telecommunications companies that supply cable TV and other paid-for video content. Both of these provide incentives for ISPs to reduce customer copyright infringement, even where they are protected from secondary liability.

In some cases, large rights holders have merged with telecommunications providers such as NBC Universal and Comcast. These conglomerates have the same types of incentives for copyright enforcement as did Sony after it purchased Columbia Pictures Entertainment in 1989 (and later Metro-Goldwyn-Mayer). Rights holder groups are also adept at using music and film stars to lobby politicians, with the author of one independent review of intellectual property policy for the U.K. government later complaining that "politicians often do and say silly things when they come into contact with celebrities" (Gowers 2008).

Civil society groups have campaigned relentlessly for stronger user protections to be included in new copyright laws, with varying success. The Electronic Frontier Foundation led a successful campaign for a DMCA provision that allows the librarian of Congress to exempt certain classes of works from anticircumvention provisions, where users are being "adversely affected . . . in their ability to make noninfringing uses" (sec. 1201(a)(1)(c)). As eastern European countries implemented EU law while becoming members, members of the European Digital Rights coalition campaigned for them to make maximum use of flexibilities in the directive to protect user rights, particularly over anticircumvention rules (Brown 2003). But generally civil society has been kept out of or sidelined in the negotiations leading to copyright law revisions (Litman 2009) and has had to battle for influence in legislatures and courts. At the OECD, the civil society coalition refused to approve Internet policymaking principles developed in a multistakeholder process, since they included liability for copyright infringement in some circumstances for intermediaries (Civil Society Information Society Advisory Committee 2011).

The successful campaign against the 2012 Stop Online Piracy Act (SOPA) introduced in the U.S. House of Representatives demonstrated the political impact of a coalition including Internet technology companies, nonprofit Web sites such as Wikipedia, civil society groups, and the broader user community. SOPA would have given rights holders wide powers against ISPs, search engines, domain name registrars, payment processors, and advertising companies. However, coordinated action, including traditional lobbying, online petitions, consumer boycotts, and a one-day blackout of popular Web 2.0 sites, brought support from President Obama and caused the bill to become stalled in Congress. Rights holders, unused to this level of political pushback, complained that "misinformation" was fueling the campaign. News International chairman Rupert Murdoch complained that "Obama has thrown in his lot with Silicon Valley paymasters who threaten all software creators with piracy, plain thievery" (Wortham and Sengupta 2012).

The SOPA backlash from the user community was strong enough to threaten other legislative attempts to strengthen copyright provision, with several European governments pausing their ACTA ratification processes and the European Commission referring it to the EU Court of Justice for assessment of its compatibility with fundamental rights (Brand 2012). An unprecedented campaign by European civil society groups led the European Parliament to reject the agreement, preventing its ratification by any EU member states (European Digital Rights 2012).

Table 4.3 summarizes the various actors and their contribution to copyright policy. While rights holder associations were successful during most of the development and diffusion of the Internet in shaping policy in their interests, overreach on SOPA led to a setback. It is not yet clear whether this represents a fundamental change in the balance of interests or just signals the need for a change of political tactics.

Outcomes

Copyright policy has traditionally been settled in "dark, smoky rooms" between major corporate stakeholders, facilitated by government (Litman 2001). This produced reasonably stable outcomes so long as these stakeholders were themselves the major target of regulation. Litman characterized this as a process in which publishers, movie studios, recording companies, and TV broadcasters "jointly controlled the playing field" and that it was now "nearly impossible to wrest that control away" (2009, 313). The result was often concentrated markets in information goods. Upstart market entrants were the main innovators, breaking in using radical new technologies and often initially paying little attention to copyright concerns (Wu 2010).

Table 4.3
Institutional political economy

Key actors: national, regional, global	Rights holder associations (International Federation of the Phonographic Industry, Motion Picture Association), U.S/EU/Japan operating at national, EU and international (WIPO, ACTA) level. Have forum-shifted to avoid civil society (WIPO, to WTO, to ACTA). Technology industry and nonprofits.
How legitimate and accountable?	Much policy laundering, forum shifting, exclusion of civil society, bullying of developing world, fantasies that "the answer to the machine is in the machine," not the business model.
Multistakeholderism	Civil society involvement at WIPO weakened anticircumvention measures in Internet treaties (see Drahos 2003) but led to forum shift. Activists had to fight to involve legislators (in the United States and EU) in ACTA debates.
Key technical actor buy-in	Early TPMs produced by small software companies ineffective. Hardware (Trustworthy Computing Group) and operating system vendors now more involved, but still have limited effectiveness. Some ISPs have fought against three-strikes and blocking, although these may be in the interests of large ISPs as they raise entry barriers/reduce neutrality.
Lessons	Code distracted attention from business innovation for more than a decade. Graduated response has been pushed through with little multistakeholder involvement, resulting in policies widely criticized as contrary to freedom of expression. SOPA reaction could be a turning point.

This pattern was reproduced online during the late 1990s and 2000s. Individual developers and start-ups developed MP3 storage and P2P distribution systems that became highly popular but were subject to extremely adverse legal decisions. They gained legitimacy when adopted by companies such as Apple and Spotify that were eventually able to overcome great resistance from the major record labels, revolutionizing the music market. Innovative business models squashed by rights holders during the 2000s, such as My.MP3.com (Ginsburg 2001), have been resurrected in forms that give less control to right-holders.

The production of copyright policy in private, government-facilitated corporate discussions worked reasonably well when the main affected parties had at least partial representation. It has become increasingly problematic as sanctions against unrepresented users have become the main topic of smoking-room discussion. It violates a core democratic right of interested parties to participate, in the words of the U.N. Committee on Economic, Social and Cultural Rights, in "any significant decision making processes that have an impact on their rights and legitimate interests" (Helfer and Austin 2011, 513).

This has also been a problem at the international level. After becoming frustrated with the influence of developing countries at WIPO, major rights holders shifted debate to the GATT trade discussions. Here they successfully pushed the process that led to TRIPS (Drahos and Braithwaite 2002). During a decade of discussions at WIPO over a proposed broadcasting treaty, civil society and developing country representatives complained of exclusion from key decision-making processes, a lack of transparency, and even of public interest briefing papers being thrown into a trash bin in the rest room (Gross 2007). Negotiations over ACTA took place in secret for two years between rich-world economies, with negotiating texts circulated by the U.S. government to industry representatives but withheld from civil society groups as "classified in the interest of national security" (Love 2009).

Even academic copyright experts complain of being ignored. Amsterdam University's Institute for Information Law wrote to the European Commission in 2008, warning that two studies it carried out for the commission had been "almost entirely ignored" in a way that "seem[s] to reveal an intention to mislead the Council and the Parliament, as well as the citizens of the European Union," and that "reinforces the suspicion, already widely held by the public at large, that its policies are less the product of a rational decision-making process than of lobbying by stakeholders" (Hugenholtz 2008). Two independent reviews for the U.K. government felt the need to emphasize that policy should be based on evidence and not "lobbynomics" (Gowers 2006; Hargreaves 2011a). Litman argued that "the copyright war has been intensely polarizing. The conflict has been protracted and venomous. The middle ground seems to have disappeared" (2009, 317).

This is not only a theoretical problem. The exclusion of major stakeholders (users and bodies responsible for fundamental rights and, to a lesser extent, ISPs and technology companies) from negotiations over Internet era copyright reform has produced unbalanced and impractical outcomes at the national and international levels. And it has allowed rights holders to block innovative new business models, which could have increased revenues for creators while better meeting consumer needs, but perhaps threatened short-term revenues (Patry 2009).

Governments and rights holders have found it extremely difficult to extend effective copyright regulation from a relatively small number of companies to the billions of individual users of the Internet. A U.K. government review found that downloading was the most common offense committed by ten to twenty-five year-olds and that 63 percent of downloaders had full knowledge that it was illegal (Gowers 2006). Courts cannot process quickly enough lawsuits against the vast numbers of unauthorized sharers of music, and mistakes and disproportionate punishments seen in such cases have caused enough negative publicity for the recording industry to cause it to focus on more automated, code-based strategies.

These strategies, however, have generally been blunt attempts to bludgeon users of copyrighted work into compliance rather than nudge them toward legal use of work. The first has been to file an automated blizzard of lawsuits and takedown notices against individuals using software to detect sharing of copyright works. This software has proven to be "notoriously inaccurate, leading to lawsuits against people who don't even have computers or who are dead" (Patry 2009, 13) and even against computer printers. Entirely original videos have been taken down from sites such as YouTube as infringing. It can be expensive and time-consuming for affected individuals to have suits dismissed or work put back up, especially if a fair use or dealing defense is involved (Patry 2009).

Motion Picture Association of America president Dan Clickman reportedly responded to these problems by stating, "When you go trawling with a net, you catch a few dolphins" (Doctorow 2007). But such an untargeted approach is hardly appropriate where, in three-strikes systems, inaccurate allegations could lead to individuals' disconnection from the Internet and all of the online services they rely on (Yu 2007).

While courts have found against the suppliers of software and services enabling large-scale infringement using P2P file sharing (most notably in the *Grokster* and *Pirate Bay* cases), this has not been enough to stop individual developers from continuing to supply such software. Indeed, P2P systems have continued to evolve in the face of legal action, removing the central points of failure that enabled Napster to be closed down by the Californian courts.

The legal protection of TPMs has done little to stop the unauthorized access to and sharing of protected work, but has had a negative impact on competition, interoperability, innovation, and security research. TPMs can stop the design and production of compatible or interoperable devices that allow access to protected content, while blocking scientific research into the quality of security mechanisms. They stop users from exercising their fair use or dealing rights, since machines are unable to judge the sometimes subtle factors that courts would assess in allowing these exceptions (Electronic Frontier Foundation 2010), meaning, for example, that the World Blind Union is still finding that TPMs are preventing the visually impaired from using text-to-speech software to access protected e-books.

TPMs can even sometimes threaten the safety of users' computers and the Internet more broadly—to the point where officials from the U.S. Department of Homeland Security warned that "in the pursuit of protection of intellectual property, it's important not to defeat or undermine the security measures that people need to adopt in these days" (Mulligan and Perznowski 2007, 1174).

Consumer resistance eventually resulted in the abandonment of TPM restrictions on most downloaded music, although it is still a central part of the strategy of the movie industry, where it may better fit consumer desires to rent rather than own films. It is not yet clear whether the greater efforts to provide consumer-friendly legal services for online movie access will be sufficient to avoid the widespread infringement suffered by recorded music once sufficient bandwidth becomes widely available to consumers.

Freedom of expression can be greatly damaged by TPMs that prevent lawful uses of copyrighted work, or the blocking of Internet sites or users alleged to be infringing copyright without a full judicial proceeding (La Rue 2011). The DMCA encourages Web sites to immediately take down content when served with notice, but users are rarely in a position to make use of the DMCA's put-back provisions (Lemley 2007).

Demands from rights holders that ISPs disconnect customers and block access to allegedly infringing sites are particularly dangerous for freedom of expression. In a report to the U.N. Human Rights Council, the U.N.'s special rapporteur on freedom of expression said he was "alarmed by proposals to disconnect users from Internet access if they violate intellectual property rights" (La Rue 2011). The European Commission vice-president for fundamental rights, Viviane Reding (2012), responded to the ACTA debate with a statement that "copyright protection can never be a justification for eliminating freedom of expression or freedom of information. That is why for me, blocking the Internet is never an option."

But Pamela Samuelson's comment still rings true: "all too often in recent years, when courts have perceived a conflict between intellectual property rights and free speech rights, property has trumped speech" (2001). The First Amendment has a limited impact on private action, although it can be argued that copyright enforcement implicates this (Yu 2010), but European governments have no such excuse given their "positive duties" to secure their citizens' rights under the European Convention on Human Rights.

Large rights holders have spent nearly two decades trying to alter the nature of the Internet and personal computer to fit business models relying on scarcity and the control of copies, with little success. After trying all of the alternatives, some have finally begun to work seriously with innovators developing technologies that can remunerate creators without taking control of individuals' PCs or Internet connections.

These alternatives include systems such as YouTube's content ID fingerprinting system, which allows rights holders to choose whether automatically detected infringing videos should be investigated and taken down or, alternatively, to share in the advertising revenues generated by such videos. "All-you-can-eat" subscription services such as Spotify give paying customers streaming access to very large libraries of licensed musical work, coming close to the "celestial jukebox" envisaged in the early days of the Internet. Major Chinese search engine Baidu struck a deal with Universal, Warner, and Sony to allow users access to a large catalogue of works on an advertising-supported basis (Xinhua 2011a). And a review for the U.K. government suggested the development of a "digital copyright exchange," which would enable the automated trading of licenses and reduce the cost of dispute resolution (Hargreaves 2011a, 28).

Many of these technologies could have been developed much earlier given cooperation from rights holders. The BBC complained that it took "nearly five years" to put together the licenses required to launch its iPlayer service (Ofcom 2006). Technology start-ups complain that licensing nego-

Table 4.4
Outcomes and divergences

Transparency	Unclear causation from present system—Hargreaves (2011a) analysis very useful; e.g., digital copyright exchange. More transparency to more just solutions?
Enforcement	Problem of the second user—individuals can be a network and succeeding infringements impossible to police (as well as 'fair use'). Enforcement against corporations possible and legal business models and licences are effective enforcement in the sense of recompense.
	3 Strikes preposterous
Interoperability	DRM closes off interoperability—iTunes prior to unlocking, for instance.
Efficiency	Levy one option to avoid enforcement?

tiations can take an inordinate amount of time, have inconsistent results, and sometimes result in threats of legal action (Hargreaves 2011a). The evolution of digital copyright policy provides an abject lesson in the damage caused to innovation and the public interest of allowing self-interested industry groups to drive policy, excluding other stakeholders and basing regulatory decisions on "lobbynomics."

The outcomes and divergences of policy are summarized in table 4.4.

5 Censors

The debate over control of harmful and illegal material on the public Internet has developed from early discussion in the United States over online obscenity, which led to the Communications Decency Act of 1996. It now spans totalitarian regimes' firewalls, such as China's Golden Shield network blocking system and its 2009 Green Dam project to install filtering software on all new PCs, to democracies' self-regulatory actions, such as the U.K. Cleanfeed-Child Abuse Image Content system and German search engine self-regulation (Marsden 2011).

European nations and U.S. attorneys general (McIntyre 2013) have moved away from a self-regulatory approach toward a coregulatory approach in which ISPs and police cooperate in mandatory filtering of inadvertent viewing (as well as production, consumption, and sale of illegal content), with content blocking widened from child pornography to hate speech to extreme speech (Powell and Hills 2010). The institutionalization of this state-sanctioned and audited approach presents significant new challenges to freedom of expression on the Internet and has led to calls for an Internet bill of rights in the European Parliament, U.S. Congress, and elsewhere (La Rue 2011).

Public Policy and Market Failure

Social Impact of Technology

One requirement driving the Internet's original design was the ability to survive thermonuclear war (Baran 1964; Ziewitz and Brown 2013; Cohen-Almagor 2011). Whether a deliberate design feature or unintended consequence, the Internet's routing system means that data packets can take a wide range of routes from sender to recipient, reducing the ability of intermediate points to block communications (Clark, Field, and Marr 2010; Kleinrock 2010; Leiner et al. 1998).

This technical detail has had a remarkable impact on the availability of information in developed and emerging economies. While many countries take steps to block access to certain types of content within their own borders (York 2010), censorship is harder to achieve online than with physical newspapers and books and with radio and TV broadcasts. The Internet has enabled much greater worldwide access to news and opinion than any previous medium. However, it has also made it harder for governments to block individual access to content "in the interests of national security, territorial integrity or public safety, for the prevention of disorder or crime, for the protection of health or morals, for the protection of the reputation or rights of others, for preventing the disclosure of information received in confidence, or for maintaining the authority and impartiality of the judiciary" (European Convention on Human Rights 1951, sec. 10.2).

Most governments have placed requirements on ISPs and other Internet intermediaries within their own jurisdiction to block access to certain content that is illegal under national laws, by statute and more informal pressure. This almost universally includes child abuse images; incitement to violence, and genocide denial in many countries, particularly in Europe; "glorification" of terrorism; and, in a smaller number of countries, sites encouraging suicide or anorexia. Repressive regimes block a much wider range of sites about controversial issues that might pose a threat to the government (Deibert et al. 2010).

The legitimacy and acceptability of such interventions raise ethical as well as practical questions. Who has the right to judge whether particular content should be shown? When does the intervention amount to inappropriate or unethical censorship?

The EU's approach has been fragmented, partly due to the division of policy responsibility among the three commissioners for the information society, fundamental rights, and home affairs. The last has proposed mandatory blocking of online gambling, child (and adult) pornography, suicide sites, and terrorism supporting Web sites. A leaked January 2011 commission document on online gambling revealed that Domain Name System blocking, the preferred approach, could be used for gambling as well as child pornography blocking (neither approach tackles the source of offending material, only user access). Civil society group European Digital Rights (2011) reported that "the document explicitly recognises that blocking is 'technically challenging and costly' and that blocking will leave a 'significant' residual level of illegal sites publicly available . . . and that regular updating of a blocking list will be 'costly.'"

The U.S. government is severely constrained by the U.S. Constitution in trying to prevent the publication of almost any type of information. However, administrations such as Richard Nixon's (regarding the leaked Pentagon Papers, a sensitive history of U.S. operations in Vietnam) and George W. Bush's (over the existence of the National Security Agency warrantless wiretapping program) used FBI investigations and legal actions in an attempt to stop the publication of politically sensitive news.

The Obama administration attempted to stop the online distribution of over 250,000 State Department cables allegedly leaked by a U.S. soldier to the WikiLeaks site. WikiLeaks threatens state secrecy or censorship of reporting of its own activities (Benkler 2011a). WikiLeaks collaborated with several European newspapers and the *New York Times* in publishing redacted versions of these cables. They showed the extent of U.S. influence over other countries and, perhaps more pertinent, the graphic accounts from U.S. ambassadors and other senior state officials of the extraordinary levels of corruption in countries as diverse as Saudi Arabia, India, and Kazakhstan. In response, the U.S. government threatened to put the WikiLeaks founder and director, Julian Assange, on trial in the United States and arrested the presumed provider of the cables, U.S. Army soldier Bradley Manning.

As an Australian national, Assange can hardly be described as a traitor to the United States, despite the numerous outraged accusations from congressmen and media commentators. Following the precedent in the Pentagon Papers case (*New York Times Co.* v. *United States* 1971), it is also unclear that Manning would be found guilty of the most serious charge, breaching official secrecy without just cause, under the U.S. Espionage Act 1917.

The assistant secretary of state for public affairs, Philip J. Crowley, resigned in March 2011 after he made remarks in a small seminar at the Massachusetts Institute of Technology about the treatment of Manning in custody: "The exercise of power in today's challenging times and relentless media environment must be prudent and consistent with our laws. . . .

What is happening to Manning is ridiculous, counterproductive and stupid, and I don't know why the [Department of Defense] is doing it" (Smith 2011).

Fundamental Rights

Free speech has been a key part of the U.S. Constitution since the 1791 adoption of the First Amendment, and protected in the 1789 French Déclaration des droits de l'Homme et du Citoyen as "one of the most precious of the rights of man." Article 19 of the Universal Declaration of Human Rights (UDHR) states that:

Everyone has the right to freedom of opinion and expression; this right includes freedom to hold opinions without interference and to seek, receive and impart information and ideas through any media and regardless of frontiers.

This right has been interpreted robustly in relation to online communications. The U.N. special rapporteur on freedom of expression, Frank La Rue, told the U.N. Human Rights Council that the Internet's "unique and transformative nature" enables individuals to exercise a range of human rights and promotes "the progress of society as a whole" (2011, 1). He expressed deep concern that "mechanisms used to regulate and censor information on the Internet are increasingly sophisticated, with multi-layered controls that are often hidden from the public" (9). And he found that "states' use of blocking or filtering technologies is frequently in violation of their obligation to guarantee the right to freedom of expression," since they were not clearly established in law, were for purposes not listed in the International Covenant on Civil and Political Rights, used secret blocking lists, were unnecessary or disproportionate, or lacked review by a judicial or independent body. He also found that imposing liability on ISPs and other intermediaries for illegal content "leads to self-protective and overbroad private censorship, often without transparency and the due process of the law," concluding that "censorship measures should never be delegated to a private entity" and "no one should be held liable for content on the Internet of which they are not the author" (13).

The European Convention on Human Rights and EU Charter of Fundamental Rights protect freedom of expression using very similar language to the UDHR, but Europe's highest courts have heard few cases about government censorship of the Internet. The European Court of Human Rights has shown greater tolerance of laws criminalizing denial of genocide and incitement to racial hatred than would be expected in the United States, for obvious historical reasons.

In 2003, the Council of Europe drew up an additional protocol to its Cybercrime Convention (ETS no. 189) that requires criminal sanctions for the distribution of "racist and xenophobic materials" (Council of Europe 2003). Its Committee of Ministers has recommended that filtering should generally be left to individual users and national blocking systems "assessed both before and during their implementation to ensure that the effects of the filtering are proportionate to the purpose of the restriction and thus necessary in a democratic society" (2008).

The Assembly of the Council of Europe issued a resolution in 2011 welcoming "the publication, in particular via the WikiLeaks site, of numerous diplomatic reports confirming the truth of the allegations of secret detentions and illegal transfers of detainees published by the Assembly in 2006 and 2007. It is essential that such disclosures are made in such a way as to respect the personal safety of informers, human intelligence sources and secret service personnel" (2011b, sec. 9). The second sentence is presumably in response to the leak and later publication of unredacted U.S. State Department cables in early September 2011.

Repeated U.S. congressional attempts during the 1990s to censor Internet "indecency" were struck down in ringing terms by U.S. courts. The Supreme Court upheld a Philadelphia court ruling that "as the most participatory form of mass speech yet developed, the Internet deserves the highest protection from governmental intrusion. . . . Just as the strength of the Internet is chaos, so the strength of our liberty depends upon the chaos and cacophony of the unfettered speech the First Amendment protects" (*American Civil Liberties Union* v. *Reno* 1997). The furthest the courts have allowed Congress to go is to require libraries and schools receiving specific federal funding to install Internet filters under the Children's Internet Protection Act of 2000.

Iceland's crowd-sourced new national constitution contains robust protection of freedom of expression and the freedom of the media and Internet (Republic of Iceland 2011, Articles 14–16), in response in part to the Icelandic Modern Media Initiative of 2010, proposed by parliamentarian Birgitta Jónsdóttir (Santo 2011). Article 14 states in part: "Censorship and other comparable impediments to the freedom of opinion must never be enacted into law. . . . The access to the Internet and information

Table 5.1
Public policy and market failure

Social impact of technology	Ubiquitous use of broadband gives rise to call for parental controls. Widespread use of blogs and other types of political expression causes state concern leading to censorship. Both have increased since 2000, with users split between those opposed to private censorship mediated by state and others' apparent preference for a walled garden safety environment.
Policy drivers—entry barriers, network and scale effects, competition	Censorship imposes entry costs through technology choice for blocking. Deep packet inspection equipment for traffic monitoring is a dual-use technology, also capable of surveillance and blocking.
Fundamental rights in policy design	Appeal and due process almost entirely lacking. Overall frameworks subject to little democratic scrutiny.
Lessons	Privatization of censorship endemic (even in China coregulation is the claimed model). Greater regional and international transparency standards needed (La Rue 2011).

technology shall not be limited unless by a court verdict and subject to the same conditions as apply to the limits of the expression of opinion." As the youngest parliamentary constitutional standard (albeit with the oldest parliament), it is intended to present a model for a third millennium constitution, as compared with earlier French, U.S., and indeed universal models.

Table 5.1 summarizes these public policy and economic issues. States have increasingly pressured private intermediaries, especially ISPs, to limit access to a wide range of content, from political debate in authoritarian regimes, to gambling sites, to images of child abuse in almost all countries. These controls are often opaque and lacking in due process and democratic scrutiny.

Types of Code Regulation

Electronic Frontier Foundation cofounder John Gilmore famously stated, "The Net interprets censorship as damage and routes around it" (Elmer-DeWitt, Jackson and King 1993).

Many governments have attempted to prevent this rerouting by requiring ISPs to partially block access to foreign Internet sites, or preventing users from accessing computers connected to the Internet. Examples include proposals by Iran for a "halal" Internet with extremely limited connectivity to other countries, the infamous and leaky "Great Firewall of China," or the Australian single filtered point of international connectivity of the late 1990s (Deibert et al. 2008, 2010).

In 2011, the Egyptian, Libyan, and Syrian governments switched off both Internet and mobile telephony networks in the midst of revolutionary upheaval. A more effective, random, and violent example is the late 1990s Chinese government practice of arresting a random selection of cybercafé users simply for being on the Internet, and interrogating them (Keller 2000).

Assuming that countries choose to allow citizens to use the Internet, there are at least three points of control. The first is self-censorship by the user. This can be in the form of using software filters on end systems to prevent access to most obscene or politically sensitive content, or simply through exercising self-restraint out of habitual fear of state surveillance.

This fear can be less constraining in the Internet environment, where pseudonymity and anonymity are common features and encryption can make traffic extremely difficult to monitor. Recognizing this, many governments both democratic and autocratic have proposed removing such features. These policies are designed to ensure that all users can always be personally identified when using the Internet by such requirements as pre-registration and barring access for suspected pseudonymous individuals.

Corporations have carried out the same policies for security or advertising purposes (to prevent spam or ensure more closely targeted advertisements), with the result that many individuals' identities were at risk of disclosure via Facebook to authorities during the Arab Spring in 2011, though rival social network Twitter provided somewhat more robust user identity control (Brown and Korff 2011).

Chapter 7 describes how deep packet inspection can block encrypted connections, permitting only content transmitted "in the clear." Governments can address corporate willingness to control identity by simply making real identity registration a condition of licensing corporations. China has used such conditions to exclude many U.S. corporations, substituting local versions of Skype, social network QQ, search engine Baidu, and other rivals to international applications and services.

Use of real names exposes users to both the risk of political reaction to comments and the prospect of loss of personal data when companies fail to protect that real name registration. South Korea abandoned its policy of requiring user registration linked to national identity number on large Web sites (Index on Censorship 2011) after a data breach exposed 35 million users' personal information (Xinhua 2011b). The leading international human rights bodies issued a joint condemnation of mandatory policies on real names in 2005 (U.N. Special Rapporteur 2005), repeated in 2011 (Akdeniz 2011; La Rue 2011).

The identity of users can also be revealed following court proceedings. U.K. authorities and individuals have been able to secure Twitter, Google, and Facebook account holders' details through what are known as Norwich Pharmacal orders that make these international (California-based) sites codefendants in actions before English courts (Caddick and Tomlinson 2010). U.S. John Doe orders produce similar results.

Beyond users lie ISPs. The user's local ISP will generally operate under license from the national government and can therefore be controlled with some ease. Upstream ISPs can apply filters when accepting traffic from another ISP; for governments that is a particular concern when the handover is an international gateway.

There are various procedures to ensure filtering, all relying on a combination of:

• Upstream labeling (using standards such as the World Wide Web Consortium's now-obselete Platform for Internet Content Selection, PICS) applied by content creators to allow users to apply filters to unwanted content ("blacklisting") or to access only trusted content ("white listing")

• Flagging of potentially harmful sites by users and ISPs, with users of the ISP contacting a hot line (a contact center designed to report and investigate the complaint), with lists of sites maintained by hot lines and police agencies.

In *American Civil Liberties Union* v. *Reno* (1997), the U.S. Supreme Court decided that the virtually unanimous will of Congress to censor the Internet by mandatory filtering was unconstitutional chilling of speech. *Reno* led directly to the emergence of Internet Content Rating Association (ICRA) in 1999 from PICS and the U.S. Recreational Software Advisory Council system for computer games (Lessig and Resnick 1998; Machill, Hart, and Kaltenhauser 2003). The Communications Decency Act inspired standards experts to attempt to introduce a wide-ranging labeling scheme for Internet content, the PICS. Resnick and Miller (1996) explain that "the World Wide Web Consortium intended to create a viewpoint-independent content labelling system, and thus to allow individuals to selectively access or block certain content, without government or content provider censorship." As a scheme, its urgency was somewhat reduced by the Supreme Court's *Reno* decision.

The Communications Decency Act was almost immediately replaced by the Child Online Protection Act 1998, which established the Commission on Child Online Protection, whose 2000 report forms the basis for the Family Online Safety Institute's educational approach to child protection from harmful content. The 1998 act was suspended and overturned, and finally the government's last appeal was refused a hearing by the Supreme Court in early 2009. The lack of market adoption of ICRA has been attributed in part to lack of incentives for Web sites unless rating can interoperate with other standards, or more radically unless rating is made mandatory.

Campaign for Democracy and Technology cofounder Daniel Weitzner stated that CDT broadly supported the W3C decision to develop PICS, the Electronic Freedom Foundation was ambivalent, and the ACLU against it, but, he continued, "What was at stake for the industry was their chance to prove they didn't have to be treated like the mass media, and that was the result in the *Reno* decision. . . . The coordination was between the early Internet industry, some part of the civil liberties community and the White House—Gore, Magaziner, Clinton—who gave their blessing right after the *Reno* decision appeared" (Marsden 2011, 114). This was classic industry-led self-regulation that "worked in that it was the right approach, but not as regards interoperability with other incentives for individual website owners."

Co-implementation on child abuse images is clearly not a self-regulatory issue. Where real issues existed, there were some differences between the market-driven U.S. approach ("not self-regulatory but technology will provide the tools") and EU coregulatory standards-based approach toward ICRA. Weitzner concluded, "I don't think there were ever clear expectations set by policymakers as to results, nor were there adequate resources provided for deployment. To my mind that is putting a figleaf on the problem" (Marsden 2011, 114).

Tracking the progress of such labeling standards sheds light on the manner in which technical standards can be used to create content classification and, ultimately, content standards. At this interface, standards bodies are technical fora with clear influence on content standards, an excellent example of the influence of technology standards on policy.

Filtering and labeling was the obvious tool to ensure that end users had the choice of which content to view without censorship (Berman and Weitzner 1995). It became the default solution to child protection with PICS, an immediate response to the threat of legal classification of indecent content in the United States. It emerged from a meeting organized by the World Wide Wide Consortium in June 1995 to discuss technical solutions for Internet content regulation (Shah and Kesan 2003). Support for the development of Web site quality labels became part of the European Safer Internet Action Plan 1999–2002. Its scheme was taken up, promoted, and adapted by ICRA, and by 2005 it was adapted for use on mobile Internet sites. While support for ICRA included government funding and adoption by some Web sites, most Web sites choose not to label their pages.

In Europe, hot lines were the preferred approach to notify ISPs about potential illegal child pornography (all other illegal content being the responsibility of the notice and takedown regime), with the first hot lines established in 1996. The Internet Watch Foundation hot line had a coregulatory arrangement with police forces in the United Kingdom, though a more formal regulatory arrangement was needed in other countries. The hot lines inspected the material and passed to police for prosecution any material that on scrutiny appeared to be illegal. This case-by-case approach was replaced in 2002 by the removal of entire Usenet groups, leading to broader censorship as it was recognized that some innocent material was bound to be removed.

A blunt approach to blocking Web content is to block all traffic to and from specified Web servers (based on their IP address, or by misdirection of their domain name). Pennsylvania took this approach with a law passed in 2002 (18 Pennsylvania Statutes sec. 7330) that required ISPs to block access to servers within five business days of a notice from the state attorney general.

A district court blocked the enforcement of this law as contrary to the First and Fourteenth Amendments and because it found that orders targeting fewer than 400 sites had resulted in the blocking of nearly 1.2 million innocent sites (*Center for Democracy and Technology* v. *Pappert*, 2004). This occurred because Web servers commonly host more than one Web site—in one case examined by the court, over 10,000 sites. Similar overblocking problems have been seen with government and court orders blocking sites such as YouTube in India, Pakistan, and Turkey (Deibert et al. 2010).

In 2003, British Telecom (BT), the largest retail and by far the largest wholesale ISP in the United Kingdom, decided as a matter of "corporate social responsibility" to design a more sophisticated system, internally named Cleanfeed, to block its users from accessing overseas child pornography, which had been largely eradicated from the United Kingdom (primary hosting locations then were the United States and Russia). In order to ascertain which specific Web pages and images to block, it used a list of uniform resource locators (URLs) supplied by the industry-funded Internet Watch Foundation, which became known as the Child Abuse Image Content (CAIC) list.

BT's method of dealing with the blocking of specific URLs was a more targeted approach than others adopted by Nordic and Scandinavian ISPs, and discussion ensued in the European Telecommunications Standard Institute about creating a standard for its method of blocking URLs (Marsden 2011). Other ISPs had used DNS blocking, and the CAIC list is harder to circumvent, although users determined to view banned material can use proxy servers and connect to servers using encrypted links or nonstandard ports.

Cleanfeed blocks only what is explicitly blacklisted rather than an entire domain. However, the chaotic result of an attempt to block an image on Wikipedia in early 2009 revealed both the problematic governance and lack of transparency of the CAIC list, the ad hoc nature of Internet Watch Foundation procedures, and the ability of users to reverse-engineer the blocking system (McIntyre 2010; Clayton 2005).

Cleanfeed's success has led others to propose the system be used for purposes other than child pornography, a mission creep that has resulted in European Commission discussion. In the United Kingdom, it was first proposed in 2007 that Cleanfeed/CAIC blocking be made mandatory, then that "extreme" adult pornography be blocked, as well as terrorism-supporting Web sites. In Australia, the proposed national system for mandatory filtering of all hard-core pornography—adult, child, extreme and otherwise—has also been named Cleanfeed (though the plan first made in 2007 was delayed until at least mid-2013 at the conclusion of a convergence of communications review.)

Table 5.2
Types of code and code regulation

Layer	Application or network or both. For example, Chinese ISPs use Golden Shield to filter at entry point to network (and nation), supported by filtering software in client PCs. Western nations typically at network (e.g., Cleanfeed) and filters at client level.
Location	Clients for filters, manufacturers, and ISPs for transport-level filters.
Enforcement of code	National: Egyptian nihilist plug pulling, but negation of code. "Chilling effect" of police enforcement. Golden Shield national solution.

The U.K. government has now persuaded major ISPs to ask new customers whether adult content should be blocked on their own connection (Curtis 2011), and may require that they also ask this question of existing customers. Moreover, Justice Richard Arnold made plain in *Twentieth Century Fox* v. *BT* (2011) that the relatively low cost of using Cleanfeed to block retail customers' access to the Newzbin file-sharing index was what convinced him to impose an injunction, and which is likely to pass muster with the European Court test in *Scarlet Extended* (2011).

We summarize the types of censorship code in table 5.2. This operates mainly at the network layer at users' access ISPs, and at the application layer on users' end-systems in filtering software.

Institutional Political Economy

Kreimer (2006) restated governments' dilemmas in regulating Internet content: "Even where speakers are theoretically subject to sanctions, the exponential increase in the number of speakers with potential access to broad audiences multiplies the challenge for censors seeking to suppress a message" (13). Given the bottleneck control over the user experience provided by ISPs, co- and self-regulatory initiatives populated by these critical actors are central in Internet content regulation (Marsden 2011).

European ISP filtering has emerged from EU-funded labeling and anti-pedophile sexual image reporting hot lines. European funding for hot lines to remove suspected child pornography through reports to the police in each member state continues with multiyear EU funding.

The best-known and oldest example is the U.K. Internet Watch Foundation, but these institutions exist throughout Europe. McIntyre (2010) has considered the U.K. example alongside Ireland, which has a similarly freestanding body. Other European governments have instituted a more formal coregulatory structure with direct reporting to the police. Coordination mechanisms such as the EC Safer Internet Forum play an important role, together with European organizations representing hot lines, national ISP associations, user awareness nodes (Insafe), and ICRA.

Civil society freedom of speech and anticensorship organizations play a role in trying to prevent overzealous censorship. Empirical studies of ISP blocking of content (in the claim of breach of copyright) suggest such a danger is real (Deibert et al. 2010). Conventional labeling and rating methods may not be easily applicable to inappropriate user-generated and posted content.

In 2010 the European Commission proposed a directive that would require EU-wide blocking of sites containing child abuse images. The impact assessment focused wholly on crime and child protection rather than including wider free expression and cost–benefit impacts (Staff Working Document 2009), admitting that Article 21 on blocking access to child pornography on the Internet is not within Council of Europe Convention CETS No. 201, which the remainder of the proposal is meant to fully implement. Blocking proved the main cause of controversy, with critics claiming it to be expensive, pointless, and a diversion from the more effective prosecution of offenders (European Digital Rights 2011).

The proposed directive required that "blocking of access shall be subject to adequate safeguards, in particular to ensure that the blocking is limited to what is necessary, that users are informed of the reason for the blocking and that content providers, as far as possible, are informed of the possibility of challenging it." However, such adequate safeguards were not detailed at all, a lacuna in view of state privatization of censorship and known previous inaccuracies and errors in blocking lists. By contrast, European commissioner Viviane Reding (2009) has stated, "We will only be able to reap the full social and economic benefits of a fast moving technological landscape if we manage to safeguard the openness of the Internet" in her speech calling for an EU version of the U.S. Global Online Freedom Act.

After ferocious opposed lobbying by advocates of child protection against digital rights, the European Parliament's Civil Liberties Committee voted by 50 to 0 to remove blocking provisions from the directive (European Digital Rights 2011).

Regulation Using Financial Intermediaries

Commercial application providers, as well as charities that have significant bandwidth costs or rely on Internet-based fundraising, can be effectively censored by regulation of payment or hosting intermediaries. Three somewhat effective examples were targets of U.S. government action: individuals listed in the database of a company that had been used to process payments to commercial providers of child pornography; users of gambling sites based in the small Caribbean island state of Antigua; and readers of the anonymized political source site WikiLeaks. We take these in turn chronologically as the form of censorship in each case became more complex and arguably less successful (as the WikiLeaks material remains available freely even when WikiLeaks itself suffers financial hardship).

In the first case, in 1999, customer details were obtained from a credit card payment processor in the United States, with enforcement taking place in both the United States and Europe (notably the United Kingdom) against several thousand individuals. The identities were clearly available, and payment in itself was represented by police as a motive to commit an illegal action. Several suicides resulted from the publicity stemming from the police operations (McIntyre 2013).

In the second case of offshore gambling, in which a 2006 law banned financial intermediaries from processing payments to or from gambling operators, the case was more complicated for three reasons. First, the underlying activity was illegal only for residents in particular geographies (notably the state of New York, whose attorney general, Eliott Spitzer, was energetically involved in prosecution of the case), but was not illegal in the location where the companies were based. Second, by securing the compliance of the credit card companies, the U.S. government arguably exceeded its jurisdiction in that not all transactions and account holders could be proved to be within the jurisdiction and therefore committing a crime. Third, this activity was shown to be illegal under world trade law, notably in a case before the World Trade Organization (Wu 2007). It was somewhat ironic that the United States should be arguing that several

Chinese government activities against U.S. corporations for engaging in behaviors that are illegal and considered immoral in China should reflect almost exactly the legal arguments that the United States made before the World Trade Organization appellate tribunal (WT/DS285/AB/R 2005). The United States signaled that it was closed for gambling to non-U.S. actors (Wohl 2009).

With the added complication that British citizens have been arrested when in transit through Texas airports for breach of U.S. gambling regulation, it is clear that unlike child abuse images, out-of-jurisdiction gambling sites are much more difficult to regulate. Scott (2007) notes, "The opportunistic arrest of the in-transit chief executive of the UK-based internet gambling company *Betonsports* in Texas in July 2006 is reported to have triggered the company's withdrawal from the US online market and the chief executive's dismissal." This airport transit arrest may remind Internet scholars of the arrest of Felix Somm Munich, the managing director of CompuServe Germany, in 1998, due to his company's failure to block customer access to child pornography (Bender 1999).

Scott (2007) examines case studies of attempts in the United States to prohibit gambling and the U.K. acceptance in the Gambling Act 2006 of the Gibraltar-based offshore status of many key corporate actors. He states: "Achieving compliance with regulatory objectives is challenging enough within domestic regimes where behavioural responses are difficult to predict. But, where that regime involves cross-border business activities, the complex relationships between regulators, businesses and consumers may conspire to frustrate the intentions of the policy makers . . . the near impossibility of preventing determined punters from engaging in internet gaming."

The third case, of WikiLeaks, is even more convoluted. It is not clear that its activities are illegal, whether inside or outside the United States. It is not clear that the U.S. government took any direct action to curtail its activities. It is also uncertain which types of state actions against its founder, Julian Assange, might have been incidental or deliberate attempts to disincentivize the organization from full pursuit of its activities.

The notable elements of the WikiLeaks dispute with the United States and other governments are threefold: U.S. pressure on corporations dealing with WikiLeaks; European governments' legal pressure on Assange and WikiLeaks; and Arab and other countries' reaction to the exposure of corruption and thus proof of the political danger they faced from the transparency of political processes offered by WikiLeaks and, more broadly, the Internet.

First, the United States apparently put executive pressure on U.S. corporations not to host WikiLeaks servers and successfully obtained information related to the Twitter and e-mail accounts of WikiLeaks sympathizers and presumed collaborators, including an Icelandic member of parliament (Zetter 2011). There was no official communication from the State Department, but politicians such as Senator Joe Lieberman had openly threatened both Assange and the hosting company for his content, Amazon Cloud Services, with retribution for what Lieberman referred to as Assange's "treason." Amazon terminated its WikiLeaks hosting agreement unilaterally, claiming that denial of service attacks on WikiLeaks had created a breach in Amazon's terms of service and that it was ending the contract to protect its other clients.

WikiLeaks relocated its servers to Swedish ISP Bahnhof, with a forty-seven-minute hiatus in service. It responded on Twitter, stating, "If Amazon are so uncomfortable with the First Amendment, they should get out of the business of selling books." Various U.S. financial corporations then stopped cooperating with the WikiLeaks Foundation, among them PayPal, MasterCard, Visa, and Bank of America. U.S. government employees were warned not to view WikiLeaks cables, and the U.S. Air Force computer network blocked the newspaper partners.

The assistant secretary of state for public affairs stated, "We do not control private networks. We have issued no authoritative instructions to people who are not employees of the Department of State" (MacAskill 2010). However, the lack of a direct call to financial and hosting partners of WikiLeaks did not prevent extralegal pressures being applied effectively (Benkler 2011a).

Where direct orders were made by the U.S. government for details of WikiLeaks' linked social media account holders, only Twitter is known to have resisted the executive order, though it was forced to reveal details in March 2011 following a court hearing (Parr 2011). The arguments rejected by the federal judge were presented by those objecting in the case: Icelandic Member of Parliament Birgitta Jonsdottir, Dutch activist Rop Gongrijp, and U.S. security researcher Jacob Appelbaum, together with interveners the Electronic Frontier Foundation and the American Civil Liberties Union.

European authorities reacted to WikiLeaks ambiguously. The Swiss government–owned PostBank suspended Assange's personal account as the conditions for its establishment were fradulently ignored, since he is not a Swiss citizen. In Germany, PayPal refused to accept donations for the Wau Holland Foundation that supported WikiLeaks through donations.

The third governmental reaction to WikiLeaks in censorship terms was that of repressive regimes whose embarrassing secrets were leaked in the confidential cables. These governments broadly censored access to the WikiLeaks site and the various mirror sites that were created after November 28, 2011. Within a week of the first denial-of-service attack on WikiLeaks, there were over a thousand mirror sites in operation. The responses ranged to outright censorship in Zimbabwe and many Arab countries (Black 2010), as well as banning newspapers responsible for the cable releases, effectively a countrywide equivalent of the U.S. government filter.

There were two unexpected results of this blatant censorship, both a symptom of the new political reality of online organization. The first was the Distributed Denial of Service attacks by hacker group Anonymous against the governments of Tunisia and Zimbabwe, as well as various U.S. government sites and financial institutions. The attack took place throughout the two months after the cables were released. The second was the uprisings in Tunisia and Egypt, which had strong censorship but also a strong Internet-literate middle class that had accessed the cables illicitly. Electronic media played a small but significant part in these upheavals.

It is also clear that both text messaging and Internet access were suspected by the Egyptian authorities of being major causes of the earlier revolt in Tunisia, as the Egyptian government chose to shut down mobile networks and Internet access in January 2011, including networks that were majority owned by U.K.-based multinational Vodafone. This was regulation of censorship by private actors: "Companies can find themselves under duress from governments to operate in ways that go beyond legally accountable law enforcement activities" (Global Network Initiative 2011).

Vodafone and others were following direct government censorship orders under the terms of their licenses. The position of mobile ISPs is crucial in this respect, as the number of broadband mobile users has already exceeded fixed broadband users, with a particularly high proportion of mobile users in authoritarian regimes and emerging democracies.

Table 5.3
Institutional political economy

Key actors: national, regional, global	ISPs, international intermediaries, multinational content companies, largely local user groups. Coders multinational (e.g., W3C PICS). Surveillance-industrial complex.
How legitimate and accountable?	Accountability requires transparency to users. Private action subject to little accountability (e.g., put-back provisions). Engineering ethics an undeveloped area.
Multistakeholderism	Little representation for nongovernmental organizations in censorship discussion, with corporate-government discussions largely private. Some discussion apparent (e.g., in hot line governance).
Key technical actor buy-in	ISP-level filtering prevalent since emergence of large-scale spam e-mail problem in early 2000s, continued by BT technical initiative. Need for standards and best practices to ensure minimal collateral damage from blocking, particularly where technology sold to totalitarian regimes' ISPs.
Lessons	Private censorship accompanied by government encouragement, sponsorship (e.g., hot lines). Democracies increasingly need political control of export of technology conducive to repression.

Table 5.3 summarizes this institutional political economy. The key actors are technical and financial intermediaries, law enforcement agencies, and content producers. Civil society groups have played a limited role, although child protection groups have been a high-profile voice for restrictions on child abuse images.

Outcomes

Technologies of censorship can be used for commercial and political control. Deibert et al. identify four phases of regulation, from openness prior to 2000 to denial of access and to control (2008, 2010). This chapter has described the critical decisions made in 1996 and 1997, with the decision to allow ISP liability to be limited. Prior to that, Internet development was a legal mess, if a code success.

The developments since 1997 have been toward increasing commercialization led by advertising revenues (notably with the development of Yahoo! and Google search and the Facebook social network site), yet direct censorship has been relatively limited, governments apparently largely favoring indirect controls through ISPs and these new intermediaries. The failure of the PICS initiative through ICRA was an unfortunate illustration of the limits of self-regulation when free riding was not disincentivized. Its success would have required much greater levels of participation by Web site operators, who had little incentive to do so.

Government attempts to substantially increase the levels of online censorship have largely taken place by encouraging private ISPs to limit access to suspect material for their own customers. Where there is no direct contractual relationship between ISP and content provider, no explicit possibility to enforce regulation applies, and the ISP is responsible for content only when it has been given notice of its potential harmful or illegal nature. At that point, it may take down such content prior to investigating the complaint: notice and takedown (NTD) under the Electronic Commerce Directive (ECD) and, for copyright-infringing material, the DMCA. ISPs that act as "mere conduits" (Article 12, ECD) have no liability if they follow such rules, nor do content hosting services, subject to some exceptions (Article 14, ECD).

Such regimes have been criticized as a "shoot first, ask questions later" approach in which ISPs have little incentive to investigate the complaints of alleged pornographic, defamatory, or copyright-infringing content (to name the three most common categories for NTD). The role, effectiveness, and impact on ISP competitiveness of filtering is also essential to the roles of NTD regimes under ECD. The suggestion that other interlocutors, notably search engines and P2P systems, provide alternative routes for users to share potentially illegal or harmful content, raises the issue of the reform or amendment of the ECD to embrace these categories of content intermediaries.

The real fork in the road in the past ten years has arguably been the development of large-scale filtering technologies, which provided for some measure of national—through access ISP—jurisdiction. Thus, the landmark *UEJF et LICRA* v. *Yahoo!* case of 2000 in France established filtering by IP address and the beginning of national jurisdiction outside the United States (Reidenberg 2002). Filtering software imposed by government appears to have run into both practical and financial difficulties, with the Australian mandatory filter delayed by government (Australian Associated

Press 2010) and Chinese attempts to impose mandatory filtering by July 2009 also abandoned in favor of a public institution filter for schools and cybercafés. The latter Green Dam technology prospects are uncertain (BBC 2010).

In 2012, Twitter and Blogger, widely lauded for their promotion of free expression, announced they had introduced systems that allowed content to be blocked in specific jurisdictions after requests from national authorities. This was claimed to be preferable to content being blocked globally (York 2012).

More broadly, the Internet as used by political dissidents has been subjected to government demands on intermediaries. Governments required access to e-mail and social media accounts in order to censor content, as well as Web site takedown. There is a crisis in corporate governance for multinational information intermediaries including:

- ISPs such as BT
- Mobile ISPs such as Vodafone
- Equipment manufacturers such as Cisco
- Collecting societies such as Société d'Auteurs Belge
- Search engines from Yahoo! to Google (Marsden 2008; Deibert et al. 2010).

Yahoo! suffered a crisis of confidence in regulation in both its failure to convince French courts that it could identify national users in the *UEJF et LICRA* v. *Yahoo!* case and its six-year failed court battle to persuade California courts to prevent standing of the French judgment in California (Reidenberg 2005). More dramatically Yahoo! handed over dissident records to Chinese police in 2001, resulting in the ten-year imprisonment for political dissidence of Wang Xiaoning and others (Goldsmith and Wu 2006).

As a result, companies sought guidance on their activities in countries with differing human rights approaches, whether in Europe, where racist extremism and genocide denial are offenses, or in China, where free speech faces severe obstacles. Viviane Reding discussed whether European law should ban European information technology companies from activities in repressive regimes and concluded that it was unnecessary. A year later, the European Parliament (2010) condemned Nokia Siemens Networks, a gigantic European multinational telecoms and Internet company, which had sold monitoring center control equipment to Iran, where it was used to control mobile text messages in the protests after the 2009 presidential election there.

Attempts have been made continually by U.S. Congressman Chris Smith to introduce a global online freedom act (H.R. 3605 [2011]) "to prevent United States businesses from cooperating with repressive governments in transforming the Internet into a tool of censorship and surveillance, to fulfill the responsibility of the United States Government to promote freedom of expression on the Internet, to restore public confidence in the integrity of United States businesses, and for other purposes." This is intended to prevent the activities of such companies as Yahoo! in China and Lucent Alcatel or Cisco in China and the Arab world. It has failed to reach a full House vote, as was the case with its predecessors in 2009 and 2007 (111th Congress: H.R. 2271 and 109th Congress: H.R. 4780). The European effort of 2009 also failed in Parliament.

Where legislation failed, so also has private U.S. court action under the Alien Tort Statute of 1789, which permits action against U.S. companies for damages incurred as a result of their collaboration with repressive foreign governments, intended originally for collaboration with the former colonial power. Hu Kunming (2007) reports that Yahoo! settled with dissidents and their families on November 13, 2007, in part to avoid further poor publicity in the United States after Congressional Foreign Affairs Committee inquiries into their collaboration, and that of Microsoft and other U.S. multinationals, with Chinese censors. Yahoo! also agreed to establish a fund to assist dissidents placed in such circumstances in the future. In 2010, Google finally withdrew from China after various censorship incidents and highly suspicious hacking of activists' Gmail accounts. In 2011, Cisco was sued by several activists under the Alien Tort Statute for its activities in providing filtering allegedly specifically marketed as efficient in finding banned Falun Gong images (Sui-Wee Lee 2011), but the actions have made little progress.

Censorship of political dissidence is not confined to noted repressive regimes. In late 2011 it was reported that South Korea's state censors were removing 10,000 Web sites a month accused of various immoral and dissident purposes such as nebulous claims of preventing social harmony, including that of the independent academic member of the "standards commission." South Korea in 2007 had required all users of popular Web sites (those with readership of more than 100,000 users a day) to register their real names in order to comment, but announced in 2011 that it would abandon this policy after the massive CyWorld data breach that lost the personal data of the majority of the population (Xinhua 2011b). This is not to be overly sanguine about Internet censorship, but to realistically assess its success in avoiding the extremes of censorship evident elsewhere in the more traditional media.

The pseudonymity and anonymity of the Internet, together with user encryption, means that determined and skilled users can generally avoid detection when avoiding censorship. However, the collaboration of Western multinationals with repressive governments puts ordinary users at risk. While human rights declarations, corporate responsibility charters, and proposals for legislation are welcome, and the undermining of the more reactionary elements of state censorship in pursuit of consenting adults continues, the direction of censorship appears to be toward greater attempts to control users, even as the number of users, and thus difficulty in mass censorship, is rising.

Secretary Clinton's (2010, 2011) confused but clarion call for some types of Internet freedom establishes in international statecraft that foreign sovereign censorship is for most purposes discouraged by the United States. Communications, and digital technology in part, has played a significant role in political change such as the Arab Spring of 2011. However, caution needs to be exercised, as both the Middle East and North Africa and earlier democratic movements owe much more to university education, economic changes wrought by globalization, and the incompetence of rulers than they do to Twitter, Facebook, or text messages. (Recall that the overthrow of the European Communist regimes was achieved in 1989–1990 without modern digital technology.)

Nevertheless, a combination of the Internet, mobile networks, and satellite television, including, notably, Al-Jazeera has fashioned the latest claim of digital technologies of freedom following de Sola Pool (1983). If the railways, telegraphs, intercontinental private shipping, and electricity created incredible social and economic changes in the nineteenth century, with attendant political uprisings (Spar 2001), so the Internet appears to be creating its own vortexes and currents in the international political economy (Marsden 2004).

Private censorship is barely discussed in 2011 Clintonian doctrine, except as a result of direct government action, such as that exerted on Vodafone's Egyptian operations (Arthur 2011a). She condones a coregulatory type of censorship, for example, that exerted against Amazon's cloud computing hosting in the face of furious political pressure. This followed the WikiLeaks exposé of U.S. condoning of many dozens of murderous tyrants worldwide in full knowledge of the scale of their corruption, torture, and other abuses of suffering populations. Notably, she insisted that the United States has taken no direct extralegal action against Wiki-Leaks, which is correct only in the narrowest sense (Ingram 2011). Therefore, types of private censorship for political advantage or pecuniary gain are condoned by the Clinton doctrine.

In response to Secretary Clinton's criticism, China has made a great play of its adherence to the UDHR and has published a white paper on its citizens' freedom to use the Internet: "Chinese citizens fully enjoy freedom of speech on the Internet. The Constitution of the People's Republic of China confers on Chinese citizens the right to free speech. . . . Vigorous online ideas exchange is a major characteristic of China's Internet development, and the huge quantity of BBS posts and blog articles is far beyond that of any other country" (People's Republic of China 2010, sec. III).

Kingma (2008) argues that the tendency toward re-regulatory policy extends beyond child protection into online gambling, among other areas, where it is felt that risk regulation has overliberalized controls on gambling markets (Mikler 2008). In as contested and complex an environment as online child protection or gambling, where realistic solutions involve a great deal of interference and state regulatory control over individual behavior, it is unsurprising that the types of legitimacy and effectiveness that have long been the norm offline have been abandoned in favor of stylistic and superficial calls for self-regulation, in the knowledge that the problems are insoluble. The EU has varying standards of gambling regulation, ranging from very liberal laws in, for instance, the United Kingdom to more onerous regulations and even prohibitions against offshore gambling in Sweden and Italy. There is an impasse in the EU regarding the regulation of gambling (Hornle 2010; European Digital Rights 2011).

Table 5.4
Outcomes and divergences

Transparency	Blocking lists private, obscure reasons for removal, no generic reporting duty on ISPs.
Enforcement	More consistent put-back would help to make enforcement fairer. Private censorship removes user rights. General classes of content censored (e.g., Usenet). Blind alley as bad guys can always access. Enforcers should go to source: arrest producers.
Interoperability	Cleanfeed better approach compared to DNS blocking collateral damage. Iran's "halal Internet" worst of all possible worlds, with not even interconnection.
Efficiency	Blocked illegal content remains partially accessible. Significant costs imposed on intermediaries.

We summarize these outcomes in table 5.4. Even in democratic states, the operation of blocking systems is often opaque and a disproportionate interference with freedom of expression.

Gambling, WikiLeaks, and political repression may be smoking guns for censorship, but ubiquitous traffic management policies may encourage deployment of technologies that permit discrimination at far more subtle levels, using deep packet inspection, than these crude examples (Peracchio 2011). We turn to this subject in chapter 7.

6   Social Networking Services

The growth of social networking services (SNS) and user-generated content has heightened concerns over privacy, copyright, and child protection and raises new questions about the scope and focus of Internet regulation. Regulators' concerns over ordinary citizens' use of the Internet have led to calls for specific regulatory instruments that address the use of such sites and the risks and activities that affect users (Boyd and Hargittai 2010; Palfrey, Gasser, and Boyd 2010).

The degree of interoperability of code is vital in the regulation of users' information on such sites, as well as the access of friends, family, advertisers, spammers, stalkers, and other actors to those users. This chapter builds on previous chapters' findings, recent literature, and regulatory proceedings to assess the extent to which the more conventional issues-based regulatory instruments, such as the Electronic Commerce Directive (ECD), are being supplemented by generic social networking regulation, supplemented by appeals to an extralegal and possibly nebulous civic responsibility of SNS, a type of corporate social responsibility to shape these sites' code to support public policy objectives.

Public Policy and Market Failure

Social networking tools on the Internet did not begin with Web 2.0, and bulletin boards (Usenet) and intranets predate the commercial Internet (Ziewitz and Brown 2013). There have been two generations of online SNS claimed, though most are simply hybrids, and the distinction is as much a matter of investor and media distinction as reflecting techno-socioeconomic changes among users (Ofcom 2008; Boyd and Ellison 2007):

1. First-generation World Wide Web based, emphasizing social search applications for online dating (e.g., Match.com), online trading and classifieds (e.g., Craigslist), online auctions (e.g., eBay), and reunion (e.g., Friends Reunited, Classmates.com).

2. Web 2.0 from 2002 (OECD 2007), using new software functionality and broadband domestic connections, explicit professional (e.g., LinkedIn), elite (e.g., ASmallWorld), and social (e.g., Bebo, MySpace, Facebook) networking applications based on referral through mutual friends or interests.

DiPerna (2006, 7) described SNS as "connector" sites and identified interrelated characteristics, discovery, and coordination: "Connectors make discovery more powerful and accurate through social search and trust-building applications."

Market Development

The range of SNS is broad, but most easily divided into those that are open to anyone and walled-garden, invitation-only sites. Mass adoption of broadband drove the second generation of SNS, and South Korea's Cyworld was the first of the Web 2.0–type of mass participation SNS. By 2003 the incumbent ISP had bought Cyworld; by 2011 it had 33 million accounts, more than half the South Korean population.

Communities of combined services and connector sites have proved commercially very successful, with English-language examples including Yahoo!, Google, Microsoft Network, and Facebook since its 2011–2012 expansion into content partnerships. While some popular sites have withered, notably Yahoo!-owned Geocities, America Online (AOL), and MySpace, the largest commercial networking federations of sites have more than half a billion daily users and several petabytes of data available to profile and sell advertising to those users. In figure 6.1, various types of social networks are modeled against their commercial or public (as opposed to private) characteristics.

Most SNS have been agglomerated into a federation of search engine, vertically integrated content, free online e-mail, chat, and video hosting, a common feature to more established SNS owned by Yahoo! Microsoft, and Google (as well as CyWorld in Korea and QQ in China). Unusually, Facebook developed specifically as an SNS before vertically integrating with

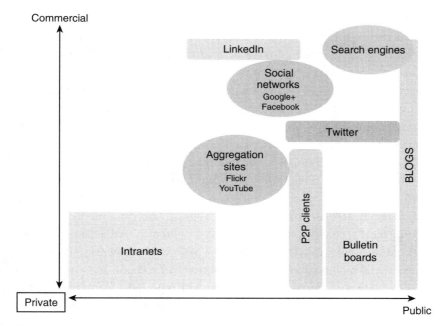

Figure 6.1
User-generated content regulation mapped using axes public/private and private/commercial (adapted from Marsden et al. 2008)

these services, notably with Skype IM and Bing search through its minority shareholder Microsoft. Professional networks such as LinkedIn and monetized virtual world Second Life are more niche-tageted than advertising-driven SNS and aggregation sites. Other popular self-regulated SNS include Flickr (a photo-sharing service) and YouTube (a video-sharing service now owned by Google).

Media sharing services are not communities as such; there is less interaction between members and therefore less regulated behavior specific to the networks. This case study therefore focuses on full SNS, notably the behemoth Facebook. Facebook claimed to grow from 12 million to 1 billion active monthly users between the end of 2006 and the end of 2012 (Facebook 2012). In China, QQ claimed 820 million users in mid-2011 (Hartje 2011). The earlier SNS (including those now owned by Microsoft and Yahoo!) also have substantial reach, with ComScore (2011) claiming that two-thirds of European online users use Microsoft sites at least once a month.

Public Policy

For social networking entrepreneurs with commercial Web sites, the audience of users is a commodity to be sold to advertisers, which makes the terms of use for such users a subject for regulation as a private space (Smythe 1977; McStay 2011). Critics have accused SNS of treating users as a commodity to be exploited, with the potential cost of switching and unsubscribing by exploited users, or simply their inertia to do so, the best hope of the network owner. Private law governs such relationships with terms of use (ToU), though the rapid unilateral changes to such terms and their complexity and obscurity make any meaningful user consent largely illusory. LinkedIn is a professional social network with about 50 million users that floated on stock markets in 2011. Shortly after its flotation, it unilaterally changed the advertising preferences for account holders without notifying users: those who were alerted by fellow users had to opt out of social media advertising retrospectively. Facebook and Google Buzz have a history of such decisions. Cyworld reported a data breach that exposed all of its members' data to the police, but only after two days of internal investigation: "Intruders accessed systems containing its main databases on Tuesday, obtaining names, email addresses, phone numbers and resident registration numbers of its users" (Ramstad 2011).

Information provided to SNS by users commonly becomes tradable to third-party advertisers by the social network, and the latter also claimed copyright permission over information such as photographs and had retained that information without return should the user terminate or be terminated from the account. Such concerns are almost as old as the public Internet, with, for instance, Yahoo! attracting much criticism in 1999 for a change in Geocities users' ToU after it had acquired the then-popular social network and Web hosting company. In response, Yahoo! posted an amended version of the ToU: "Yahoo does not own content you submit, unless we specifically tell you otherwise before you submit it" (Napoli 1999). More recently, Facebook and other SNS agreed to conform to European law and permit users to remove their data, though controversy exists over the permanent deletion of such data by the SNS (Office of the Data Protection Commissioner, Ireland 2011). In response to a February 2009 change in Facebook's ToU that led to user protest, CEO Mark Zuckerberg (2009) stated: "A lot of the language in our terms is overly formal and protective of the rights we need to provide this service to you. Over time we will continue to clarify our positions and make the terms simpler."

Edwards (2008) has raised the important practical question of reversion: Can users secure return of your information, and its deletion by the SNS and third-party contractors, in the event of the contractual arrangement with the SNS terminating without fault on either side?

The most popular SNS, including Facebook, Baidu, and Google+, insist that users reveal their real identity as a matter of its ToU. As a result, anonymity is theoretically impossible. In reality, many users attempt to circumvent the "real names" policies of such networks, though the largest networks have introduced policies and policing of pseudonymity and invalidated accounts where such policies are suspected to have been violated. This is claimed to be for security reasons, but it is also more commercially attractive to advertisers to know users' gender, sexual preference, cultural preferences, and age in order to target advertising more successfully.

The requirement for real identities would suggest that robust controls are possible to prevent children from accessing adult content. Children under age thirteen are not permitted to use Facebook, as a response to the additional protections required by the U.S. Children's Online Privacy Protection Act (COPPA). In reality, children circumvent these restrictions by entering an inaccurate birthdate on the initial subscriber information register. The costs and loss of advertising revenues associated with compatibility appear to be the outstanding issue for Facebook rather than any ethical consideration that an adult content site may be inappropriate for children. Facebook in 2012 made clear that branding and advertising may depend in the future on better regulatory compliance, notably in access for minors.

Age verification has been a key approach for improving child safety, but with little consensus on the best approach (Thierer 2007). A very high proportion of children under age thirteen appear to use Facebook, which is against the ToU. A survey of 23,000 European children found that by ages of eleven to twelve, 48 percent of children have a social network profile, rising to 72 percent by ages thirteen to fourteen (Livingstone et al. 2010).

The U.K. Children's Charities' Coalition on Internet Safety (2010, 3) stated:

12. Far from having an incentive to collect accurate data about them, very many web sites have a material interest in not knowing the real ages.

13. The foregoing observations are particularly true in relation to the so called "free internet" i.e. financed largely through advertising. . . .

21. Consideration should be given to requiring all companies to perform a "child safety audit" prior to the release of any new product or service on to the internet, particularly if it is going to be made available on the "free internet".

John Carr, a consultant in Internet child protection, argued that European concerns for user privacy and child safety can create a new environment in which regulation emerges on an individual company basis: "Our job is not to anguish over the rights of small companies and barriers to competition. If that means making it too expensive for small companies, then that's the cost of being in the business" (Marsden 2011, 81). This approach differentiates Europe from U.S. self-regulation and raises the classic regulatory issue as to whether a race to the top (quality) or the bottom (removing any protections) results in the absence of government intervention. It may be that recruiting specialists in child safety is an entry barrier to new start-ups: venture capital may neither fully understand the policy environment nor invest the money for a start-up. New social networking start-ups may be unable to secure funding, which means there may be a real innovation issue.

The U.K. Child Exploitation and Online Protection Centre (2007, 11) claims: "Web 2.0 . . . has changed the way children and young people interact online, affording them more creative control over their online experience. . . . There is a strong positive association between opportunities and risks in this context; increasing opportunities for online interaction also present challenges for those tasked with the regulation of online content, behaviour and offline consequences." While it is no doubt true that opportunity presents problems and solutions (European Network and Information Security Agency 2007), it also allows mass user self-regulation using Web 2.0 tools to report abuse and flag and label content.

SNS have membership and use rules, which entitles them to suspend or expel members accordingly. Members can report and even rate the content or comments of others. There is substantial self-policing by residents of these communities. That is not to deny that much unilateral action takes place by corporations without user involvement or consent, but much useful community-based norm resolution also occurs.

Table 6.1
Public policy and market failure

Social impact of technology	Enormous success of SNS. Mass diffusion of SNS creates concern for child protection and exclusion from adult networks and privacy.
Policy drivers—entry barriers, network and scale effects, competition	Costs of providing safer environment nontrivial. Network effects and better brand experience created dominance for Facebook over MySpace, AOL, MSN, Google.
Fundamental rights in policy design	Significant private actor business model with little regulatory action until 2009. Rapidly developing field.
Lessons	Nudge toward self-regulation became audited public demand by the European Commission in 2008–2009. Still apparent that regulation most likely is the result of failure to achieve adequate privacy standards.

Table 6.1 summarizes the public policy concerns arising from the very success and ubiquity of online SNS. A study of SNS ten years ago would have centered on user-generated regulation (Mayer-Schönberger and Crowley 2005), bulletin boards, and virtual community Second Life, and our own previous studies in this area have made user-generated regulation our focus (Marsden 2011; Marsden et al. 2008). The dominance of commercial SNS over broadband connections and governments' response since about 2003 makes this case study a mixed examination of user-centered, commercial-centered, and government-based responses to the code that enables SNS—what may be called the "mass age of the social network."

Types of Code Regulation

The growth of virtual communities in SNS has created large-scale test beds of experimentation in participation, norm formation, feedback effects, and better technical and regulatory design. Though the techniques are familiar from earlier community formation, the growth of participation in Web 2.0 platforms has created technical and socioeconomic policy challenges.

Entry barriers to design of and participation in new virtual communities depend on the network architecture chosen (e.g., open versus closed choices, development of quality of service, agreements for hosting with mobile networks). As Facebook (2012) stated in connection with the mobile ecosystem: "There is no guarantee that popular mobile devices will continue to feature Facebook, or that mobile device users will continue to use Facebook rather than competing products. We are dependent on the interoperability of Facebook with popular mobile operating systems that we do not control, such as Android and iOS, and any changes in such systems that degrade our products' functionality or give preferential treatment to competitive products could adversely affect Facebook usage on mobile devices" (13).

SNS depend entirely on the ecosystem in which they operate, and subtle changes in code change the control settings, reducing the time that users spend inside the SNS environment, and consequently advertising income, leading Facebook to warn investors of the risk of "making it easier for our users to interact and share on third-party websites" (12). Such is the precarious SNS balance between interoperability on the Web and associated mobile platforms and control of the user experience.

The inventor of the World Wide Web, Tim Berners-Lee, has been a leading critic of the potentially fragmented, anticompetitive nature of dominant SNS. In a 2010 article, he warned: "Once you enter your data into one of these services, you cannot easily use them on another site. Each site is a silo, walled off from the others. . . . The isolation occurs because each piece of information does not have a URI. Connections among data exist only within a site. So the more you enter, the more you become locked in." As a result, he believes that SNS become "a central platform—a closed silo of content, and one that does not give you full control over your information in it. The more this kind of architecture gains widespread use, the more the Web becomes fragmented, and the less we enjoy a single, universal information space." The clear implication is that sites such as LinkedIn and Facebook are potentially problematic closed monopolists and that Google+ would be a solution only if its business model was not equally closed. One of the fathers of the Internet, Vint Cerf (now working at Google), echoed this critique (Sabbagh 2011).

Interoperability is a challenge for users and third-party application providers wishing to use SNS. While AOL had to open access to its Instant Messenger (IM) in the terms of its merger with Time Warner in 2000 and Windows IM became interoperable with Yahoo! IM in 2006 (though not for video chat), Facebook was intended to be a closed network, though Windows IM users since 2010 have had the ability to message with Facebook IM account holders, and Microsoft-acquired Skype was added to

Facebook in 2012. Microsoft's purchase of Skype IM service will make interoperability a more significant issue for policymakers and application providers going forward.

The key code concern is with commercial and centralized networks—the model for Facebook, Orkut, LinkedIn, and Google+. As the EU-funded research project Socialnets pointed out, a peer-to-peer (P2P) architecture can aid the privacy and security of a network, particularly relevant in view of the numerous data breaches and deliberate privacy invasions by centrally architected networks that aim to leverage users for advertising purposes (Botgirl 2011; Searls 2011). PATH and Safebook (Leucio Molva, and Önen 2011) illustrate the extra levels of user autonomy available with a more distributed architecture. FreedomBox (2011), founded by Free Software Foundation general counsel Eben Moglen, is a further example.

In particular, it is noteworthy that many of the most popular commercial SNS joined the Open Social Alliance of interoperable application programming interfaces (APIs) in 2007, launched by Google, with seven iterations until the end of 2010. As the market developed, the Open Social Alliance partners lost out to Facebook in market share, as well as Chinese and other country-specific sites. Open Social aimed to make interoperability easier in four domains: the general JavaScript API; people and friends; publishing and accessing user activity information; and Persistence, a simple key value pair data service for server-free stateful applications. By contrast, Facebook built a proprietary platform in much the same way as Apple's AppStore, a walled garden with standards to which developers needed permission to develop.

Facebook runs several APIs to which third-party developers must write, created to enable Facebook to control the user and developer experience. The Open Graph protocol enables developers to integrate their pages into the Facebook graph API. Facebook uses Open Graph to harvest data rather than exporting and interoperating with independent other sites. It uses its "iframes" API to allow third-party developers to create applications that are hosted separately from Facebook but operate within a Facebook session and are accessed through a user's profile, thus bringing advertisers to Facebook. Since iframes essentially nests independent Web sites within a Facebook session, their content is distinct from Facebook formatting. Facebook Connect is a set of APIs that enable Facebook members to log onto third-party Web sites, applications, mobile devices, and gaming systems with their Facebook identity, which became generally available in 2009.

User-Generated Regulation

With the increasing consumer-citizen use of the Internet, new services and new business models have been created for those prosumers who create as well as consume content. There are many user-created environments in which bottom-up rules have claimed to be set (Wu 2003a) but are ruled in legal terms by user contractual ToU, not by government regulation. Their regulatory effect is voluntary and not necessarily supported or recognized by government (Ellickson 1991; Murray 2006). Difficulties with self-organization include user inertia to default settings; the decision by e-commerce providers to make Web sites almost impossible to use selectively for average users; and "the myth of the superuser," that is, the belief that users are technically competent and will self-select (Sunstein 2002; Weinberg 1997). SNS have incentives to make options available to privacy fundamentalists, but not to make them too easy for the average user to change away from defaults that favor the platform (Preibusch and Bonneau 2011). As Kim, Tang, and Anderson state (2012, 1), deciding whether to engineer privacy and security into Facebook and other SNS creates a "dilemma for operators: will they tighten their privacy default settings, or will the improvement in security cost too much revenue?"

Given the number of users and viewers of SNS, it is of limited effectiveness to regulate the posters of content directly, a lesson that legislators absorbed in the 1990s. The regulation of these systems takes place at corporate and user levels in the same way as Usenet sites were first regulated in the early 1990s. That does not mean that there is no innovation in their regulatory structure: virtual worlds, for instance, have built up elaborate self-regulatory models (Noveck 2006; Mayer-Schönberger and Crowley 2005).

In Europe, the primary regulatory mechanism is notice and takedown (NTD) under ECD Articles 12 to 14. This does not require ex ante monitoring, but does require content hosts to take down users' content that they have been informed of (given "notice") either breaches of law or otherwise offends their ToU, though there can be no obligation to monitor (*SABAM* v. *NetLog* 2012). There is thus a shift of liability. ECD provides clarification of the applicable liability regime to Internet intermediaries (with no strict liability), sets out the exoneration conditions for certain types of intermediary activity (transmission or storage of third-party content), and does not affect the liability of the actual content provider (which is left to national law). The host's limited liability is to ensure that users are able to use the service only under conditions or terms that explicitly permit the content host to take down material that is illegal, often extending this power to material that is offensive, of an unsuitably adult nature, and so on.

European courts, especially in France, have reinterpreted the ECD hosting provisions to create liability for content on the part of eBay, and in Italy a local court found similarly against Google Video (OECD 2011b). Whether these cases are overturned on appeal, the current national judgments create cost-of-business restrictions for auction and video hosting sites.

An example of user-generated regulation using NTD is the video-sharing site YouTube. On YouTube, the editorial controller, if such exists, is the person who posts the content. For regulatory purposes, YouTube users post the content, and the YouTube Web site reacts ex post on receiving complaints regarding breaches of copyright or offensive content (*Viacom et al.* v. *YouTube* 2010). This is fundamentally different from traditional broadcast regulation, where the editorial controller (the broadcaster) is responsible for the content ex ante, that is, before it is offered to the public. YouTube claimed as early as 2006 that it removes objected-to video within fifteen minutes (China People's Daily 2006). However, later cases suggest that such immediate action is not comprehensive (Marsden 2011, 75).

Some SNS display far greater responsiveness to empowering users to create and regulate content, report abuse, and maintain their privacy. Some offer increased security and protection from harmful content for users who desire, or in any case receive, walled gardens, that is, less open Internet experiences. The launch of Google+ in 2011 was intended to provide greater user control and privacy compared with the earlier Google Buzz network, as well as market leader Facebook.

Table 6.2 summarizes the key concerns with social networking site design and code. SNS concerns arise mainly in the proprietary contractual arrangements made between SNS and third-party application providers, with abuse of user data a prominent example of the fact that enforcement

Table 6.2
Types of code and code regulation

Layer	Application (including third-party applications and media partners); platform.
Location (manufacturers, ISPs, servers, clients)	Server side with some mobile-based features.
Enforcement of code	Terms of use enhanced by contractual terms with thirty-party application providers and media partners.

is a private legal remedy that admits of no overriding public policy objective.

Institutional Political Economy

The key actors in social networking are the SNS themselves, typically commercial sites that sell advertising, as well as the application developers who work with the sites; advertisers; users individually and as groups; and governments representing the interests of those users, especially on issues of privacy, child protection, and cyberbullying.

Developers are effectively regulated by code as well as partner agreements they have with the SNS, and Facebook, for instance, has exercised significant control over the business models of applicant developers such as Zynga (owners of the multiuser interactive game Farmville). Advertisers can use SNS to advertise according to user information on interests, which raises issues about user privacy, but because the information is provided to the advertisers by the social network selling the advertising opportunity, it is the social network's role that is critical.

Users require security and privacy as well as the attractions of SNS and are placed in a position of vulnerability due to the personal data they supply and share with friends. The network effects of social sites are such that membership becomes a self-fulfilling element of socializing offline as well as online, where other members of their peer group use the network. As a result, there are strong dependencies for users on the social network, and governments have actively monitored and lobbied SNS.

Multistakeholder forums have been convened by both European and U.S. governments, with the most formal forum that of the European Commission. In the United States, both Facebook and Google responded to concerns raised in a 2011 presidential summit on SNS and cyberbullying of teens (Jennings 2011) by introducing new systems to take down content more expeditiously. Facebook launched its safety pages in late 2010.

Guidelines for SNS were created in 2009 in Europe, and the Council of Europe in 2010 drafted a Recommendation of the Committee of Ministers on human rights and SNS and in 2011 issued draft guidelines for SNS (Council of Europe 2010, 2011). The rights affected are listed as privacy (Article 8 of the European Convention), free expression (Article 10), and data protection. In terms of self-regulatory initiatives, the Global Network Initiative asked the Centre for Democracy and Technology to produce guidelines on user rights and SNS (2011).

The European Commission pursued a strategy to encourage SNS to self-regulate by making this the subject of its fifth annual Safer Internet Forum, in 2008, establishing the multistakeholder Social Networking Safety Task Force. Commissioner Reding (Speech 08/465, 5) stated, "The Internet industry should take a pro-active role in protecting minors using their services. I am a supporter of industry self-regulation regimes as long as they are broadly accepted by stakeholders and provide for effective enforcement." She particularly mentioned the U.K. Council for Child Internet Safety Code of Practice (2008) in the United Kingdom, its Danish equivalent, and the agreements made by MySpace and Facebook with the U.S. attorney general.

The European Commission described itself as the broker of the Safer Social Networking Principles signed on European Safer Internet Day 2009 (European Union 2009), indicating a strong political will for parties to collaborate, and to publicly audit company commitments and results of the principles (Donoso 2011). This followed the commission's brokering of the European mobile content code of conduct in 2007 (European Union 2007), which formed a template for the creation of the 2009 Social Networking Principles. The parties driving the self-regulatory activities, apart from the industry signatories and the commission, were the members of the Safer Internet Forum, largely children's charities across Europe.

The commission used an agency and research center to engage with stakeholders using a survey and report on recommended actions, as well as consulting itself in the months prior to announcement of the self-regulatory guidelines (European Network and Information Security Agency 2007; Wainer and Miltgen 2009; European Commission 2008). In June

2011, the European Commission formed a new "collaborative platform" and invited stakeholders to investigate "a review of the current industry self-regulatory agreements in the field" (European Union 2011b).

The social network commitments to the principles were audited annually, with the 2011 results criticizing Facebook for its slowness in responding to complaints and its lack of resources to combat complaints of breaches of the principles. These are the principles in summary (O'Connell et al. 2009):

• An easy-to-use and accessible "report abuse" button, allowing users to report inappropriate contact from or conduct by another user with one click and SNS commitment to examine and, where appropriate, take down such content expeditiously and review such policies and implementation regularly

• Ensuring privacy for full online profiles and contact lists of minors

• Ensuring that private profiles of users under the age of eighteen are not publicly searchable

• Guaranteeing that privacy options are prominent and accessible at all times

• Preventing those under age from using their services

In 2011 38 percent of all nine to thirteen year olds in Europe used Facebook, showing that the final principle was far from being complied with, with 70 percent of Dutch children on Facebook (European Union 2011b).

The United States adopted a more self-regulatory approach, though not without substantial federal interest. The federal government in 2009 convened an interagency task force on bullying, staged a national summit in August 2010, and launched the stopbullying.gov Web site in 2011. In 2011, the President and First Lady convened a summit on online bullying at the White House, to which the key SNS sent representatives. Self-regulation was undertaken in response to fears that the incoming Obama administration and Democrat majority in Congress would introduce a comprehensive federal data privacy law, though this did not transpire during the period of 2009 to 2012.

Previous European regulatory interaction with U.S.-headquartered search engines illustrates the increasing extraterritorial reach of the EU's privacy regime. A 2008 opinion from EU data protection commissioners recommended a six-month limit on the retention of search records linked to individuals and reaffirmed the applicability of the European data protection law: "Search engine providers must delete or irreversibly anonymise personal data once they no longer serve the specified and legitimate purpose they were collected for" (European Digital Rights 2008). Google responded that it would anonymize records after nine months and added a link to its privacy policy on its home page. Until 2007, Google had kept identifiable records permanently, and its failure to change policy, together with fears that Facebook and other commercial rivals would operate a similar policy, led Commissioner Reding to argue in the proposed data protection regulation: "To enforce EU law, national privacy watchdogs shall be endowed with powers to investigate and engage in legal proceedings against non-EU data controllers" (Reuters 2011). Yahoo! had followed Google's lead in 2008, though claiming it would delete some search data within three months, not Google's nine months (Helft 2008).

Finally, the Council of Europe established guidelines for SNS (2011) for adoption in 2012. It stated in 2011 that "amendments to the drafts should in particular concern a strengthening of the position on blocking and filtering of search engines, a clear support for anonymous profiles on social networking services while taking into account the fear of civil society and industry of ex-ante obligations with regard to content" (Committee of Experts on New Media 2011). Furthermore, the committee "agreed not to pursue consultation with the industry on the draft self-regulatory guidelines" given the limited time left to agree a new draft. The elements under discussion were to ensure anonymous use of SNS, a concern that had become much more pressing after the Arab Spring of 2011, during which activists' use of social media sites had led repressive governments to attempt to identify the users in order to censor their activities (see chapter 5).

It is clear that significant political capital has been expended by governments to encourage greater self-regulatory responsibility by SNS, together with emphasis on preventing abuse. The involvement of multiple stakeholders is evident and has been encouraged by government, though the civil society involvement has focused on child protection rather than online rights. The divergent approach of civil society between those in favor of more regulation to protect children (U.K. Children's Charities' Coalition on Internet Safety 2008) and those encouraging self-regulation

Table 6.3
Institutional political economy

Key actors: national, regional, global	ISPs, intermediaries, multinational content, largely local user groups. Coders in Silicon Valley. Child protection groups.
How legitimate and accountable?	User-generated regulation offers some control. Generally opaque terms and application mean users vulnerable to private action without appeal.
Multistakeholderism	Little formal multistakeholder consultation by corporates. Restricted to publicity of most egregious privacy breaches and lobbying of government
Key technical actor buy-in	Walled-garden Facebook approach meant third-party application developers dependent on Facebook. More open environments supported; significant research effort in interoperable social media to prevent high-walled gardens.
Lessons	User-generated regulation in social media proved largely mythical in face of commercial pressures to reduce privacy for third-party advertiser use. Civil society fragmented and ineffective.

but with concern over data privacy (European Digital Rights 2008) has led to a fragmented lobby in terms of the focus of their attention to government action.

Table 6.3 summarizes the actors' roles in the regulation of SNS. The dialogue is between two extreme positions. First is the deregulatory zeal of the venture-capital-fueled SNS themselves and their development ecosystem, in their increasing tendency to claim benefits from user-generated regulation (as a nudge mechanism, which has proven somewhat mythical in its effect). Opposing the unregulated trading of information is the responsibility of child welfare groups as a proxy for wider user concerns about the abuse of personal data.

We can conclude that commercial pressures to reduce privacy for third-party advertiser use thus far have evaded any real political traction to introduce regulation and that fragmented civil society has been largely ineffective in encouraging greater regulatory intervention.

A clear understanding of the sociopolitical role of the new technologies supporting virtual communities and SNS is needed, together with an analysis of what features the Internet should bring to this arena and an identification of which communication channels provide the means to promote them to the general public (Pollett et al. 2011). In surveys users have identified the inherent capability to attribute cross-platforms levels of popularity, priority, and trust to create greater trust in their intermediaries. For instance, search engines support effective information search and discovery from heterogeneous sources, but privacy concerns and the legal implications in using and combining such information are rarely taken into account. Similarly citizens and communities' opinions and discussion are typically uncontrolled. There is a need for configurable authentication mechanisms that can be easily tuned to the specific application requirements, for instance for controlled anonymity.

The public nature of social networking space is not yet a legally accepted concept. York (2010) has assessed ToU and blocking for Facebook, YouTube, Flickr, Blogger, and Twitter and compares them to the U.S. cases *Marsh* v. *Alabama* (1946) and *New Jersey Coalition against War in the Middle East* v. *J.M.B. Realty Corp.* (1994) holding that shopping malls must permit leafleting on societal issues, subject to reasonable standards set by the malls (Marsden 2011). York sees this as extending to Facebook in the online environment and suggests that Facebook could be held to generally accepted public standards in the degree of free speech that it offers.

The question is therefore whether SNS pose a special case, where user rights demand protection as a right to either belong to or to grant access to a dominant SNS. This is a more complicated question than simply one of consumer rights, as it would be an extension of requiring ISPs to grant users access to those networks as a type of free speech. It may also open the question of third-party application developers' rights to interoperate, or even to "must-carry" rules similar to cable network rules that require broadcast television stations to be rebroadcast on cable.

Outcomes and Divergences

Regulators are moving toward new policies and regulations to enforce compliance with data protection law by SNS following earlier specific regulatory attention paid to search engines. The November 2010 settlement of a class action suit (Darlin 2010) brought by aggrieved Gmail users on the social network Google Buzz (rapidly remedied by Google after public outcry) demonstrates that courts will take action at least in egregious cases of invasion of privacy. In 2011, Google settled its Federal Trade

Commission (2011) case on the same matter, accepting biannual inspections of all products in a privacy audit that would last until 2030. Google put $8.5 million into an independent fund to be used to support organizations promoting education about privacy on the Web. Google had already said: "We will also do more to educate people about privacy controls specific to Buzz. The more people know about privacy online, the better their online experience will be" (Darlin 2010).

As a California corporation with an Irish subsidiary, Facebook owes fealty to European privacy rules only to the extent that its operations may be affected by negative national rulings that would deny it service. As a result, it took a very liberal (i.e., minimal) approach to privacy with its users' data (Facebook 2010; Constine 2010), attracting substantial opprobrium over a period of years but little evidence of declining use. Australian communications minister Stephen Conroy said in May 2010 that Facebook "had a complete disregard for users' privacy" (AAP 2010). Facebook in 2011 adjusted and improved privacy standards for third-party developers in response to calls for it to regulate application developers' access to users' friends' data, made by the American Civil Liberties Union and others in 2009 (Security Blog 2011).

The most notable outcomes of a regulatory action against SNS have been the biennial reviews over a twenty-year period from 2011 that both Google and Facebook agreed to (Facebook 2012). Google allowed the privacy audit to extend from its Buzz SNS, against which the original complaint was filed, to all of its products. Facebook also agreed to an audit in July 2012 by the Irish regulator, to which it answers under European data protection law. This formal review, designed to assess Facebook compliance with a 2011 comprehensive assessment, required these main improvements:

1. A mechanism for users to convey an informed choice for how their information is used and shared on the site, including in relation to third-party applications

2. Broad update to the data use and privacy policies on user transparency

3. Transparency and control for users through the provision of all personal data held to them on request and "as part of their everyday interaction with the site"

4. Deleting social plug-in data held on users and nonusers "much sooner than presently"

5. Increased transparency and controls for the use of personal data for advertising

6. Notification of facial recognition or "tag suggest" that "will ensure Facebook Ireland is meeting best practice in this area from an Irish law perspective"

7. Enhanced ability for users to control tagging and posting on other user profiles

8. Enhanced ability for users to decide on addition to groups by friends

9. Better Facebook compliance management and governance function in Dublin "to ensure that the introduction of new products or new uses of user data take full account of Irish data protection law" and consequently European law (Office of the Data Protection Commissioner, Ireland 2011).

These extensive new controls accompany the transformation of Facebook into a publicly traded company and Google's increasing competition with Facebook in SNS with Google+. Controversy over the two companies' privacy breaches had become headline news by 2012, with particular concerns expressed over the degree to which they were trading data with third-party advertisers and developers.

The German state privacy regulator for Schleswig-Holstein in summer 2011 required its Web sites to prevent the implementation of Facebook's "Likes" tracking software, which can track users' Web history in real time, as users were not requested and not able to opt out of the service (JWZ 2011). Schleswig-Holstein declared that it is a violation of European data privacy law for a European Web site to include a nonprivacy-protecting Like button on their Web site, as Facebook does not yet fully comply with European data privacy requirements. In response, the German news site Heise Online introduced a local version of the Facebook Like button, which allowed users to consent to data being tracked before those data could be transferred to Facebook. Facebook blocked this move, stating: "The manner in which [Heise.de] have incorporated the Heise.de Like Button violates our Platform Policies," citing: "8th Platform Policy: You must not use or make derivative use of Facebook icons, or use terms for Facebook features and functionality, if such use could confuse users into thinking that the reference is to Facebook features or functionality." Facebook thus retaliated against the German Web site, effectively placing its commercial terms ahead of the explicit instruction from the German state regulator. The outcome of this case will set a further precedent for European sovereignty over a U.S. social network. That the Data Protection Directive applies to U.S. sites' use of Europeans' personal data is well established.

The image of increasing attention by SNS to their social responsibilities is incomplete, and in one assessment, the European Commission (European Union 2011c) reported, "Only Bebo and MySpace ensure that minors' profiles are accessible only to their approved list of contacts by default. Only Bebo, MySpace, Netlog and SchuelerVZ ensure minors can be contacted by default only by their approved list of contacts." It pointed out that "56% of 11–12 year olds and 78% of 15–16 year olds say they know how to change privacy settings on their social network profile." (see European Union 2011b). Donoso (2011, 24) outlined the problems of Facebook in terms of child protection as including: "reports of inappropriate content/ contact are not answered. Profiles of minors are not set to 'private by default.' Some advertising can be considered as not appropriate for minors. The mechanisms to avoid re-registration of underage users are inefficient." He also identified a "Lack of information on existing parental control mechanisms." This suggests both more transparency is required from Facebook, and that its advertising needs more careful targeting to prevent children receiving adult content.

The bandwagon tipping effect of the most successful SNS Facebook caused a race to the bottom when Facebook became the runaway Western leading SNS. This contrasts strongly with the baseline for data protection that was examined in the first case study in this book, where relatively high European legislative standards for data set a benchmark to which companies from other regions, notably the United States but also competitive outsourcing destinations such as India, had to aspire in order to process the personal data of European users. SNS therefore provides an excellent test case in unregulated environments, where the key difference with the overall data protection regime is that governments slowly woke up to the privacy-invasive habits of SNS advertising and third-party data harvesting. Attempts to nudge companies away from their core business advantage—that of trading the personal data of users creating the maxim "if you're not paying for it, you're the product"—were failures, and Bebo proves a satisfying proof that unregulated profit-seeking behavior will usually defeat more public-leaning business models in this space. In 2011 and 2012, regulators appeared to be taking much stronger action against both Google and Facebook to ensure that SNS were more respectful of user privacy rights.

The Council of Europe human rights commissioner in 2011 stated, "Indexing by search engines, as well as targeted advertising by application developers and online merchants, are just two of the known manifestations of 'dataveillance' by third parties. It remains to be seen whether other forms of 'profiling' may also be able to take place via SNS" (Hammarberg 2011). Commissioner Hammarberg noted the Hamburg State data protection commissioner's concerns regarding Facebook's friend finder feature. He also announced that the Council of Europe Convention for Protection of Personal Data (which parallels the Data Protection Directive EC/95/46), would undergo a process of "modernization" to address social networking among other concerns.

The Article 29 Working Party issued an opinion on correct use of personal data by Web sites (Opinion 5/2009) that focused in part on SNS. As with the radio frequency identifier and behavioral advertising code regulation analyzed in chapter 3, they have increasingly considered aspects of social network design that affect privacy. As Edwards and Brown (2009) explain, "Aspects of the code itself provide equally important means of achieving a delicate balance between users' expectations of data security and privacy and their desire to share information" (Edwards and Brown 2009,1). The default settings of user privacy preferences particularly influence this balance. Edwards and Brown (2009) suggested "a legal regime requiring that defaults be provided at the most privacy-friendly setting" and "automatic expiration of data," also suggested by Mayer-Schönberger (2009).

The European commissioner for justice in September 2011 specifically focused on SNS as a security threat: "The increasingly sophisticated use of the internet and social media by violent extremists adds an extra layer to security challenges" (Georgieva 2011). It was not clear whether she was referring to Islamic militants or the neofascist opponents responsible for the mass killing in and around Oslo in July 2011. In reaction to the U.K. lootings of August 2011, the U.K. prime minister called for powers to suspend SNS in cases of actual knowledge of potential gang coordination, yet earlier in the year, he had ordered a review and signaled support for less regulation of social media over so-called superinjunctions and had welcomed the role of social media in the Arab Spring. A leading

Table 6.4
Outcomes and divergences

Transparency	Most important SNS deliberately opaque in software updates and privacy policy changes. Little evidence of good practice.
Enforcement	Individual reuses of data not susceptible to corporate-type enforcement. Nudges and defaults ("distributed enforcement" more useful. Policy on child protection moving toward offering greater user involvement in safety.
Interoperability	Open social: Why can't users move data and interconnect? Note portability is insufficient.
Efficiency	Corporate governance conformity to best practices arguably best outcome. Has the Federal Trade Commission or European Commission achieved this through its recent scrutiny?

commentator noted that "the result is an incoherent set of prime ministerial demands for more and less communication regulation, in effect calls for both more and less censorship at the same time" (Sabbagh 2011). Cameron's home secretary (the interior minister) later signaled that this reaction would be replaced by less draconian plans for cooperation rather than direct censorship.

The lessons drawn can be summarized as lack of transparency, enforcement (despite some improvements), and efficiency of enforcement (see table 6.4). Because Facebook and Google have previously been deliberately opaque in privacy policy changes, they present little evidence of good practice. Where good practice and therefore higher entry barriers for new users existed, as arguably occurred with Bebo, the SNS paid the price in market failure. Where individuals have reused data, user-generated regulation ('nudges and defaults') can be more useful than corporate policies: what might be termed "distributed enforcement." With recent U.S. and European policymaker interventions, policies toward child protection are moving toward greater user involvement in safety, with the ability to report to the police. The question remains: Why can't users move data and interconnect? Portability as enforced in Ireland is insufficient for this purpose, a problem we consider in the concluding chapter.

The connection with the telecommunications standards debates over platform control of content providers is overwhelmingly important. The following chapter has the same open or controlled metanarrative as in this one.

7 Smart Pipes: Net Neutrality and Innovation

As the Internet first became a mass medium during the 1990s, many companies (notably AOL, followed by mobile operators) tried to maximize advertising revenue by building "walled gardens" for their customers, to keep users within affiliated Web pages. However, they could not keep up with the rapid innovation and diversity of the rest of the Internet and the growth of dedicated search engine Google. Most were forced by their customers to become increasingly interoperable with the rest of the Internet (Ziewitz and Brown 2013).

The same commercial pressures, with additional state sovereignty concerns and capacity pressures on network operators, are again driving a partitioning of the Internet into more controlled private domains. Facebook is providing social tools that encourage its users to access external content from within its own platform. Many ISPs are deploying sophisticated traffic management tools that allow some types of data (e.g., real-time voice calls) and content sources (specific Web sites that have paid for privileged access) to be prioritized. While this can reduce congestion and security threats to networks, it can also be used to protect existing monopoly services and new proprietary services (Mims 2011).

The motivation to make the networks more intelligent (to create "smart pipes") is to reduce congestion to protect users' experience and, indirectly, the business of the ISP. The monopoly motive is directly concerned with the ISPs' profits and not directly with user welfare, especially where users have little transparency or ability to switch to another provider. Mobile networks have been particularly active in blocking voice over Internet Protocol (VoIP) and even rival texting services. This has led to political campaigns for network neutrality, the principle under which ISPs must give equal treatment to comparable traffic flows across their networks and not block any application without user consent (Wu 2003b; Lemley and Lessig 1999).

Conventional U.S. economic arguments have always been broadly negative to the concept of network neutrality, preferring the introduction of tariff-based congestion pricing (David 2001). Hahn and Wallsten (2006) explain that network neutrality "usually means that broadband service providers charge consumers only once for Internet access, don't favor one content provider over another, and don't charge content providers for sending information over broadband lines to end users." This is the focus of the problem: network owners with vertical integration into content or alliances have greater incentives to require content owners (who may also be consumers) to pay a toll to use the higher-speed networks that they offer to end users (Economides and Tåg 2007). Note that all major consumer ISPs are vertically integrated to some extent with proprietary video, voice, portal, and other services.

The Federal Communications Commission in the United States has acted on several network neutrality complaints (notably those against Madison River Communications, an Internet service provider, in 2005 and Comcast in 2008) as well as introducing the principle in part through several merger conditions placed on dominant ISPs, but it delayed its report and order on network neutrality until its eventual publication in the *Federal Register* in September 2011. It was instantly challenged by various interested parties and would be litigated in the winter of 2012–2013. Development of European legal implementation of network neutrality principles has been slow, with the European Commission referring much of the detailed work to the new Body of European Regulators of Electronic Communications (BEREC), which was developing an extensive work program on network neutrality in 2012 (BEREC 2011). At the European member state level, statements of principle in favor of network neutrality have been made in, for instance, France, but no legislation was enacted before the end of 2011 (Cave 2011).

Public Policy Objectives

Network neutrality comprises two separate nondiscrimination commitments (Marsden 2010, 24): one of universal service and another of common carriage. Backward-looking "network neutrality lite" claims that Internet users should not be disadvantaged due to opaque and invidious practices by their current ISP. The argument is that a minimum level of service should be provided that offers open Internet access without blocking or degrading specific applications or protocols—an updated form of universal service (Mueller 1998). That provides a basic level of service that all subscribers should eventually receive. Forward-looking "positive network neutrality" describes a practice whereby higher quality of service (QoS) for higher prices should be offered on fair, reasonable, and nondiscriminatory (FRAND) terms to everyone, a modern equivalent of common carriage (Noam 1994). The type of service that may be entitled to FRAND treatment could result in short-term exclusivity in itself, as, for instance, wireless and mobile cell towers may be able to carry only a single high-definition video stream (Talbot 2006) at any one time and therefore a monopoly may result. As common carriage dictates terms but not the specific market conditions (Cherry 2006; Marsden 2011), transparency and nondiscrimination would not automatically result in a plurality of services.

ISPs have argued that there is little public interest in controls over the operation of private networks and that regulation will stifle innovation in network management, the development of new services, and, ultimately, investment in new network capacity. Regulators such as Ofcom in the United Kingdom have accepted much of this laissez-faire position, arguing only that basic consumer protection and competition policies are required to ensure an efficient market in services (Kiedrowski 2007).

Public Policy and Fundamental Rights

Network neutrality is a more political issue than most telecommunications regulators are used to, as technologies of censorship are at stake (La Rue 2011). BEREC (2010, 20) explains: "Freedom of expression and citizens' rights, as well as media pluralism and cultural diversity, are important values of the modern society, and they are worth being protected in this context—especially since mass communication has become easier for all citizens thanks to the Internet." It adds that because economic regulators are narrowly focused, "intervention in respect of such considerations lies outside the competence of BEREC."

This lack of competence is often, but not always, a result of the legislative competences allocated by national parliaments to regulators. The explicitly technoeconomic remit of most telecoms regulators in Europe gives them limited functionality in assessing rights-based issues such as data protection and freedom of expression. However, the so-called converged regulators of broadcasting and telecoms such as AgCom in Italy and Ofcom in the United Kingdom have no such legislative block on assessing human rights, and any reluctance to make such assessments is likely to be a result of organizational culture as well as the perceived groupthink of market-oriented technoeconomists. With increasing EU attention to rights-based issues, as a result of the incorporation of the Charter of Fundamental Rights within the Lisbon Treaty (in effect from December 1, 2009), national regulators have been slow to react to the fundamental rights concerns raised in this debate. The Court of Justice decisions in *SABAM* v. *NetLog* (2012) and *Scarlet Extended SA* v. *SABAM* (2011) force them to confront the issue in future.

Forms of private censorship by intermediaries have been increasing over the past decade even as the law continues to declare those intermediaries (mainly ISPs, but increasingly also video hosting companies such as YouTube, social networks such as Facebook, and search providers such as Google) to be "three wise monkeys." These intermediaries are not subject to liability for their customers' content under the "mere conduit" regimes of the United States and EU so long as they have no actual or constructive knowledge of that content: if they "hear no evil, see no evil and speak no evil" (Marsden 2010). Deep packet inspection (DPI) and other advanced traffic management techniques will give ISPs much more granular knowledge of what their customers are downloading and uploading on the Internet. ISPs could filter out both annoying and illegal content. For instance, they could "hear" criminal conversations, such as those by terrorist sympathizers, illegal pornographers, harassers, those planning robberies, libelous commentary, and so on. They could also "see" illegal downloading of copyrighted material. They could be obliged to cooperate with law enforcement or even copyright industries in these situations, which would create even greater difficulties where that speech was legal in one country but illegal where it was received (Deibert et al. 2010).

Traffic management techniques affect not only high-speed, high-money content but, by extension, all other content too. You can build a high-speed lane on a motorway only by creating inequality, and often those "improvements" slow down everyone currently using the roads. The Internet may be different in that regulators and users may tolerate much more discrimination in the interests of innovation. To make this decision on an informed basis, it is in the public interest to investigate transparently both network neutrality "lite"' (the slow lanes) and network neutrality "heavy" (what rules allow higher-speed content). For instance, in the absence of regulatory oversight, ISPs could use DPI to block some content altogether if they decide it is not to the benefit of ISPs, copyright holders, parents, or the government. ISP blocking is currently widespread in controlling spam e-mail, and in some countries in blocking illegal images, as we described in chapter 5.

One of the main claims by ISPs wishing to manage Internet traffic is that Internet traffic growth is unmanageable by traditional means of expansion of bandwidth and that therefore their practices are reasonable. In order to research this claim, regulators need access to ISP traffic measurement data. There are several possible means of accessing data at Internet exchange points, but many data are private either because they are between two peers that do not use an exchange or because they are carried by a content distribution network (CDN). No government regulator has yet produced any reliable data, and carriers' own data are subject to commercial confidentiality.

A common ISP mechanism to reduce network congestion is to set caps on the monthly bandwidth available to each customer. This was the default in most countries prior to the introduction of broadband modems in the late 1990s. Only in countries with unmetered local calls, such as Canada and the United States, was Internet use "all you can eat" (Oftel 2000). With the introduction of broadband cable in Canada, the Canadian Radio-Television and Telecommunications Commission permitted monthly download caps on users. This was justified by the shared resource used by cable modem subscribers in the local loop (Geist 2011). The commission (2011) reiterated its permission for caps, justified by reference to its responsibilities to ensure competition under Telecommunications Act 1993 Section 7. Comcast in the United States created a 250 GB cap (Burstein 2008), which was considered more transparent than its previous use of DPI and other techniques to prevent peer-to-peer (P2P) transfers.

Most caps relate to maximum download capacity and are assessed independent of the maximum download speeds that users can receive, the latter being the headline rates that are generally used in broadband

Table 7.1
Public policy and market failure

Social impact of technology	Use of monitoring of traffic still largely hidden from fixed end users. Mobile broadband and streaming video growth likely to increase user concerns.
Policy drivers—entry barriers, network and scale effects, competition	QoS technology imposes nontrivial network costs that increase with scale, though deployment expertise offers scale economies. Security dual use reduces costs.
Fundamental rights in policy design	Notable by the absence of rights from early deployment, discussion on this issue is growing with regulatory oversight.
Lessons	Permitting technology development without privacy and expression oversight can lead to invasive technologies. Telecoms regulators inadequate to discuss rights-based policies.

advertising to consumers. OECD (2008) found that of 215 broadband packages sampled, almost half would result in users' exceeding their monthly caps within three hours at advertised maximum speeds. Countries that were at the bottom of the OECD tables for bandwidth provision, Australia and New Zealand, have adopted the radical step of commissioning a national fiber local loop to replace their incumbent telephony monopoly. Public intervention is by no means a taboo in broadband investment, and the European Commission has repeatedly approved all nonurban public investment in fiber deployments proposed by member states, while Australia is building a publicly funded national fiber wholesale network. The lessons of public policy and market failure are illustrated in table 7.1.

Types of Code Regulation

Most voice calls and video today use a dedicated copper telephone line or cable line; tomorrow they may use high-speed fiber lanes on Internet connections, which could make a good business for ISPs that wish to offer higher capability for managed services (such as high definition video with guaranteed quality of service) using DPI. It is both smart pipes' intelligent networks and the greater capacity of fiber-optics that enable such services. Not all ISPs will do so, and it is quite possible to manage traffic less obtrusively by using the DiffServ protocol to prioritize traffic streams within the same Internet channel. The DiffServ protocol specifies a simple, scalable, and coarse-grained mechanism for classifying and managing network traffic. Waclawsky (2005) stated in regard to ISP traffic management protocols that "this is the emerging, consensus view: [it] will let broadband industry vendors and operators put a control layer and a cash register over the Internet and creatively charge for it." The Third Generation Partnership Project (3GPP), the standards body for 3G mobile telephony, has been working since 2000 on a set of standards called IMS (IP Multimedia Subsystem 2006): an operator-friendly environment intended to generate new revenue by way of DPI. In 2005, fixed-line carriers and equipment vendors created IPSphere (2006), a new set of standards for network intercession in IP application flows. Both sets of standards support the ability to filter and censor by file type and content provider on the Internet. In an extreme case, one could degrade all content that is not tagged as paying a premium carriage fee. This enables the carrier to discriminate and decide which content to delay and which to permit to travel at normal speeds to the end user. Users can encrypt all traffic to prevent inspection in the same way that firewalls on Intranets were evaded using Port 80 and other techniques (Clayton, Murdoch, and Watson 2006). (Port 80 is the hypertext transfer protocol's usual port on a computer modem; thus routing traffic through this port makes it highly unlikely to be blocked).

Until recently in the United States, the Internet had been subject to telecommunications regulation only for interoperability and competition, building on inquiries that regulated computer data transfer by the Federal Communications Commission (Werbach 2005), and the design principle of end-to-end described by Saltzer, Reed, and Clark (1984), which dominated early Internet design. That principle itself was superseded by the need for greater trust and reliability in the emerging broadband network by the late 1990s, particularly as spam e-mail led to viruses, botnets and other risks. As a result, end-to-end has gradually given way to trust-to-trust mechanisms, in which receipt of the message by one party's trusted agent replaces the receipt by the final receiver (Clark and Blumenthal 2011). This agent is almost always the ISP, and it is regulation of this party that is at stake in network neutrality. ISPs are not only removing spam and other hazardous materials before they reach the (largely technically uneducated) subscriber; they also can remove other potentially illegal materials on behalf of governments and copyright holders, to name the two most active censors on the Internet, as well as prioritizing packets for their own benefit.

Given the difficulty in assessing whether network layer innovation is necessary, network engineers' calls to avoid neutrality regulation are strikingly vehement. Handley (2011) suggested that the role of standards organizations, especially the Internet Engineering Task Force (IETF), is to provide "tussle space" (Clark et al. 2002) for ISP and content provider business models to emerge, notably by ensuring that protocols permit application layer innovation. He points out that network neutrality is problematic for the standards community because it involves legal and economic issues that are outside the IETF core competence, offers rival business models to which IETF must be agnostic, and has different ramifications in different countries. For instance, U.K. ISPs have widely deployed DPI, whereas in the United States and Germany, DPI is much less often deployed.

Initial treatment of network neutrality discussed four "Net freedoms" (Federal Communications Commission 2005) for end users: freedom to attach devices, run applications, receive the content packets of their choice, and receive "Service Plan Information . . . meaningful information." Even now, scholars are suggesting that freedom to innovate can be squared with design prohibitions (van Schewick 2010), despite over a decade of multibillion-dollar protocol development by the ISP community resulting in the ability to control traffic coming onto their networks (Waclawsky 2005) and wholesale rationing of end user traffic (Odlyzko and Levinson 2007). Berners-Lee (2006) explained: "There have been suggestions that we don't need legislation because we haven't had it. These are nonsense, because in fact we have had net neutrality in the past—it is only recently that real explicit threats have occurred." Berners-Lee was particularly adamant that he does not wish to see the prohibition of QoS because that is precisely the claim made by some U.S. network neutrality advocates—and opposed by the network engineering community.

Deep Packet Inspection and Traffic Management

In order to manage traffic, new technology lets ISP routers (if so equipped) look inside a data packet to "see" its content, using DPI and other techniques. Previous routers were not powerful enough to conduct more than a shallow inspection that simply established the header information—the equivalent of the postal address for the packet. An ISP can use DPI to determine whether a packet values high-speed transport—as a television stream does in requiring a dedicated broadcast channel—and offer higher-speed dedicated capacity to that content, typically real-time dependent content such as television, movies, or telephone calls using VoIP.

Avoidance of DPI and other inspection techniques by encryption was a concern for Clark et al. (2002, 9): "Encrypting the stream might just be the first step in an escalating tussle between the end user and the network provider, in which the response of the provider is to refuse to carry encrypted data" (though he imagined only an authoritarian national monopoly ISP engaging in such behavior). Handley (2011) agrees and argues that standards bodies can designate the protocols to build the playing field, not to determine the outcome, particularly because design is not value neutral. He uses the session initiation protocol (SIP, specified in the IETF's RFC 2543) as an example of a standard that can be used by both network neutral ISPs and those desiring more intrusive traffic management, avoiding the dilemma that IETF becomes "stuck between [DPI], and innovation-inhibiting regulation." Note that "SIP is designed to be independent of the lower-layer transport protocol" (RFC 2543, 1999, 1).

The main public policy problem with DPI is its potential for surveillance and privacy invasion; with regulation, it eliminates the "tussle space," and government has to pick winners, as well as encourage rent-seeking behavior by those potential winners. Handley (2011, 11) lists five types of prioritization that have the potential to discriminate against particular applications, of which DPI is worth further attention, if only because it is the most expensive and intrusive of the technologies listed, and therefore ISPs have a particularly acute choice between investment in bandwidth capacity and in DPI to control the level of traffic at existing bandwidth. To some extent, there is a binary choice, and at the margin "either we end up with a network where innovation can only be within narrow bounds, constrained by yesterday's common applications, or the regulators eventually step in and prohibit broad classes of traffic prioritization" (Handley 2011, 16). Crowcroft (2011) makes the additional point that there has been little innovation within the network architecture for thirty years and that neutrality regulation might make this problem worse. He concludes that "we never had network neutrality in the past, and I do not believe we should engineer for it in the future either" (12).

The applications standards community is less sanguine about network-layer discrimination than the network engineers, perhaps unsurprisingly as it is their services that stand to receive discriminatory treatment. The end-to-end applications argument has been made forcefully by World Wide Web inventor Tim Berners-Lee (2011), and it is worth recalling that he made WWW standards royalty free and nondiscriminatory as a design choice in the creation of the World Wide Web Consortium in 1994 (Marsden 2011). He argues strongly against application discrimination, though he is careful not to argue for legislation prohibiting QoS that does not discriminate in this way.

Similarly, Handley places faith in nondiscrimination by application via the Re-feedback of Explicit Congestion Notification (Re-ECN) protocol developed by Briscoe (2008). However, development and deployment of draft protocols (see RFC 2009) as solutions in an area that directly affects free speech is a heroic endeavor for a politician, however logical to an engineer. Given the range of issues, the ITU Focus Group on Future Networks (2010) concluded that much wider liaison both within ICT industry standards bodies and with neighboring and converging areas was essential to determine future network architectures.

DPI equipment can also be used for blocking specific content, as requested by many governments. If a government is willing to require ISPs to install DPI equipment, dual-purpose technology that can be used for much more than law enforcement purposes, do ISPs have an incentive to use that equipment to its maximum commercial effectiveness? This is a matter of pressing and legitimate public policy. This problem of when QoS tools may be used arose in the context of behavioral advertising when British Telecom entered into secret subscriber trials with Phorm, a U.S.-based targeted advertising corporation in 2006, though in the wake of the controversy, U.K. ISPs have ceased to trial with Phorm (McStay 2011) and it appears to have exited the European market in favor of the regulatory environments in the new markets of South Korea and Brazil (Clayton 2008; Marsden 2010).

DPI and other techniques that let ISPs prioritize content also allow them to slow down other content, as well as speed up content for those that pay (and for emergency communications and other network-preferred packets). This potentially threatens competitors with that content: Skype offers VoIP using normal Internet speeds; uTorrent and BBC's iPlayer have offered video using P2P protocols. Infonetics (2011) states: "Although residual concerns over Net neutrality and operators' proclivity for all-you-can-eat services have made U.S. operators hesitant to do any widespread deploy-

Table 7.2
Types of code and code regulation

Layer	Varies but typically network and transport layers
Location (manufacturers, ISPs, servers, clients)	Hardware and software vendors' DPI solutions; ISP traffic management solutions
Enforcement of code	Termination monopoly held by ISPs—nontransparent term of use for end users

ments . . . the DPI market is growing at a healthy pace in other parts of the world. We anticipate particularly dramatic growth in emerging markets." They add that "operators across all regions plan to use DPI to enable value-added services, such as content-based charging and premium services that provide a guaranteed quality of service for applications like video streaming." This demonstrates the dual use of the technology, to both rate-limit and control the user experience for security and cost rationalization, as well as to provide faster secure service for premium content.

Encryption is common in these applications and partially successful in overcoming these ISP controls, but even if all users and applications used strong encryption, this would not succeed in overcoming decisions by ISPs simply to route known premium traffic to a "faster lane," consigning all other traffic into a slower nonpriority lane (a policy explanation simplifying a complex engineering decision). P2P is designed to make the most efficient use of congested networks, and its proponents claim that with sufficient deployment, P2P could largely overcome congestion problems. Table 7.2 illustrates the types of code and code regulation discussed in this section.

Institutional Political Economy

This policy field displays a plurality of market actors (content and carriage disguise the various interests within and between those sectors, such as mobile networks and vertically integrated actors) and a profusion of formal (state and supranational) as well as informal (standard-setting) regulators. It exhibits advanced examples of regulatory capture, especially in the more static and matured regulatory environment of telecoms.

The arguments surrounding network neutrality revive the surveillance-industrial complex (ACLU 2004) argument of long standing between civil society advocates of free speech and expression on the Internet together with almost all noncommercial and some commercial content companies, and large ISPs and some commercial content providers. To briefly reprise the ACLU argument, the claim is that companies (and individuals, though this category is less relevant here) are pressured to voluntarily or compulsorily provide consumer information to the government; government processes and searches private data on a mass scale; and some companies are pushing the government to adopt surveillance technologies and programs based on private sector data, investing in the private sector's surveillance capability. We consider each in turn.

Large telecoms and commercial content companies largely oppose network neutrality, in that payment on a priority basis supports a cable TV type of model and protects their investments in commercial video rights and lower bandwidth networks. The argument is that noncommercial players and domestic users are unwilling to invest in better services and need to be rationed in order to be persuaded to pay for higher quality. There is some truth in this claim, but also in the counterclaim that ISPs and large content providers may be using technical means to protect their existing monopoly or oligopoly services, including telephone service and premium TV channel provision. (Consider: if voice over the Internet is effective, why would any consumer pay for a telephone service or telephone calls? A similar argument applies to video.) In Canada, Telus has argued that rationing access by metering billing for consumers is ineffective because it has substantial competition, suggesting that a truly competitive market would produce increasing capacity offers to consumers (Geist 2011).

The use of "throttling" technology (by which a network administrator slows down non-preferred packets)—essentially P2P applications being slowed by use of Sandvine technology—was at issue in the Federal Communications Commission (FCC) order (2008) against Comcast, a major cable broadband ISP. A Comcast deposition to the FCC stated that BitTorrent throttling began in May 2005. Comcast's claims not to have throttled and blocked traffic when exposed in May 2007 had been misleading. The FCC ordered Comcast to do the following within thirty days:

1. Disclose to the commission the precise contours of the network management practices at issue here, including what equipment has been used, when it began to be employed, when and under what circumstances it has

been used, how it has been configured, what protocols have been affected, and where it has been deployed;

2. Submit a compliance plan to the commission with interim benchmarks that describe how it intends to transition from discriminatory to nondiscriminatory network management practices by the end of 2008

3. Disclose to the commission and the public the details of the network management practices that it intends to deploy following the termination of its current practices, including the thresholds that will trigger any limits on customers' access to bandwidth.

Most damning, the FCC found that "Comcast has an anti-competitive motive to interfere with customers' use of P2P applications." This was because P2P offers a rival TV service delivery to cable, which the FCC found "poses a potential competitive threat to Comcast's video-on-demand (VOD) service." The Comcast use of DPI to discriminate between providers of P2P was also condemned in strong terms: "Comcast's practices are not minimally intrusive, as the company claims, but rather are invasive and have significant effects." The commission concluded that Comcast's conduct blocked Internet traffic, rejected Comcast's defense that its practice constitutes reasonable network management, and "also concluded that the anti-competitive harms caused by Comcast's conduct have been compounded by the company's unacceptable failure to disclose its practices to consumers."

The FCC justified its regulatory authority to issue the Comcast order and open Internet order (Federal Register 2011), invoking its Title I ancillary jurisdiction under the Communications Act to regulate in the name of national Internet policy as described in seven statutory provisions, all of which speak in general terms about promoting deployment, promoting accessibility, and reducing market entry barriers. On these grounds, Comcast in 2008 brought a suit to the court of appeals to overturn the order, succeeding in 2010 (Frieden 2011). The FCC ruling against Comcast's attempts to stop P2P by sending phantom reset packets to customers reflects another easy case, as obvious as the VoIP blocking in Madison River in 2005. Comcast announced a 250 GB monthly limit in early September 2008, replacing its previous discretionary terms of use reasonable caps (Burstein 2008). Comcast also replied by explaining its use of Sandvine technology and its plans to introduce a "blunter weapon" in its future shaping of traffic. Comcast responded to the FCC network neutrality ruling by claiming that it engineers its own VoIP product with QoS and avoids the public Internet.

The "open Internet" and network neutrality consultations launched by the European Commission in 2010 produced over 300 responses, fairly evenly divided between industry and users, the former generally in favor of discrimination and the latter opposed. (The consultation was described as *open Internet* in an attempt to prevent political rows that characterized the use of the term *net neutrality* in the United States.)

There was very little input by content providers, but a great deal by ISPs and relevant equipment manufacturers. Ofcom in the United Kingdom had fewer than 100 responses to its so-called network neutrality consultation earlier in the same year. By contrast, the 2009–2010 inquiry in the United States produced almost 30,000 responses, though many of these were very similar or identical. The level of interest was also reflected in an online petition in favor of network neutrality signed by almost 2 million individuals. In the United Kingdom, by contrast, the use of online petitions at the prime minister's Web site was more exercised by the by-product of network neutrality: behavioral advertising trials and a petition condemning the secret trial by Phorm produced almost 10,000 votes. Though public opinion is fickle, it was clear in summer 2011 that a very large group of Netherlands voters were very upset that KPN Mobile threatened to use DPI (Preuschat 2011) to block WhatsApp, which produced the political support for its network neutrality law. We may expect to see more protest behavior by "Netizens" who do not agree with network neutrality policies, especially where ISPs are seen to have failed to inform end users fully about the implications of policy changes. Regulators and politicians are challenged publicly by such problems, particularly given the ubiquity of e-mail, Twitter, and social media protests against censorship. Research into social activism against corporate control of the Internet is a growing research field (Powell and Cooper 2011; Hart 2011).

The total responses do not reflect the degree to which policymakers listen to the various responses, and the general bias toward business constituencies was reflected in the composition of the speaker panels for the European Parliament and Commission joint hearings on network neutrality and the open Internet organized in Brussels after the conclusion of the consultation in November 2010. The vast majority of speakers represented industry prodiscrimination interests, with only members of the European Parliament, content provider BBC, and a single civil society stakeholder presenting dissenting views from the commission-organized morning session. The afternoon session was more balanced due to the presence of many consumer-oriented members of the European Parliament. The U.K. government organized a private network neutrality summit in March 2011, at which two user groups were invited, together with the Taxpayers Alliance. This reflects the wider view of telecoms policymakers that civil society organizations are outsiders to the usual telecoms economic discussion and raise intractable problems. Telecoms policymakers in government are only slowly learning the need for rights-based dialogue.

Net Neutrality, Censorship, and Developing Countries

The problems of development and the global digital divide are intimately connected to network neutrality (Internet Governance Forum 2008). Internet connectivity is still very expensive for most developing countries, despite attempts to ensure local Internet peering points (exchanges) and new undersea cables, for instance, serving East Africa. Flooding the developing world's ISPs with video traffic, much of which comes from major video production countries such as India, Nigeria, and the United States, could place local ISPs in serious financial peril. Casualties in such undertakings include countries blacklisted by major ISPs for producing large amounts of spam.

The second development problem that the network neutrality debate centers on is the wireless or mobile Internet. Most developing countries' citizens have much lower bandwidth than the West, and most of their connectivity is mobile: India is probably the poster child for a country with at least ten times more mobile than fixed phone subscribers. In the next several years, Internet users in the developing world will test the limits of mobile networks, and capacity as well as price might determine the extent to which they can expect a rapidly developing or a Third World Internet experience.

Universal service is still a pipe dream for many in the developing world, and when that arrives, the definition it is given will determine the minimum threshold that ISPs have to achieve. As Mueller (2007, 7) states, network neutrality "must also encompass a positive assertion of the broader social, economic and political value of universal and non-discriminatory access to Internet resources among those connected to the Internet."

The types of non network neutrality employed in West Asia and North Africa in winter 2010–2011 were politically rather than economically motivated, that is, by political censorship designed to prevent citizens' access to the Internet, as seen in chapter 5. Mueller (2007) argues that the tendency of governments in both repressive and traditionally democratic regimes to impose liability on ISPs to censor content for a plethora of reasons argues for a policy of robust noninterference. That is especially valuable in countries where there is much less discussion of how government deployment of ISPs as censors can endanger user privacy and freedom of expression. Mueller suggests that the network neutrality metaphor could be used to hold all filtering and censorship practices up to the light, as well as other areas of Internet regulation, such as domain name governance.

Table 7.3 summarizes the political economy concerns raised in the network neutrality debate, in which large corporate interests sought to capture the policymakers' agenda, with a vociferous lobbying campaign in the United States and a muted one in Europe (Sluijs 2010), led by civil society groups aiming to preserve the open Internet. It is notable that the

Table 7.3
Institutional political economy

Key actors: national, regional, global	Telecoms regulators; ISPs, intermediaries, content companies, largely local user groups. Coders in multinational corps. Security-industrial complex re DPI.
How legitimate and accountable?	Telecoms regulators accountable through parliaments; self-regulatory solutions unaccountable except through telecoms regulators (where applicable).
Multistakeholderism	Organized opposition to corporate blocking of applications in United States, Netherlands, and France; less attention paid elsewhere. Some effect on European Parliament amendments to telecoms package 2009.
Key technical actor buy-in	Organized by corporate vendors, notably Alcatel-Lucent, and Sandvine. Mobile industry at forefront of QoS efforts. Technical community supportive of drive toward QoS and managed services. Technical opposition to QoS bans. Also lobbied for greater bandwidth solution with minimal QoS.
Lessons	Highly technical issue meant little traction for policy initiatives to shape code except in egregious cases. Much of technical community active in control environment.

European telecoms regulators, and government officials, were initially deaf to the human rights concerns raised. The European Data Protection Supervisor (2011a) then explained its concerns in this area, which concerned data protection and the impact on privacy of the widespread deployment of DPI.

Outcomes

Unsurprisingly, network neutrality regulation has been fiercely resisted by the ISPs that wish to discriminate and charge nonaffiliated content providers higher prices or throttle popular existing services. Neutrality regulation to date has relied mainly on a series of declarations and merger conditions. Mergers afford regulators the opportunity to introduce such relatively minor adjustments, as merger parties are eager to conclude the overall deal and trade off the relatively minor inconvenience of controls on traffic management in the interests of successful approval. In the same way as consumers—even with perfect information—may not view traffic management as the primary goal of their subscription to broadband (and are thus easy targets for restrictive conditions so long as industry standards prevent real choices among ISPs), so ISPs may make strategic choices to accept some limited traffic management conditions as a price of approval. The failed 2011 merger of AT&T Wireless and T-Mobile illustrated the propensity to argue for enforcing network neutrality through merger conditions, as did the merger of Level 3 and Global Crossing, important tier 1 backbone providers with extensive content delivery networks, and the Level 3 legal dispute with Comcast (Frieden 2011).

In the discussions to amend the E-Communications Framework by Directives 2009/136/EC and 2009/140/EC, large, well-resourced European incumbent ISPs saw the opportunity to make common cause with mobile operators (Wu 2007) and others in an alliance to permit filtering. Politicians in 2012 were reviewing the ECD (European Commission 2012) and implementing local laws that favor, for instance, their copyright industries, such as the Digital Economy Act 2010 in the United Kingdom and the Haute autorité pour la diffusion des oeuvres et la protection des droits sur internet law in France (EC 2011b). Regulations are erecting entry barriers with the connivance of the incumbent players, with potentially enormous consequences for free speech, free competition, and individual expression (Akdeniz 2011). This may or may not be the correct policy option for a safer Internet policy (to prevent exposing children to illegal or offensive content), though it signals an abrupt change from the open Internet (Zittrain 2008). It is therefore vital that regulators address the question of the proper approach to network neutrality to prevent harm to the current Internet, as well as begin to address the heavier questions of positive or tiered breaches of network neutrality.

Privacy inquiries can also have an impact on regulatory control of traffic management, with the U.K. government threatened with legal action by the European Commission for implementation of the EU data protection framework that allowed the secret and invasive behavioral advertising practices of British Telecom and Phorm in 2006. The introduction of network neutrality rules into European law was under the rubric of consumer information safeguards and privacy regulation, not competition rules, and the U.S. Congress has been exploring privacy rules and controls on ISP behavioral advertising activities.

Although network neutrality was the subject of FCC regulatory discussions and merger conditions from 2003 (Frieden 2011), its status has remained unclear, with no legislation passed by Congress, and FCC actions reserved to isolated examples of discrimination that were litigated. President Obama was committed to network neutrality regulation from his Senate career in 2006 and during his first presidential election campaign (Marsden 2010). A Notice of Proposed Rule Making by the FCC extended a consultation on network neutrality over 2009–2010. This process was finishing just as a court of appeals in April 2010 judged that the FCC's regulatory actions in this area were not justified by its reasoning under the Communications Act 1996 (*Comcast* v. *FCC* 2010). The successful Comcast appeal meant that the FCC had three legal choices: reclaim Title II common carrier authority for ISPs under the 1996 Telecommunications Act, ask Congress to relegislate to grant it Title I authority, or try to assert its own Title I authority subject to legal challenge (Frieden 2010). It adopted this last course in its Order of December 23, 2010 (FCC 2010), which was challenged before the courts in 2012 (Frieden 2011). This stay of regulatory action in a general election year leaves the FCC in suspended animation in 2012 (Marsden 2010; Donahue 2010).

The EU institutions in late 2009 agreed to impose transparency and network neutrality "lite" conditions on ISPs in directives that had to be implemented in national law by May 2011. BEREC (2010) noted that legal provisions in the directives permit greater symmetric regulation on all operators, not simply dominant actors, but asked for clarification on these measures: "Access Directive, Art 5(1) now explicitly mentions that NRAs are able to impose obligations 'on undertakings that control access to end-users to make their services interoperable.'" The wider new scope for solving interoperability disputes may be used: "The potential outcome of disputes based on the transparency obligations can provide a "credible threat" for undertakings to behave in line with those obligations, since violation may trigger the imposition of minimum quality requirements on an undertaking, in line with Art 22(3) USD."

The European Commission in 2011 consulted on the future of the Universal Service Obligation (EC 2010), which may be extended to 2 Mbps broadband (affecting member state law some years later), marking a new line in the sand in Europe for minimum service levels. That may also require commitments to offering that access to the open Internet, not a throttled, blocked, walled-garden area.

Internet Interconnection, Content Distribution Networks, and Managed Services

It is not only in the last mile or in the consumer's ISP that network neutrality may be affected by policy decisions to differentiate traffic. Internet peering (the cost-free exchange of traffic by similarly sized ISPs) has been largely replaced by paid interconnection (Faratin et al. 2008), and in 2010 a dispute between Comcast and Level 3 was claimed by the latter party to involve a network neutrality dispute disguised as an interconnection dispute (Clark, Lehr, and Bauer 2011). A European dispute between Orange and Cogent in connection with Megavideo traffic involved similar claims. (Orange is the largest network provider in France, Cogent is a multinational tier 1 Internet provider, and Megavideo is a video-hosting company that uses Cogent networks for distribution.)

The timing of the dispute as Comcast was bidding to buy the television network NBC caused some suspicion that Level 3 was leveraging the political pressure on Comcast at a critical stage of the merger review. There have also been claims that Comcast may leverage its Internet access business to stream NBC programming at a discount to nonaffiliated programming, which led to a specific merger condition prohibiting such differentiation (Frieden 2011).

Network neutrality lobbyists intervened only partially successfully in the NBC/Universal merger of 2010, the abortive AT&T/T-Mobile merger of 2011, the AT&T/Southwestern Bell and Verizon/GTE mergers of 2006, and the auction of 700 MHz frequencies of 2007. In all these cases, there were significant resources deployed by the pro– and anti–network neutrality lobbies in Washington, D.C. It is difficult to assess the importance and public support for each lobby given the intimate connections between the lobbies and the politicians on both sides of the debate.

A 2011 dispute in Canada regarding the conduct of Shaw Communications, a West Coast ISP, revived these concerns, as the company appeared to indicate that its online movie subscribers would not exceed bandwidth caps with its affiliated service as opposed to competitors such as NetFlix. Shaw put out a statement explaining that the initial marketing material was in error and that Internet streaming of its own service would contribute to the bandwidth cap, but a dedicated cable-only service would not, much as AT&T uVerse uses the same physical fiber to deliver video service and data service, the former as "managed services" and the latter as non-managed IP (Anderson 2011). The difficulty for regulators will be to identify which data are a managed service and which are the straightforward IP stream.

Further questions for regulators will include whether ISPs can provide content distribution network services to content providers in competition with third parties. CDNs such as Akamai provide a virtual ISP access service by locally caching content for content customers close to the local telephone exchange, by investing in tens of thousands of servers distributed across networks and geographies. This is sometimes described as OTT (over-the-top) video service. Google has built a very large proprietary CDN for its own traffic, notably its video YouTube service, and other large content carriers such as the BBC and Facebook may follow suit. A further question arises because these CDNs are almost entirely downloading content to customers rather than acting as peers, and therefore creating a very large traffic imbalance. As a result, we can expect to see paid interconnection increasing and peering decrease (Marsden 2010).

Current telecommunications laws typically allow for disputes between public carriers, mainly ISPs. Search engines, video hosting sites, and CDNs are not public carriers but private carriers, and therefore their relations with ISPs are regulated by contract law rather than regulators, with the latter having no legislative mandate to affect those private parties' relations. Calls for search neutrality or regulation of CDNs may therefore be effective lobbying discussion but do not relate to current telecoms regulation (Frieden 2011).

ISP transparency regarding network management practices has been the main component of these policies, although best regulatory information practices have yet to emerge. Faulhaber (2010) has suggested four basic principles based on examination of other industries' information regulation: "(1) disclose all information relevant to customer choice, 2) to which customers have easy access, 3) clearly and simply, and 4) in a way that is verifiable" (738). Stronger consumer confidence could be built if information was cross-compared by an accredited independent third party that is not reliant on broadband industry funding, such as a consumer protection agency. This could be carried out at arm's length by a self- or coregulatory agreement (BEREC 2011; Marsden 2012).

The FCC and European Commission position is that only "reasonable network management" should be permitted and that end users should be given clear information on this reasonableness (Faulhaber 2010). Both have relied on nonbinding declarations to make clear their intention to regulate the reasonableness of traffic management practices. The Canadian Radio-Television and Telecommunications Commission has relied on inquiries (to the dissatisfaction of consumer advocates). Norway (Norwegian Code 2009) and Japan have nonbinding self-regulatory declarations that thus far have not been enforced. In 2011, Singapore instituted a network neutrality requirement that ISPs do not block third-party applications, which is also the subject of the law passed in the Netherlands in March 2012 (Marsden 2012).

Wireless Network Neutrality

Wireless (in European terms, mobile) is a particular concern for network neutrality, and it was controversy over blocking by a mobile operator that led to the Netherlands law. Mobile remains a poor substitute for the fixed Internet (Noam 2011), and mobile smart phone users in 2010 downloaded only an average of 79 megabytes per month (Cisco 2011). Mobile is a trivial proportion of overall Internet traffic by volume, but it commands massive premiums over fixed traffic for the services provided. Cairncross (1997) explored how switched voice telephony was being replaced by VoIP, the new technology that offered extraordinary efficiencies for both voice and data. In 2000, European governments auctioned off spectrum for that IP traffic to be carried by the extraordinarily profitable mobile oligopolies that had achieved spectacular growth in the 1990s. In 2010, 1 percent of all IP traffic was carried over mobile networks. A substantial part of mobile traffic is intended in the future to be handed off to femtocells (a small, low-power cellular base station typically found in households or work premises rather than in public networks), WiFi cells, and other fixed wireless infrastructure, piggybacking on the relatively stable and mature fixed Internet that is expanding at approximately its historical growth rate of 50 percent annually to meet capacity (Cisco 2011). Despite this empirical evidence to the contrary, a cliché in network neutrality discussions is the "explosive growth" of the Internet (Cooper, Soppera, and Jacquet 2011).

Regulations passed in licensing mobile spectrum can affect network neutrality at a fundamental level. Interoperability requirements can form a basis for action where an ISP blocks an application. Furthermore, wireless ISPs may be required to provide open access, as in the FCC auction of 700 MHz upper block C frequencies—used for 4G cellular data and worth almost $5 billion at auction—in 2008 (Rosston and Topper 2010) or in more general common carriage requirements traditionally imposed on public networks since before the dawn of modern communications, with railways and telegraphs. The FCC (2010) specifically asked for answers to regulation of managed specialized services and wireless network neutrality in 2010, and it announced that it was prepared not to enforce its proposed regulation on wireless services in the near future (FCC 2010). This means that the faster-growing and more competitive U.S. market will be less regulated than the more sluggish and less competitive European market.

European telecommunications regulators group BEREC explained, "Mobile network access may need the ability to limit the overall capacity consumption per user in certain circumstances (more than fixed network access with high bandwidth resources) and as this does not involve selective treatment of content it does not, in principle, raise network neutrality concerns" (2010, 11). It explains that though mobile will always need greater traffic management than fixed ("traffic management for mobile accesses is more challenging"), symmetrical regulation must be maintained to ensure technological neutrality: "There are not enough arguments to

Table 7.4
Outcomes and divergences

Transparency	Refusal to create transparency a critical element in early U.S. cases. European work on creating greater transparency through regulation.
Enforcement	Network neutrality "lite" solutions to prevent protocol, application blocking so far limited to statute in Netherlands, and regulatory declarations (e.g., in Canada, the United States). Bandwidth or service plan capping resulted.
Interoperability	Vendor off-the-shelf solutions adapted to ISP but little transparency on policy.
Efficiency	Coregulation often suggested as best option, with full transparency and ability for users to switch, accompanied by code solutions.

support having a different approach on network neutrality in the fixed and mobile networks. And especially future-oriented approach for network neutrality should not include differentiation between different types of the networks." It concludes that mobile should be subject to the network neutrality "lite" provisions available under Directives EC/136/2009 and EC/140/2009, listing some breaches of neutrality: "blocking of VoIP in mobile networks occurred in Austria, Croatia, Germany, Italy, the Netherlands, Portugal, Romania and Switzerland" (3). Reding (2012, para. 4) stated, "This 'Internet freedom provision' represents a great victory." Commentators are not convinced that the 2009 law on network neutrality was being effectively implemented (Marsden 2012; European Data Protection Supervisor 2011).

Table 7.4 shows the outcomes and divergences of the policy process.

The Future of Network Neutrality and the Open Internet

The pace of change in the relation between architecture and content on the Internet requires continuous improvement in the regulator's research and technological training. Regulators can monitor both commercial transactions and traffic shaping by ISPs to detect potentially abusive discrimination. An ex ante requirement to demonstrate internal network metrics to content provider customers and consumers because of a regulatory or coregulatory reporting requirement may be a practical solution. The need for better research toward understanding the nature of congestion problems on the Internet and their effect on content and innovation is clear (Marsden 2012).

Chapter 6 showed us how the state security apparatus has co-opted private actors, notably ISPs, to enable it to carry out surveillance of the entire civilian population and to counter the twin bogeymen of content censorship: pedophilia (which is better pursued by arresting abusers) and "glorification of terrorism" (ditto). In this chapter, we saw how ISPs have taken those technologies of control to throttle content requested by their own users, which competes with their own or affiliated content. This is done to extract greater profits from users and content providers and to slow Internet growth to more manageable levels. This will have a substantial—if unmeasurable—effect on the freedom to innovate for start-up entrepreneurs. We also saw in chapter 4 that copyright industries have used the state and private control technologies to attempt to stem the flow of material shared freely online.

The security-industrial complex is now a substantial industry in advanced economies, with significant legal and less legal export potential to dictatorial regimes. Its technologies of control and lobbying power, the latter largely obscured from public gaze, can only increase over the coming decade, a serious threat to individual human freedoms on the Internet.

8   Comparative Case Study Analysis

In this book, we have examined five hard cases of code-based systems in which self-regulation has had limited effect in producing key public goods:

Privacy and data protection   A reliance on firms' disclosure of privacy-related behavior and consumer education has done little to protect privacy. More interventionist EU data protection rules for controllers of personal data have had a significant global impact, but this regime is now being supplemented by code rules for radio frequency identifier (RFID) tags and behaviorally targeted advertising in an attempt to improve the efficacy of privacy protection.

Copyrights and the incentivization of creativity   In contrast, rights holders since the 1990s have encouraged governments to provide statutory code regulation protecting technical protection measures and, more recently, imposing graduated response and Web blocking powers against infringers. This case illustrates the dangers of blunt code regulation imposed following government capture by concentrated industries, which has seen a distortion of the aims of copyright law, the sweeping aside of delicate social balances protecting disadvantaged groups, and forum shifting from the World Intellectual Property Organization (WIPO), to the World Trade Organization (WTO), to the Anti-Counterfeiting Trade Agreement (ACTA).

Censors and freedom of expression   Blocking and labeling systems have been introduced mainly through pressure from governments for ISP self-regulation, often without an adequate representation of civil society groups that could promote freedom of expression. Repressive regimes have encouraged self-censorship through the use of intensive surveillance of online forums.

Social networks and user-generated content   These newer domains of online interaction have seen a regulatory focus on privacy and child safety, with protections based on user consent to terms of service and minimal, crowd-sourced regulatory signals.

Smart pipes   There has been some regulatory support for network neutrality, which combines elements of universal service and common carriage to support application-layer innovation and freedom of expression. Architecting a low barrier-to-entry Internet that supports fundamental rights is a key concluding policy challenge.

Our aim throughout this book has been to identify the regulatory and governance mechanisms that have enabled the production of public goods such as security and freedom of expression, while enabling the continued rapid development of the Internet, and to understand how these processes can be protected as the Internet becomes a multilingual mass market artifact. We have taken a holistic approach to capture the roles of technology and services, business models, market structure and conduct, and governance (regulation, self-, and coregulation, standards, and other nonstate forms of control).

Understanding governance contributes to a better understanding of success and failure of Internet systems more generally. Activities at one layer of the protocol stack—and one disciplinary approach—may be driven by and affect those at others. Failure may be gaps, duplication, conflict as well as solution at the wrong level, poor function, inappropriate adoption, distorted development, or poor integration between different platforms or protocols.

The critical risks of a failure to develop governance more effectively arise from two directions:

• From the technical design community, a sensitivity failure to account for user adoption practice in creating better feedback loops can lead to system design that results in suboptimal adoption. Examples might be lack of privacy by design, misalignment of user practices and design solutions, or adoption rates below optimal (especially where universality is a desired and otherwise achievable policy option).

• From the social scientific, economics, and legal community (and government policymakers whose advice is largely drawn from their ranks), a failure to create better dialogue with the engineers in the Internet community can result in a governance failure in which user groups perceive critical governance flaws in standards creation. The result of this could be ill-conceived legal mechanisms designed to control rather than develop the future Internet, or a widespread reimposition of national borders and state censorship rather than enhancing human rights and a vibrant public sphere.

More fundamental questions need to be asked about the space for regulation of code, accepting both its importance as a regulatory tool and the overarching legitimacy and efficacy concerns that it poses. Zittrain (2006, 2008) and Ohm and Grimmelman (2010) have written about the key impact on Internet innovation of the technology's open or "generative" quality, with high reconfigurability enabling user-led innovation (Von Hippel 1976) and rapid market entry thanks to high levels of standards use and interoperability and few chokepoints or gatekeepers. However, we have seen through the case studies in this book that governments' attempts to intervene after proof of dominance has been shown is invariably a second-best compromise between a desire to avoid overly hasty regulation and a failure to realize the effect of technology on neighboring policy areas.

For instance, in the two decades since the Web browser first included cookies that are left on user computers, the European authorities have failed to persuade American companies to introduce meaningful prior consent for their users. The attempt to solve the network neutrality problem through competition law and consideration of abuse by dominant actors appears bizarre in the face of the herculean technical standards efforts since 2000 to achieve a "cash register on the Internet and charge for it" (Waclawsky 2005), which has made ISP actors unsurprisingly resistant to any regulatory nudges away from this emerging business model.

Cross-Sectional Comparison of Case Studies

Our case studies demonstrate what is by now obvious: code and law are interdependent, and law cannot control code without unforeseen consequences. Law must therefore comprehend its effects on code, and vice versa: programmers need to understand the limits of law and its potential to affect their architectures. Smarter regulation provides nudges and tweaks to coders, users, and companies, as well as using market incentives, standards, and government procurement policies.

We asked in each case study how different levers work at different layers. In legal terms, that means examining the extent of vertical integration and bottlenecks. However, as we are dealing with human rights such as free expression, that also means compatibility with those fundamental rights— and how civil society can push governments toward regimes that have a better outcome for them.

We asked in each case if stakeholder input to policy has been meaningful or a Potemkin village square to which neither corporate nor government actors pay real attention (Marsden 2011). Our conclusions are in table 8.1. Note that *sledgehammer* refers to the use of that particular tool to crack a nut, an explicit and disproportionate use of force.

Our top-level concern, shown in table 8.2, is public policy response to code and institutional dynamics. In the absence of market failure, without detrimental social impact, there would be no need for regulation at all.

An overarching social impact of the Internet and related technologies has been to make the diffusion of information—whether personal data, copyrighted works, or banned materials—much more difficult to control. Regulation that depends on such control is therefore challenged, which gives rise to many of the problems we consider in the case studies.

Despite the speed of development of these markets, they all display significant monopolistic tendencies driven by network effects, even where corporate sunk cost is not an overwhelming factor—for example, social networking sites (SNS), in which user time is the most significant investment. The user is a prisoner of her own making. At the same time, ex post competition policy, postulated as the most economically efficient response to monopoly concerns, has been shown to be very defective in its speed of response to rapid market entrenchment (e.g., in the Microsoft browser case).

In several of our case studies, there were no agencies with responsibility for fundamental rights concerns such as censorship and freedom of expression. These concerns were left largely or entirely to markets, and regulators focused on economic impacts. Only in the most egregious cases (such as the U.S. Communications Decency Act, or European Commission proposals for mandatory ISP blocking) did courts or legislatures intervene.

In other case studies, existing regulators have been extremely slow to understand the implications of new technology and markets and to ensure effective protection of individual rights. This oversight on the part of poli-

Table 8.1

Best and sledgehammer practices

Example	Reflexive best practice	Sledgehammer
Encryption	Incentives for adoption of Secure Socket Layer/Transport Layer Security (SSL/TLS) to protect e-commerce, stop WiFi hacking	Clipper chip; crypto software export controls; key escrow (government attempts to require individuals to deposit or otherwise reveal encryption passwords)
Data protection	Privacy by design: Schleswig-Holstein public procurement rules favoring EuroPrise-certified software Privacy impact assessment (of legislation, government regulation, private companies)	U.S.-EU negotiated safe harbor for data protection—market entry condition—but mollified by weak enforcement
Copyrights	New business and legal models needed	Napster, KaZaA cases DRM and anticircumvention laws "Three strikes" DNS rerouting/blocking ACTA
Censors	Pre-CAIC Internet Watch Foundation Banking industry response to phishing Spam filtering and takedown	Golden Shield and Green Dam Statutory Web blocking *ACLU* v. *Reno* Superinjunctions to reveal Twitter and Google users
Social networks	Coregulatory codes of practice Enforcement action by Canadian federal privacy commissioner	Requiring real name registration, prelicensing and regulating bloggers; kill switches for social networking
Smart pipes	Instant messaging interoperability—AOL/TimeWarner merger Essential facilities, fair reasonable and nondiscriminatory, and interoperability	Network neutrality—extreme positions on both sides Google algorithm and mergers IMS and DPI as used by Phorm

Table 8.2
Public policy and market failure

	Data Protection	Copyright	Censors	Social networking	Smart pipes
Social impact of technology	Bandwidth, storage, processing capacity all doubling every 12–24 months, making it much easier for organizations to process and share personal data. E-government drives for personalization and savings; law enforcement and intelligence agency surveillance further impetus.	Perfect digital reproduction at almost zero marginal cost on user equipment has rendered copyright ineffective. Massive infringement over peer-to-peer nets, cyberlocker sites.	Ubiquitous use of broadband gives rise to call for parental controls. Widespread use of blogs and other types of political expression cause state concern leading to censorship. Both have increased since 2000, with users split between those opposed to private censorship mediated by state, and others' apparent preference for walled-garden safety environment.	Mass diffusion of social networks creates need for child protection and exclusion from adult networks. Other critical concerns over privacy.	Use of monitoring of traffic still largely hidden from fixed end users, except some early adopters with peer-to-peer and gaming applications. Mobile broadband and streaming video growth likely to increase user concerns.
Policy drivers: barriers to entry network and scale effects Competition	EU promotion of single market in data flows Personal data hoarding by information giants.	Incentivizing creativity. Grant of exclusive rights plus high returns to scale has created highly concentrated markets in music, film, software (latter with added network effects).	Censorship imposes entry costs through technology choice for blocking. DPI equipment for traffic monitoring a dual-use technology, also capable of surveillance and blocking.	Costs of providing safer environment nontrivial. Bebo decline relative to Facebook reveals tipping effect of dominant network.	Quality-of-service technology imposes nontrivial network costs that increase with scale, though deployment expertise offers scale economies. Security dual use reduces costs.

Table 8.2
(continued)

Fundamental rights in policy design	European Convention on Human Rights and EU Charter of Fundamental Rights key policy drivers.	Rights to remuneration, moral rights in Universal Declaration of Human Rights and Berne Convention.	Appeal and due process almost entirely lacking. Overall frameworks subject to little democratic scrutiny. Few institutional champions of free speech ex ante.	Little effective government policy but significant private actor business model with little or no privacy.	Notable by their absence from early deployment; rights-based discussion growing with regulatory oversight.
Lessons	Privacy is a key human right that may need significant government intervention to protect.	Policy focus has largely been on protecting rights of creators at the expense of freedom of expression and privacy.	Privatization of censorship endemic (even in China coregulation is the claimed model). Greater regional and international transparency standards needed (La Rue 2011). Focus on content producers would have longer-term impact and greater sensitivity to freedom of expression.	Nudge toward self-regulation became audited public demand by EC in 2008–2009. Still apparent that regulation is the most likely result of failure to achieve adequate privacy standards.	Technology development without privacy or expression input can lead to spectacularly invasive systems. Telecoms regulators inadequate to discuss rights-based policies.

cymakers has resulted in the subordination of user rights to both corporate and security interests, in privacy and data protection, network neutrality, social networks, and copyright. Remedying this failure to protect the fundamental rights of citizens is both an engineering and a broader regulatory challenge.

Regulation by code can increase the efficacy of regulation but should not be seen as a panacea. Copyright holders' hopes that "the answer to the machine is in the machine" led them to waste almost twenty years attempting to enforce scarcity-based business models rather than innovate toward the "celestial jukebox" that is finally emerging in products such as Spotify. Code is fundamentally a non-state-designed response that can lead to more effective solutions but will tend to undervalue the public interest and lack democratic legitimacy.

Nudges from regulators can encourage more legitimate private responses, but fundamental rights concerns often need stronger intervention, especially when business interests point firmly in the other direction or social benefits impose high private costs on corporate actors. Ideally it should be possible to design better code solutions that take into account the legitimate aspirations of users as citizens by incorporating social scientific and other nontechnical methodologies at the design stage. We return to this theme at the end of the chapter.

In table 8.3, the institutional political economy of Internet regulation shows a familiar dialogue between property right holders and governments, with multinational actors adding to their leverage through expertise and influence in technical standards bodies. There is a consequent legitimacy and transparency gap, and a struggle for civil society to raise any effective voice in the policy debates at an early enough stage to make meaningful design contributions in terms of due process in the deployment of technologies.

Effective, scalable state regulation often depends on the recruitment of intermediaries as enforcers (e.g., ISPs) in the few durable bottlenecks in the Internet value chain. The Internet has disintermediated many traditional points of control (e.g., consumer electronics manufacturers in the case of digital music reproduction equipment and publishers in the case of censors) and opened up further possibilities for individuals to interact without (yet) significant regulatory intervention (e.g., social networking sites). Such platforms can help users to act in their own interests—for example, by enabling

Table 8.3

Institutional political economy

	Data Protection	Copyright	Censors	Social networking	Smart pipes
Key actors: national, regional, global	DP regulators; consumer protection agencies (e.g., Federal Trade Commission). Coordination in EU, APEC. Police, advertisers, tech industry.	Rights holder associations; United States, EU, Japan operating at national, EU, and international (WIPO, ACTA) level. Have forum shifted to avoid civil society (WIPO to ACTA).	ISPs, international intermediaries, multinational content companies, largely local user groups. Coders multinational (World Wide Web Consortium, Platform for Internet Content Selection). Child protection groups.	ISPs, intermediaries, multinational content, largely local user groups. Coders in Silicon Valley. Child protection groups.	Telecoms regulators; ISPs, intermediaries, content companies, largely local user groups. Coders in multinational corps. Surveillance-industrial complex re. DPI.
How legitimate and accountable?	Mainly legislative creatures, hence democratically accountable. Less so outside Europe with self-regulatory solutions.	Much policy laundering, forum shifting, exclusion of civil society, bullying of developing world, fantasies that "the answer to the machine is in the machine," not the business model.	Accountability requires transparency to users. Private action subject to little accountability (e.g., put-back provisions). Engineering ethics an undeveloped area.	User-generated regulation offers some control. Generally opaque application terms and application means users vulnerable to private action without appeal.	Telecoms regulators accountable through parliaments; self-regulatory solutions unaccountable except via telecoms regulators (where applicable).
Multistakeholderism	Annual regulators' conference open to all stakeholders. RFID process explicitly multistakeholder, although industry tried hard to ignore civil society.	Civil society involvement at WIPO weakened anticircumvention measures in Internet treaties (see Drahos and Braithwaite 2002) but led to forum shift. Activists had to fight to involve legislators (United States, EU) in ACTA debates.	Little representation for free-speech nongovernmental organizations in censorship discussion, with corporate-government discussions largely private. Some discussion apparent (e.g., in hotline governance).	Little formal multistakeholder consultation by corporates. Restricted to publicity of most egregious privacy breaches and lobbying of government.	Organized opposition to corporate blocking of applications in United States, Netherlands, and France; less attention paid elsewhere. Some effect on European Parliament preelection 2009.

Table 8.3
(continued)

	Data Protection	Copyright	Censors	Social networking	Smart pipes
Key technical actor buy-in	Firefox (DNT), Apple Safari blocks third-party cookies by default (no ad network, unlike Microsoft and Google). RFID industry wrote privacy framework with some other stakeholder input; code approved by Article 29 Working Party.	Early technological protection measures produced by small software companies ineffective. Hardware (Trusted Computing Group, TCG) and operating system vendors now more involved, but still limited effectiveness. ISPs have fought against three-strikes and blocking, although in the interests of many as they raise entry barriers and reduce neutrality.	ISP-level filtering prevalent since emergence of large-scale spam e-mail problem in early 2000s, continued by British Telecoms technical initiative. Need for standards and best practices to ensure minimal collateral damage from blocking, particularly where technology sold to totalitarian regimes' ISPs.	Walled-garden Facebook approach meant third-party application developers dependent on Facebook ecosphere. More open environments supported; significant research effort in interoperable social media to prevent high-walled gardens.	Organized by corporate vendors (e.g., Alcatel-Lucent, Sandvine). Mobile industry at forefront of qualify-of-service (QoS) efforts. Technical community supportive of drive toward QoS and managed services. Technical opposition to QoS bans. Also lobbied for greater bandwidth solution with minimal QoS.
Lessons	Strong intervention from legislators and regulators is sometimes needed to counteract police and industry with interests in weaker regulation.	Code distracted attention from business innovation for more than a decade. Three-strikes has been pushed through with little multistakeholder involvement, resulting in policies widely criticized as contrary to freedom of expression.	Private censorship accompanied by government encouragement, sponsorship (e.g., hot lines). Democracies increasingly need political control of export of material conducive to repression.	User-generated regulation in social media proved largely mythical in face of commercial pressures to reduce privacy for third-party advertiser use. Civil society ineffective.	Highly technical issue meant little traction for policy initiatives to shape code except in egregious cases. Much of technical community active in control environment.

the restriction of third-party code's access to personal data on social networking sites and smart phones—but may need regulatory encouragement to do so when it is not in the platform operator's own commercial interest.

Companies can be regulated much more easily than individuals because of their tangible nature: they are easily identifiable and have assets that can be seized to prevent further malfeasance and remedy existing wrongs. Governments have found ways to maintain this despite the increasing ease of offshoring through mechanisms such as regulation of payment intermediaries (gambling) and the arrest of corporate officers who pass through their jurisdiction (gambling again).

As the Internet shifts control to individuals, this makes regulation more difficult. Because actors are often offshore or enforcement is driven by the commercial interests of corporate stakeholders (or both), there is a technocratic focus on interests of companies rather than citizens or users— often seen as the problem or the product, for instance, in copyright or social networks or network neutrality. Unsurprisingly this results in a lack of legitimacy or accountability given the objectification of the citizen. This can be summarized in the term of abuse: "the freetard" (Marsden 2010). It would be akin to politicians treating the voter as the problem. It is a worrying expansion of the traditional methods of setting copyright policy and the dominance of the private property right over other fundamental interests, particularly given that communications policy is essential to participative democracy.

The often mythical quality of multistakeholderism is proven by the extraordinary lack of real consultation that has taken place, particularly over network neutrality and copyright, most consultation being ex post and somewhat ad hoc. We return to this in the examination of code below. Ex ante policy consultation often focused on corporate concerns, behind closed doors, rather than those of citizens, which tended to be rushed and after-the-fact types of discussion regarding implementation. The impression given is that multistakeholderism was a slogan and a last-minute concern rather than an integrated element in decision making, let alone civil society an equal partner in trilateral discussion with government and industry.

Fundamental rights concerns remain, with governance of several case studies predetermining:

• Lack of concern, experience, and skills and lack of remit or enthusiasm to deal with fundamental user rights such as with copyright (economic concerns within departments of commerce and business, trade negotiators: Drahos and Braithwaite 2002)

• Censors (security concerns within interior ministries and their executive agencies and effective child protection group lobbying not matched by free speech advocates)

• Network neutrality (e.g., the technocratic and competition-oriented, narrowly defined statutory remit of a telecoms regulator)

Commercial interests dominate technical actors in policy debates, which has resulted in investment in control by dominant operators in bottlenecks rather than innovation by start-ups—again, particularly in copyright and network neutrality. Proprietary code dominates open source, standards-based solutions are limited, and therefore interoperability and wider concerns over ensuring the fungibility of code are relegated to marginal issues compared to the immediate commercial imperatives of monopolistic actors. If we had examined search neutrality or personal Internet security, we would have found similar proprietary solutions adopted rather than a search for industry consensus.

The lack of standards-based solutions in our case studies so far is a reflection of the dynamism and technological innovation in the studies, but also in the lack of impetus by market actors or regulators to negotiate and implement common standards. The former element is a feature of the period of technological development we examine, whereas the latter is a deliberate policy choice. Therefore, we see nothing inevitable about this trend toward proprietary standards. We see an opportunity for reexamination of the regulatory options in these case studies as the overarching lesson. This neither proves nor disproves Zittrain's "tethered appliance" thesis (Zittrain 2008), but it does indicate that the room for regulatory action still exists and should be reconsidered.

Monopolistic industry structure often means that users have no effective choice, for instance, over using music restricted by digital rights management (DRM) before the iTunes move to unprotected formats, or network-neutral ISPs. Where there is oligopoly, there is less or no concern for end user acceptance or resistance. It should be good business, good design, and good regulatory compliance to road-test new services and products prior to their imposition on an unsuspecting public.

Table 8.4 shows that code control over the various policy areas is maintained through various layers of the protocol stack, not merely the application layer. This is obviously the case with smart pipes, where the code innovation is designed to reach deep into the protocol stack to engage in deeper inspection of the bit stream. It also influences privacy, not least because informed consent for smart pipe–type activities is not unambiguous. It also affects censors, as network-level filtering depends on inspection that may be deeper than the packet header. By contrast, copyright enforcement, in the period before ISPs were directly involved in the activity, depended on tracing the end user by presenting to the ISP the IP address downloading suspected of infringing on material, and code enforcement of DRM. This may change as HADOPI (Haute autorité pour la diffusion des oeuvres et la protection des droits sur internet) types of regimes emerge and ISPs are required to conduct more strenuous enforcement on behalf of copyright holders, though blocking Web sites (e.g., Newzbin or Blogger) is relatively trivial for ISPs already engaged in blocking of various forms of pornography. This was a key factor in the decision by the English High Court to grant an injunction requiring British Telcoms to use its Cleanfeed system to block access to the Newzbin site. At the same time, the EU Court of Justice has found in two key decisions (*Scarlet Extended SA* v. *SABAM* 2011; *SABAM* v. *Netlog* 2012) that a general obligation cannot be imposed on ISPs or Web sites that monitor their customers' activities for illegal behavior.

For ISP censors, the mode chosen can cause substantial unintended collateral damage. The emergence of standards for Cleanfeed-type blocking may mitigate some free speech concerns and prevent the blocking of Wikipedia as in the infamous 2009 U.K. episode, in which blocking of one image by industry-standard filtering technology caused all U.K.-based edits to Wikipedia to be blocked (McIntyre 2011, 2012). Overall it is clear that both the sophistication of controlling code and its reach down into the protocol stack are at a stage of evolution not previously seen in the public Internet. There is no inevitability about even more widespread adoption of code to control user behavior and a deeper infiltration into transport layer, but that does appear to be the direction of travel.

Table 8.4
Types of code and code regulation

	Data protection	Copyright	Censors	Social networking	Smart pipes
Layer	New focus on RFIDs, browser code (do not track, cookies) and privacy by design	1990s focus on technological protection measures has largely been failure. Now three-strikes, ISP blocks.	Application or network both. Chinese ISPs use Golden Shield to filter at entry point to network (and nation), supported by filtering software in client PCs. Western nations typically at network (e.g., Cleanfeed) and filters at client level.	Application (including third-party applications and media partners); platform.	Varies but typically network or transport layer.
Location (manufacturers, ISPs, servers, clients)	Software and system architects.	Previously software and hardware vendors; now ISPs.	Clients for filters, manufacturers and ISPs for transport-level filters.	Server side with some mobile-based features.	Hardware and software vendors' DPI solutions; ISP traffic management solutions.
Enforcement of code	Threat of Data Protection Directive enforcement; revision of Data Protection Directive.	WIPO Internet treaties require anticircumvention measures. Digital Millennium Copyright Act and European Copyright Directive (EUCD) ban devices and circumvention. Haute autorité pour la diffusion des oeuvres et la protection des droits sur internet, Digital Economy Act (DEA), and infringement actions used to impose on ISPs.	National: Egyptian nihilist "plug pulling" but negation of code. Green Dam local filters; Golden Shield national solution. Heavy government pressure in the United States and EU for self-regulation by ISPs.	Terms of use—enhanced by contractual terms with third-party application providers and media partners.	Termination monopoly held by ISPs—nontransparent term of use for end user. Competition regulation.

We can see within and between case studies evidence for the hypothesis that greater multistakeholder involvement will improve the quality of regulatory design, including the technical understanding of code. The RFID code of practice went through several iterations dictated by the original regulatory requirement of a more inclusive coregulatory practice. The first version was largely written by industry, but the result was flimsy, not least because of the exclusion of academic and civil society stakeholders and refusal to incorporate rights-based concerns. It was rejected by regulators. After strong pressure from other stakeholders, a much more comprehensive version was produced and approved by data protection (DP) regulators. A second example is technological protection measures (TPMs); the first generation was woefully ineffective because small start-up companies largely wrote the code. It took the involvement of large industry players such as Microsoft to produce regulatory technologies that were not trivially circumvented, but they nonetheless largely failed to have the desired impact. A third example is Cleanfeed, which is better targeted than previous IP and Domain Name System (DNS) blocking techniques and therefore appears to be less intrusive on freedom of expression as well as being relatively broadly accepted by the industry. A counterexample is the manner in which deep packet inspection (DPI) has been introduced on some ISP networks, where the lack of user consultation led to infamous incidents such as Comcast/Sandvine's BitTorrent seeding or BT/Phorm's secret DPI and behavioral advertising trials. (Phorm's system trials used deep packet inspection of the ISP customer's Web browsing, in order to insert ads relevant to that browsing behavior, without user permission being given.) These were poster children for the failure to consider multistakeholder discussion prior to design or even implementation of innovative control technologies.

The enforcement of product or service terms and conditions by code (including the statutory terms and conditions of copyright) is usually blunt. This quickly becomes problematic when it has an impact on fundamental rights, for example, when DRM stops blind users from accessing text materials using text-to-speech software. It is a significant problem in policy areas that are central to democratic rights and where legal enforcement is hedged with all sorts of conditions that are too subtle for implementation through code (e.g., copyright fair use or dealing). For example, offering users a binary choice of acceptance of new terms of service for a social network that their entire community uses, or rejection of new conditions leading to termination of account, is no choice at all. In a similar fashion, enforcing unilateral opaque and often subjective terms for use of an ISP's service does not contribute to a meaningful exchange of views with users over network neutrality. Even exiting a service when rejecting a change of code can be difficult or impossible for the user, as, for instance, in removing personal data from a social network or ISP (both of which retain data for extensive periods, either imposed by regulation such as data retention or reduced from infinity by the pleas of data protection regulators and politicians).

Table 8.5 compares the outcomes in each of our case studies. Transparency is a prerequisite for dispute resolution. It is notable in these cases that the opacity of the implied terms and business practices of service providers has created a perception of untargeted and capricious enforcement against users. Increased transparency must be a basic regulatory requirement in order to make markets operate more effectively as well as to provide at least a baseline for users to understand their rights. The calamitous consequences of the sanction of service denial for users who have invested many hundreds of hours in creating an online identity or integrating into an online community may often be disproportionate to the types of infringement of which users are accused. This makes transparency absolutely essential to any informed regulatory bargain between users and service providers. Sanctions and even accusations of breach of terms can be poorly targeted because of the difficulty in establishing the identity of the infringer with a shared resource such as an IP address. Appeals and due process, where they exist at all, have been ill defined and underdeveloped. This should make corporations especially sensitive to the effect of enforcement actions on a wrongly accused party.

The potential for user-generated regulation has not yet been fully explored. Companies have embraced it when it can provide them with a benefit, such as protection for liability for hosting copyright-infringing content. But it has so far been ignored when benefits would instead accrue to users. For example, a take-down button for third-party tagged, posted content that prevents distribution until agreement from the subject is sought would help protect users from the spread of embarrassing photos, but would be against the general interests of social networking in increasing the quantity of content available on their networks.

Table 8.5
Outcomes and divergences

	Copyright	Privacy	Censors	Social media	Smart pipes
Transparency	Unclear causation from present system—Hargreaves (2011) analysis very useful (e.g., digital copyright exchange). More transparency to more just solutions?	Limited impact of opaque privacy policies and user education—often unintelligible to users, who often are in a poor position to judge privacy risks.	Block lists private—obscure reasons for removal—no generic reporting duty on ISPs.	Most important social networks deliberately obscure in software updates and privacy policy changes. Little evidence of good practice.	Refusal to create transparency a critical element in early U.S. cases. European extensive work on creating greater transparency through regulation.
Enforcement	Problem of the second user—individuals can be a network and succeeding infringements impossible to police (as well as fair use). Enforcement against corporations possible; legal business models and licenses effective enforcement in the sense of recompense. Three-strikes massively disproportionate.	Varied levels of enforcement by EU regulators suggest cultural factors also important. Data breach requirements and code solutions could increase privacy protection more uniformly.	Put-back would help to make enforcement fairer. Private censorship removes user rights. General classes of content censored (e.g., Usenet). Blind alley as bad guys can always access.	Individual reuses of data not susceptible to corporate-type enforcement. Nudges and defaults more useful: "Distributed enforcement." Policy on child protection moving toward offering greater user involvement in safety.	Network neutrality "lite" solutions to prevent protocol, application blocking so far limited to statute in Netherlands, and regulatory declarations (e.g., in Singapore, United States). Bandwidth or service plan capping resulted.

Table 8.5
(continued)

	Copyright	Privacy	Censors	Social media	Smart pipes
Interoperability	DRM closes off interoperability—iTunes prior to move to unrestricted MP3 format, for instance. Continued issue with e-book formats.	Broad European standards are driving a global race-to-the-top, with export controls and "adequacy" assessments driving interoperability between national regimes.	Cleanfeed better approach compared to DNS blocking collateral damage. Iran worst of all possible worlds: not even interconnection.	Open social—why can't all users move data and interconnect? Note portability is insufficient.	Vendor off-the-shelf solutions adapted to ISP—but little transparency on policy.
Efficiency	Levy one option for efficient enforcement? New business models are key.	Efficiency via internalized data controller self-enforcement? Norm enforced by law.	Answer should be to go to source: arresting producers, not blocking viewing.	Corporate governance conformity to best practices arguably best outcome. Has the Federal Trade Commission or European Commission achieved this through recent scrutiny?	Anything but telecoms trench warfare or entirely shutting off third-party innovation must beat either extreme. Coregulation suggested as best option.

Given the problems we have identified with transparency and enforcement, the minimum that we might expect end users to be able to retaliate with is to take their business elsewhere. However, absent interoperability, it may well be that the user is locked into a service that may have treated him or her in an arbitrary or unfair fashion. Therefore, in order for any type of consumer sovereignty even to be broached, some minimum level of interoperability would be required in circumstances where there is no realistic prospect of users otherwise migrating to a different service provider. A classic example is the social network, which refuses to return all personal data and to delete all evidence of the user. Another is DRM "locks" that close off interoperability—users cannot move their music collections to another service or even sometimes hardware platform, leaving them vulnerable to the shutdown of services—as happened with music services from MSN, Walmart, and Yahoo! By contrast, cookies are an interoperable way of permitting users to opt out of services, even if this is somewhat of a false choice given the extraordinary preponderance of cookies across advertising-supported Web sites. Interoperability in the cases of censors and network neutrality is more an issue between service providers.

Efficiency conclusions lead us to consider the fork in the path that has not been taken. In each of our case studies, greater attention to user rights and interoperability would have led policy in a different direction, which would have been based on greater transparency and focus on due process where enforcement was found necessary. Thus, a greater emphasis on business model innovation would have avoided much of the copyright enforcement saga of the past decade, as would maintenance of the 1990s principle of end user filtering for censorship. Network neutrality may have remained a minority concern had greater transparency been agreed on and publicized at an early stage by the ISP industry. Social networks that respected end user privacy and prevented children's membership of adult environments may have not grown as quickly, but would have created an environment in which users had greater trust and confidence that their rights would be protected (much as trust in electronic commerce is seen as key to encouraging nonshoppers online to participate in the Internet economy more fully).

These different futures may be seen as utopian, but it is important that policymakers are reminded that an alternative future can be mapped out based on their policy choices, as well as market and social developments.

That suggests that keeping such choices open is an important element of the policy environment, which is why interoperability and transparency assume such important roles in our final chapter. It also suggests that the best way to avoid the need for heavy-handed regulatory intervention is to maintain—through interoperability and standards—the potential for innovation within the Internet environment, such that the conditions for alternative futures have not been made impossible due to deeply embedded monopolistic market structures and practices.

9 Holistic Regulation of the Interoperable Internet

In the opening chapters, we described the multistakeholder environment for Internet governance and regulation, in which user groups lobbied along with business and governments. We also described the insights of new institutionalism, with exit and competition for standards becoming increasingly critical in the information economy. In chapter 2, we went on to describe interoperability as a means of lowering entry barriers and increasing consumer welfare. We also described how highly computer literate prosumers could encrypt and otherwise creatively secure an Internet experience with more freedom in both expression and access to information goods and how control technologies were deployed to limit some of this freedom. We explained that this freedom was for at-the-margin tech geeks, not the billion-plus Facebook and Google users. We described the perils of stranded citizens with little market attractiveness: those who are digitally illiterate, follow default settings slavishly, do not understand privacy policies, let alone click-wrap software licenses, and are unable to exit the environments in which they find themselves.

In this conclusion, we explain what more is needed to square the circle of Internet regulation in the broader public interest for all Internet users, not the fortunate few or the even more fortunate and fewer dominant corporations. We argue for "prosumer law" and give an example of our proposed solution to the problems of dominant social networking services. We then examine the international governance of information, especially the apparent incompatibility of human rights and trade-related concerns exposed in such multistakeholder fora as the OECD. Finally, we argue for holistic regulation of the Internet, taking a transdisciplinary perspective to solve those hard cases we have examined.

Prosumer Boycotts and the Silk Thread of Consumer Law

Descriptions of personal data as the metaphorical oil in the digital economy are wide of the mark, even for data of the deceased (Edwards 2013), unless they have seeped into the sediment. Personal data accumulate with the individual's treks into cyberspace, and therefore a better metaphor is silk, woven into the tapestry of the user's online personality. Moreover, *user* is a poor description of the potential creativity of the individual user (Von Hippel 1976; Morrison, Roberts, and von Hippel 2000) in cyberspace. The hideous ugliness of the term *prosumer* (the online creator, after Toffler 1980) should not hide the potential for the individual to move far beyond a caterpillar-like role as a producer of raw silk and encompass their ability to regenerate into a butterfly or moth.

The verb *to surf* indicates the user-generated agenda of the prosumer, as does the weaving of a web by billions of prosumer-created sites. The silk has created tapestries as rich as Wikipedia, as well as Facebook and MySpace (Benkler 2006). It is arguably the loss of the sense of ownership of "your space" that led to the latter's decline. The silkworms that turned created a death spiral (Mehra 2011), even though it was at first only a prosumer boycott (led by those who preferred to control their data cocooned in their own personal form: chrysalis or pupae). The problem is that such boycotts rapidly create a landscape of zombie users: many readers will have ancient Hotmail and MySpace accounts that are undead, unchecked, unmourned, useless to advertisers, and antithetical to positive network effects that alone can feed a successful business.

Let us then speak of prosumer law (Fernandez-Barrera 2011). Agencies regulating antitrust and competition issues have a deep cleft between their competition economists and their consumer advocates (Mehra 2011), a division that at the Federal Trade Commission had traditionally been physical as well as intellectual. Even as innovative arguments are made for intervention in high-technology networked markets, intellectual resistance runs deep (*Verizon* v. *Trinko* 2004; Meisel 2010; Barnett 2011; Manne and Wright 2011). Communications regulators have similar silos, even the yawning chasm between telecoms and broadcast regulators, the former concerned largely with network economics and technical proficiency (Laffont and Tirole 2001; Cave 2004). For instance, Spulber and Yoo (2009) introduce network theory to the study of the economics and law of telecommunications and in so doing adopt a minimalist view of the application of the essential facilities doctrine to the Internet's plumbing.

Pro-consumer arguments (Reding 2007) to the contrary in Europe are viewed as European exceptionalism by the isolated United States. The broadcast regulators should be concerned with the rights of the citizen and consumer to receive balanced information on that ubiquitous and pervasive medium (Cowie and Marsden 1999). We argue that little has been done to support prosumers as opposed to passive viewers (Directive 2007/65/EC Articles 1–2).

Essential facilities law is a very poor substitute for the active role of prosumer law that we advocate, especially in its Chicago school minimalist phase (Lessig 1998). In the late 1990s, as the Web was developing and Microsoft was crushing Netscape in what is elegantly described as its moment of "Schumpeterian emergency" (Bresnahan, Greenstein, and Hendersen 2011), it was still possible to agree with Schumpeter, Scalia, and Easterbrook (Mehra 2011) that innovative upstarts could outwit clumsier behemoths (Cowie and Marsden 1999; Lemley and McGowan 1998). This was not the real lesson of IBM and Microsoft in our view. Instead, we have portrayed an information landscape with a billion captured moths creating silk for ever fewer merchants, notably Google, Facebook, Amazon, and Apple. Allowing those moths to evolve and choose whether to exit, control their own prosumption, or continue their silken personal data capture is a key question for prosumer law.

What should such law consist of? It is not sufficient for it to permit data deletion because that only covers users' tracks; it does not entitle them to pursue new adventures, particularly where all their friends (real and imagined) are cocooned inside the Schumpeterian victor's web. It requires some combination of interconnection and interoperability more than transparency and the theoretical possibility to switch (Werbach 2010; Weiser 2009). It needs the ability for exiting prosumers to spread their wings, take their silk away from the former exploiter, cover their traces, and interoperate their old chrysalis with their new moth life. That suggests interoperability to permit exit (Burk 1999).

Consider the problem with two hard examples: network neutrality and social networking systems (SNS). In the former case, users can exit an ISP that is breaching network neutrality, subject to two as-yet-unfulfilled conditions: that full, meaningful consumer transparency is offered and that switching is trivial, in particular that consumers can leave their minimum-term contract (typically two years) because the ISP has breached its side of the bargain by introducing nonneutral practices. Because consumers keep control of their data (except for law enforcement data retention purposes) and can delete cookies, extract files hosted, and so on, then absent behavioral advertising of the deeply invasive Phorm type (using Deep Packet Inspection to track the prosumer's Web browsing, they are free to leave. Moreover, they can take their telephone number with them to their new ISP. That does presuppose there remains a neutral ISP in the environment, which is not by any means certain for the Skype-active mobile user (Sahel 2011). Regulatory action in transparency, switching, and contract exit is needed.

In the case of SNS, such a relatively easy transition is not assured. First, there is the extraction of the user's proprietary data. While the Irish regulator decision ensures that data can be returned (Office of the Data Protection Commissioner, Ireland 2011), it does not cover all the data cocooned in one piece. First, Facebook removed data to the United States without valid consent, as, for instance, in the Like button dispute in Schleswig-Holstein in 2011. Second, data were leaked promiscuously to third-party application providers, as the Federal Trade Commission (FTC) discovered. Third, the formatting of the data and the need to access friends' data (e.g., wedding and baby photos), which are undiscoverable using a search engine, mean that the user is in the position of: "You can leave Facebook, but Facebook never leaves you."

Prosumer law suggests a more directed intervention to prevent Facebook or Google+ or any other network from erecting a fence around its piece of the information commons: to ensure interoperability with open standards (Lemley 1999). We argue it is untrue to state that there is so much convergence between platforms that there is no clear distinction between open commons and closed proprietary environments (Barnett 2011), though voluntary forfeiture of intellectual property rights to permit greater innovation has always been commonplace (Bresnahan, Greenstein, and Henderson 2011; Barton 1997). It also suggests that Google's attempts to adjust search in favor of its products, if proven to extend beyond preferential puffery for Google+, are inimical to prosumer law.

Prosumerism should be a declared policy of the European Commission alongside the European interoperability framework (EIF). European electronic commerce consumer law is a marked departure from freedom of contract in European law. It is therefore not difficult to extend the EIF and the legal protection for prosumers in this direction in law, though implementation requires all member states to commit to such a step in practice as well as theory.

The European prosumer has already dealt significant creative destruction to many pre-Internet industries through such services as Linux, Skype, BitTorrent, and the VLC Media Player. It would be fitting for Europe to lead the United States in adapting Von Hippel's ideas to the case studies that we have presented here. We do not have great confidence that the United States will match rhetoric with reality in enforcing such an agenda, preferring talk of "Internet freedoms" and "bills of privacy rights" without actual regulations to achieve those outcomes. We are convinced that fudging with nudges (Yeung 2012) needs to be reinforced with the reality of regulation and coregulation, in order to enable prosumers to maximize their potential on the broadband Internet.

Hard-Wiring Interoperability into Standards?

The market and information failures of the network effects pervading the Internet were noted by the chair of the FTC as early as 1996 and have been in evidence throughout its development (Bar, Borrus, and Steinberg 1995; Lemley and McGowan 1998; Cowie and Marsden 1999). As the technology stabilizes and matures, it may be that less radical innovation lies ahead, but we see no reason for policymakers to surrender entirely to a cable television model (Lemley and Lessig 1999) for the Internet in copyright or carriage or convergence on social networking. Therefore, solutions that maintain interoperability and open standards, which drove Internet, World Wide Web, mobile, and computer innovation in the 1990s and 2000s, should be maintained against the Janus-faced comfort of a largely walled-garden, passive Internet future.

Most merger decisions throughout the period 1996 to 2011 supported interoperability and open standards, including European media mergers in the mid-1990s, the AOL/TimeWarner and Baby Bell mergers subject to Computer III requirements (as discussed in chapter 2), and European Commission abuse of dominance decisions against Intel, Microsoft, and Apple. It is our contention that similar remedies should be pursued against the new information monopolists of Google and Facebook, where abuse of dominance is found. Google and Facebook negotiated consent decrees after user privacy breaches, which commits both to agreeing to privacy audits of all products and applications every two years until 2030.

This is a less radical proposal than the separations principle of Wu (2010), who proposes a rigid separation between carriers and content and applications providers, based on historical analysis of previous communications industries—including the FCC's 1970 Financial Interest and Syndication ("fin-syn") Rules in cinematic production and distribution, as well as the concentration in the telecommunications industry resulting from the 1996 Telecommunications Act. Our analysis is similar but has shown that effective enforcement of interoperability is possible even in the face of vertical integration by incumbents. This in part reflects the view from Brussels, where less obvious regulatory capture of the political process of communications regulation takes place. National policy may be entirely captured, but even its harshest critics must admit the European Commission is more insulated by its supranational character.

Paradoxically, this may be due to a political contaminant in competition policy. European competition policy is less captured by the minutiae of price-based abuse of dominance than the United States, even though this is the direction of travel (Coates 2011). As a result, the more interesting interoperable solution in such cases as Microsoft is possible, whereas the Microsoft case was settled rapidly in the United States after the George W. Bush administration took power. It might be argued that the European targets were American firms with homes of convenience in Ireland or Luxembourg for European legal purposes, which of course and undoubtedly defuses much political pressure for leniency.

Competition policy is also not the only European or U.S. initiative. The EIF 2.0 emphasis on interoperability as a priority in both government procurement and in research and development offers a broader toolkit than competition policy alone can provide, in part a function of the fortunate placement of the former competition commissioner in the Directorate General CONNECT responsible for the EIF. We argue that a separations principle to break up monopolies across the information field is neither feasible nor entirely necessary in the European context (Cave 2004, 2011). Examples of industries switching under competitive pressures that create new market models will prevent radical separations policies from being adopted, as Facebook's success over MySpace and Apple's success in creating a music store free of digital rights management argue for interoperability, not separation. Moreover, the fight to establish interoperable electronic book standards will not be answered by structural separation, as Apple, Amazon, and others tussle to offer standards to the market.

Moreover, the interoperability approach does prevent a further regulatory arm wrestle of the type that Wu so colorfully chronicles and has pervaded the history of pre-Internet communications policy. It does depend on effective enforcement, and in this it suggests a heroic commitment to such policies at national as well as European levels, which critics suggest is beyond the European Commission's appetite for implementation (Moody 2010). Critics may argue that an approach founded largely on the relatively puny market impact of the Microsoft decision is grasping at the shortest of straws. The alternative, trench warfare based on regulatory attempts to reestablish rigid separation of functions (Kroes 2010a), is in our view both an excessive intervention given the continuing flow of innovation in the Internet ecosystem and likely to favor the politically skilled incumbents more than scrappy entrants, as we have seen in our case studies.

A comparable example is the attempt to separate retail from investment banking. This has been a far higher political priority in the wake of the vast regulatory failures in bank regulation since 1980 but shows little real progress since 2007's calamitous revelation of the extent of the larceny in the banking system in the United States and Europe (Davies 2010). We accept that a complex and interlocking EIF will depend on coordination between member states and the European Commission, a coordination shown to be spectacularly lacking in the altogether more important matter of the governance of the single European currency in 2010 through 2012. However, interoperability is technical enough, and its problems and potential hostages lie far enough away from Brussels (mainly in Silicon Valley, San Diego, and Seattle) that a heroic policy signal is possible.

The FTC may have shown the way in its treatment and settlement of the Intel case, with its emphasis on interoperability requirements as a remedy with a six-year period stated and conditions affecting interoperability and patent policy in the case of change of control, a spectacularly invasive example of interoperability being hard-wired (FTC 2010). It is coincidental and fortuitous that interoperability can also mean free software in principle (however expensive its implementation and integration with legacy systems). Politicians who (perhaps mistakenly) assume that interoperability is a free and leisurely European lunch are more likely to support that policy. However, we recognize that interoperability is neither a simple nor a cost-free option (Yeung 2012; Palfrey and Gasser 2012), nor that it should be imposed without prima facie evidence of dominant actors' refusing to provide interface information that permits interoperability.

Commissioner Kroes (2010a) referred to the arduous attempts made by antitrust authorities on both sides of the Atlantic to ensure interoperability in the Microsoft and Intel cases. The outcome was to deny those actors the tools to exclude innovative competitors from the market. Hard-wired interoperability is the most promising solution to achieve those ends, however tortuous the task.

Interoperability and SNS

One promising solution to the otherwise patchy nature of regulation is that of SNS interoperability. In earlier work we have identified high sunk costs and network effects as barriers to entry protecting dominant SNS: "The behemoth SNS can influence negotiation with ISPs absent net neutrality regulation, leading to a vertical value chain of dominance" (Brown and Marsden 2008). We proposed that "competition authorities should impose *ex ante* interoperability requirements upon dominant social utilities . . . to minimise network barriers" and identified three models of information regulation from case law:

• Must-carry obligations, which are imposed on broadcasters and electronic program guides

• Application programming interfaces (API) disclosure requirements, which were placed on Microsoft by the European Commission ruling upheld by the European Court of Justice

• Interconnection requirements on telecommunications providers, especially those with dominance—already echoed in the AOL/TimeWarner merger requirement for instant messaging interoperability.

We also recommended that "API disclosure requirements are necessary but not sufficient—the ability to program platform apps is of little use if they cannot run" (Beydogan 2010). "Must-carry obligations enable one platform to 'break in' to another (e.g., Flickr's app on Facebook). Interconnect requirements [are] most likely to lead to seamless user experience that will create real competition." This would impose telecoms interoperability and switching requirements on SNS.

Historically, broadcasters and cable operators did not necessarily enjoy good bilateral relations, viewing each other as competition—in the same way ISPs such as AOL/TimeWarner saw emerging SNS as competition. The success of both Facebook and the AppStore gives pause to those who champion an entirely open model, as consumers appear to prefer low-walled gardens, a debate endlessly reiterated since the AOL walled-garden service. Nevertheless, SNS are another example of some user preference for a relatively closed-walled-garden model.

The final outcome of such an approach continues to be uncertain even as Facebook announced its intention to become an "entertainment hub" with news, video, and music embedded in the site from 2012. This is a similar approach to that adopted by AOL, the mobile Vodafone 360, and MySpace and has previously failed. MySpace, for instance, rewrote its code to prevent the embedding of YouTube videos in 2008, causing significant user unrest. The experience of Facebook as a destination site will prove an excellent case study as its strategy develops.

The profound implications of extensions of broadcast or other regulation onto SNS would create a very different regulatory space within which SNS operate. If one views innovation as perpetual and endemic to such networks, one may oppose such regulation on those grounds. If, however, the view is that social networking growth has plateaued with the constrained environment of Facebook now dominating, then the use of competition law on the Microsoft precedent, and its extension in EIF 2.0, may suggest that interoperability is forced on that dominant network.

It is important to note that the drive by government, most pronounced in the European Commission's approach, toward more SNS regulation to conform to European legal norms as well as concerns for child protection and privacy, is conducted in an informal soft law manner (Senden 2005; Marsden 2011). Civic responsibility and the Internet is the leitmotif, from the graduated-response legislation that places enforcement in the hands of ISPs and coregulation models for harmful but legal content that affects search, e-commerce, SNS, and other intermediary providers.

"Closed-open proprietary versus free information models" depend on code choices (Zittrain 2008; Wu 2010). The concern here is not with the openness of FSF-GPL, Apache, or Linux license models directly (Guadamuz 2009), though we note their importance as contributors to the Benkler (1998) argument that peer-produced production can help create an information commons. Our concern is with wider mass participation models and their regulation, with Lessig's (2008) and Boyle's (2008) commons arguments for reform to redress the extremism of intellectual property law. The difference is that we acknowledge the role that government can play as a broker for policy solutions while recognizing that government can often be captured by regulated industries. However, antitrust and open data policies can help user empowerment (Mehra 2011), and we are more confident than Wu that the tendency toward government captured by regulated monopoly may not be the whole story.

Internet Governance Principles: Human Rights, Free Trade, or Both?

Regulators are used to acting at national scale, but effective Internet regulation requires much stronger coordination at regional and international levels. Online service providers are easier to regulate locally because they require infrastructure (Web hosting) and capital and revenues to develop (code) and operate (mainly bandwidth costs, especially with video). There are very few noncommercial cloud services; many are free to users but funded by advertising. Providers could operate outside a jurisdiction, but regulators have a nuclear option of local ISP-based blocking (e.g., Turkey commonly uses blocking against YouTube), where out-of-jurisdiction providers will not apply restrictions to local users, or more subtle options such as banning payment processing (online gambling) or purchasing of advertising space from noncompliant companies. Most of the encryption tools in use are session based (SSL/TLS) between a user and service provider, so the unencrypted data can be accessed at the provider end (Facebook messages or BlackBerry messages either at Research in Motion or corporate servers).

In standard setting, geography can still matter. Information giants can safely ignore nation-states with only a few million customers, whose national regulators impose restrictions unacceptable to those businesses. This need to build international consensus, combined with regulatory limits of technology (e.g., digital rights management), may mean that states have to compromise on some of their key policy goals (limits on hate speech, protection of scarcity-based copyright business models) and build stronger models for operational cooperation (faster takedown of child abuse images, spammers, phishing Web sites, and payment processors).

It will be critical to involve the emerging powers of the coming century (Brazil, Russia, India, China, South Africa); otherwise attempts at global cooperation will be critically undermined. However, involving more authoritarian states in negotiations can significantly harm the protection of fundamental rights and freedoms. This raises a forum-shopping conundrum: Is the Internet Governance Forum (International Telecommunication Union 2005), G20, OECD, or another body the global Internet regulation coordinator of choice? The OECD at least requires members to have market economies run by democratic institutions, but it is not a human-rights-based institution. U.S. attempts to introduce freedom of expression into the World Trade Organization (WTO) as a free trade issue may look promising, but the fate of environmental and labor standards at the WTO presages the likely outcome (Drahos and Braithwaite 2002).

The local regulatory trend has been to co-opt ISPs as enforcers—passing on infringement warnings to users, blocking access to banned sites (Cleanfeed, Newzbin), and disconnecting accused copyright infringers (HADOPI). Without extreme care, such measures will drive up the cost of Internet access, damage freedom of expression and privacy, and retard innovation. Even worse, they are unlikely to have any significant impact on the illegal distribution of child abuse images or copyrighted work. Policymakers would be well advised instead to stick with the "mere conduit" compromise reached in the U.S. Digital Millennium Copyright Act and the Electronic Commerce Directive, whereby ISPs are not liable for the data they transport—the Internet equivalent of the common carriage protections that have worked well for centuries in other network industries such as transport and telephony (Cherry 2008).

To illustrate some of the difficulties in analyzing the Internet from both a rights- and economics-based perspective, consider the OECD high-level conference of June 2011, a follow-up to its previous Internet regulation meetings in Seoul in 2008 and Ottawa in 1998. The previous meetings were dominated by electronic commerce discussions. The 2011 meeting ended with the chair's conclusions, a communiqué, and a proposal to move toward OECD guidelines (2011) for member states on Internet governance principles. The Internet Technical Advisory Committee agreed to the final text, as did the member states, the Business Industry Advisory Council, and the trade unions. The Civil Society Information Society Advisory Council (CSISAC) did not. The biggest public discussion was about intermediary liability: an excellent updated OECD report (2011c) was declassified and distributed at the conference. The word *coregulation* was not used at all in the conference, although it was the central mechanism that might have bridged some consensus and was extensively discussed in the report.

Reasonable people can disagree about as fundamental an issue as the role of ISPs and other intermediaries. CSISAC had flagged this concern in their informal part in the Seoul meeting three years earlier, asking OECD countries to "defend freedom of expression and, in this context, oppose mandated filtering, censorship and criminalisation of content that is protected under international freedom of expression standards."

The 2008 Seoul declaration that judicial due process should be followed was deleted from the 2011 communiqué. Formal opposition to ISPs as copyright police was consistent with this conviction. There were several CSISAC statements on their opposition to the communiqué, including CSISAC as a whole (CSISAC 2011), and from Knowledge Economy International, European Digital Rights initiative, Electronic Frontier Foundation, La Quadrature du Net, and others. They made clear their view of the Internet as an information commons to be kept open to innovation. Rashmi Rangnath of Public Knowledge and Milton Mueller both shared praise for the inclusiveness of OECD's process—if some concern over timing of deliberation—but regret that the proposed private censorship model for intermediaries was proposed without due process and legitimacy, including judicial process (Marsden 2011).

So many OECD speakers used different definitions of the words *freedom* and *openness* in connection with the Internet that moderator Kevin Werbach was moved to state that we are separated by a common language and to conclude that multistakeholderism is, like democracy, the "least worst system" to discuss Internet governance (Marsden 2011).

The view of governments appears to be that a form of coregulation will arrive, whether formally agreed with appropriate judicial appeal available to injured parties (as laid out in the 2008 Seoul conclusions) or as a murkier and less well regulated quicker-fix political compromise (or quid pro quo with copyright lobbyists and others). EU commissioner Neelie Kroes signaled a move toward a compact in the direction of civic responsibility, which suggests that there is now a direction of travel, if not yet a concerted push, for more ISP activity, even if she says "it is not about regulating the Internet" (Kroes 2011).

The context is also important: the communiqué was agreed by OECD members and also the Egyptian delegation on behalf of the new government. Misunderstandings of the proposed informal private censorship model by non-OECD members are very possible, to put it mildly. The United States said that the OECD and member states must do much more to explain to non-OECD members (such as Egypt and China) that the principles do not permit the types of censorship that civil society illustrated. It is exactly that liability principle and mission creep to which CSISAC so vociferously objects.

The OECD also hosted a 2011 workshop to discuss implementation of the updated OECD Guidelines for Multinational Enterprises (OECD 2011b). Cisco, Alcatel-Lucent, Vodafone, and other Internet multinationals would be well advised to take close note of point B1 in the guidelines: "Enterprises are encouraged to: Support, as appropriate to their circumstances, cooperative efforts in the appropriate fora to promote Internet Freedom through respect of freedom of expression, assembly and association online." The June OECD meeting also discussed the U.N. Human Rights Council (2011) endorsement of Ruggie's guidelines for multinational enterprises on human rights (Ruggie 2011). Point 12 established an annual forum on business and human rights, one of whose responsibilities is to examine the operation of human rights in specific sectors, likely to include communications.

Interoperability is of course linked to open data, open code, and, arguably though technologically deterministically, free speech. However, the blizzard of Internet governance principles written in the course of 2011 have their origins in law and economics or human rights, but apparently do not translate one to the other. This apparent dialogue of the deaf is also a competition policy problem (Brown and Waelde 2005; Brown 2010) and a corporate governance problem, from multinational hydrocarbon companies (Shell, BP, and others) to multimedia combines (News Corporation) (Leader 2005).

The translatability or comprehensibility of human rights language to economic law is needed more than in previous eras when the arena of international trade and competition was kept largely separate from human rights. However, the pressing need to create a dialogue between experts in the previously discrete fields is an urgent task, notably because information communication technology (ICT) brings together a fundamental growth driver and transformative technology for the global economy with its equally fundamental and transformative role in driving human communication and dialogue.

To bridge the gap between free trade and human rights standards in Internet governance, a start can be made by comparing rhetorical aims in table 9.1. We can compare the bilateral attempt by the EU and the United States to extend the WTO's Information Technology Agreement to broaden both scale and scope and eliminate nontariff barriers, which the EU has previously pushed for (IP/11/402), with the ten principles of the multistakeholder Internet Rights and Principles Coalition, which establishes at least some overlap, albeit one is written in the legal language of "trade liberalization-ese" and the other in "human rights-ese."

We have shown through our case studies that governments and companies are still not showing due regard for the rights of users, and long-overdue reform of copyright law and notice and takedown regimes in this direction is not imminent. The failure of the European institutions to reform the Electronic Commerce Directive to at least match the U.S. Digital Millennium Copyright Act in ensuring some measure of investigation and "put back" is one example. By contrast, human rights advocates have increasingly found support in the wake of the Arab Spring's demonstration of the potential of the Internet for democratic expression, and both the United Nations and regional human rights bodies have called on governments to pay more heed to private censorship and not to permit or encourage such informal censorship to take place.

In the late nineteenth and early twentieth centuries, the FTC responded to industrial trusts based on continental U.S. markets, which were replacing trade guilds at regional and local levels (Wu 2010). Internet-based informational markets are network markets of a global scale for which the WTO and World Intellectual Property Organization (WIPO) are inadequately resourced and lacking in political legitimacy (Cherry 2008). The U.S. trade representative and the European Commission's political task

Table 9.1

EU and U.S. principles versus Internet Rights and Principles Coalition

EU and U.S. Principles of ICT Trade with Third Parties	P	Internet Rights and Principles Coalition
Transparency of rules affecting trade in ICT and ICT services	1	Universality and equality: All humans are born free and equal in dignity and rights, which must be respected, protected, and fulfilled in the online environment.
Open networks for consumers to access and distribute information, applications, and services of their choice	2	Rights and social justice: The Internet is a space for the promotion, protection, and fulfillment of human rights and the advancement of social justice. Everyone has the duty to respect the human rights of all others in the online environment.
Cross-border flows of information	3	Accessibility: Everyone has an equal right to access and use a secure and open Internet.
No requirement to use local infrastructure for ICT services	4	Expression and association: Everyone has the right to seek, receive, and impart information freely on the Internet without censorship or other interference. Everyone also has the right to associate freely through and on the Internet, for social, political, cultural, or other purposes.
Governments should allow full foreign participation in their ICT services sector, through establishment or other means	5	Privacy and data protection: Everyone has the right to privacy online. This includes freedom from surveillance, the right to use encryption, and the right to online anonymity. Everyone also has the right to data protection, including control over personal data collection, retention, processing, disposal, and disclosure.
Efficient and maximized use of radio spectrum	6	Life, liberty, and security: The rights to life, liberty, and security must be respected, protected, and fulfilled online. These rights must not be infringed on or used to infringe other rights in the online environment.
Independence of regulatory authorities overseeing ICT services	7	Diversity: Cultural and linguistic diversity on the Internet must be promoted, and technical and policy innovation should be encouraged to facilitate plurality of expression.
Simple authorization of competitive telecommunications services	8	Network equality: Everyone shall have universal and open access to the Internet's content, free from discriminatory prioritization, filtering, or traffic control on commercial, political, or other grounds.

Table 9.1
(continued)

ICT service suppliers must have the right to interconnect with other service providers for access to publicly available telecommunications networks and services: cost-oriented, nondiscriminatory, and transparent rates	9	Standards and regulation: The Internet's architecture, communication systems, and document and data formats shall be based on open standards that ensure complete interoperability, inclusion, and equal opportunity for all.
International cooperation with a view to increasing the level of digital literacy in third countries and reducing the digital divide	10	Governance: Human rights and social justice must form the legal and normative foundations on which the Internet operates and is governed. This shall happen in a transparent and multilateral manner, based on principles of openness, inclusive participation, and accountability.

arguably makes them too partisan to tackle these grand challenges with legitimacy, and the International Telecommunication Union has so far been largely irrelevant.

What can achieve the aim of the production of public goods through the appropriate level of regulation of these markets? Progressive coalitions within intergovernmental organizations (e.g., Brazil and Chile within WIPO) can sometimes have an effect, but are strongly resisted by the G8 and are sidestepped through forum shifting (e.g., the Agreement on Trade Related Aspects of Intellectual Property Rights [TRIPS] within WTO and the Anti-Counterfeiting Trade Agreement). The enlarged economic policy-making community since 2009 in the G20 brings in a progressive coalition with India, Brazil, and others. But the Internet Governance Forum illustrates the limitations, as does the environmental movement (Drake and Wilson 2008; Mueller 2010).

A global Internet bill of rights should also form a baseline for analysis, and here the United Nations as well as the Council of Europe and others can play a role (Akdeniz 2011; Kleinwächter 2011; La Rue 2011). Nations could impose requirements of transparency and open participation on standards bodies through procurement power related to the produced standards. They can also use funding power and direct subsidy of standards bodies (e.g., European Telecommunications Standard Institute), suggested, if not yet convincingly implemented, in the EIF.

The sunk costs and network effects of the broadband Internet have grown stronger as information distribution has become more critical to more applications, such as voice and video calling, real-time interactive gaming, and video streaming. To maintain the Internet's openness, dominant actors need to be restricted in blocking rival content that threatens their commercial interests. As the fixed and mobile ISPs gain horizontal and vertical bottlenecks over distribution, those rules need to be more vigorously pursued to maintain some continued openness to innovation.

This modest junction between economics and human rights is only a start in reconciling the fundamental and often compatible goals that they target, especially given the public goods created by information networks (investigated by Stigler, 1999). That makes it especially important that censorship is kept to a democratic minimum and that anonymity and freedom of speech more generally are preserved. As John Stuart Mill observed in his great work "On Liberty" (1869), the majority has no more the right to silence a minority, even if that is only one individual, than that individual has the right to silence the majority.

Human rights and free markets have much to gain from the Internet's continued efficient functioning. First, it is evident that transparency and enhanced information flow at decreased cost are benefits to both economics—laboring under the weight of imperfect information as pointed out by Hayek, Arrow, and others—and human rights. The U.N. Broadband Commission for Digital Development (Gilhooly et al. 2011; Budde et al. 2011) noted that the Millennium Development Goals for 2015 depend on the Internet for both their achievement and the monitoring of their progress. Moreover, transparency is a market-based remedy that can reduce information privacy and user autonomy problems in, for instance, social networks and data protection more generally, alongside network neutrality and some measure of renewed copyright bargain between users and distributors, artists and authors. In connection with copyright and network neutrality, we note the particular importance of evidence-based policymaking rather than the extensive and even pervasive industry capture of the regulator that has characterized Internet policy to date.

Toward Holistic Examination of Internet Regulation

Hard-wiring interoperability is a radical enough option, but it goes only partway to achieving our aims in this study. An Internet open to innovation and denying dominant actors the means to reinforce their position through unfair means is a good start to ensuring choice for users. However, it neither ensures their fundamental rights nor the means to raise those fundamental issues at the design stage of new standards. We must therefore address some specific issues:

• How to introduce greater transparency and dialogue between consumer groups and other civil society stakeholders and standards experts

• How to ensure that the benefits of rapid standards making are maintained even with the additional scrutiny suggested in increasing multistakeholder arrangements

Our conclusions lead us to add our voices to those proposing multidisciplinary examination of code and law, incorporating sociolegal studies, economics and game theory, and interdisciplinary information studies drawing on socioeconomic and political analysis (Clark et al. 2005; Marsden et al. 2006). The investigation of governance and standard setting needs increasingly to draw on these interdisciplinary approaches. This is an ambitious long-term challenge, and we acknowledge that the pathway toward more holistic approaches is littered with obstacles. It includes process and the design of multidisciplinary methodologies for new protocols and standards. We argue that these decisions need engineers to consider human rights for both code and law.

There should be no appeal to technological determinism (Dommering 2006) in our calls for more holistic design of code, neither creating an inviolate sacred principle as with the end-to-end principle when the actual principle is a design fix, nor a theological dictate, nor a nihilistic (and self-serving commercial) claim such as "privacy is dead."

In consequence, the methodologies and techniques developed by regulatory communities should be structurally consistent with the new interdisciplinary scientific perspective called for by Clark et al. (2002). An integrated approach has not yet developed; the disciplines remain somewhat stove-piped in different silos. What is missing is bringing together these many solutions and approaches into a holistic and coherent scientific framework and associated evaluative and design methodologies. We can examine the effects of code on law via "Wiki government" (Noveck 2009), and WikiLeaks (Benkler 2011a), where the power of code to create a more open system of governance was at least promised. This holistic approach can be used to understand Internet development and to harness the creatively destructive force of the tussles of Internet development to stimulate the productive consequences of the Internet, improve its resilience and robustness, and use the combined technological and human systems of the extended Internet to address wider objectives in a holistic manner.

Developing a multidisciplinary catalogue of methodologies can improve comprehension of challenges to better participative decision making, including consideration of code governance approaches, such as the efforts to establish open source standards for hardware as well as software. The objective is not only to present and understand the various methodologies, but also to clarify their standing and the specific policy needs they address, and better understand the growing legitimacy problems and their potential solution or bypass. This may lead to the definition of a regulatory governance taxonomy under which the various methodologies can be classified and understood.

There is a need for the development of tools that help the wider multidisciplinary community to design legitimate holistic governance solutions. Development of these tools moves beyond traditional "dialogue of the deaf" interaction between nation-states, civil society, and expert standards bodies—including the Internet Engineering Task Force (IETF), ETSI, World Wide Web Consortium (W3C), and ITU-T — toward a better understanding of the needs and requirements for future Internet design based on broad sociopolitical buy-in (or at least better informed acquiescence) in the design process and outcomes. These are very difficult questions, not least because of the dynamic coalition forming and dissolving that takes place, as well as the opacity of links in the information ecology. Much pioneering work has been done in matching the challenges of Internet regulation to complexity theory by, for instance, Longstaff (2003), Cherry (2008), and Schneider and Bauer (2007), which promises to make these research questions easier to answer.

There is also an urgent academic mission to better explain Internet technology to legislators and regulators—to help prevent more "spoon-feeding of disinformation" to politicians by lobbyists. (Examples include copyright policy, data protection, and network neutrality.) The U.K. Hargreaves (2011a) copyright report may be a start in that direction, as is open government data standards policy (Marsden and Cave 2006), but examples of bad-faith lobbying have far outweighed good-faith impartial expert advice in the case studies.

In order to measure the success of governance design for future Internet standards, a living catalogue of standards bodies and their functions should encompass both telecoms and Internet standards but also the complex interplays and trade-offs between the various institutions and their design choices relating to software and hardware, privacy, security, and extensibility. Thus, an immediate contrast is evident between the IETF, ETSI and W3C models, for example.

The stakeholders who are influenced by standards setting go beyond those who necessarily actively participate in formal standards-setting activities. Who are the unrepresented stakeholders, such as the army of prosumers, in governance processes, and how can their interests be better represented? What impacts do approaches such as open source have on governance processes? Policy research needs to identify potential new participants in standards making and success and failure factors of differing governance approaches, including alternative or similar examples (Morris and Wong 2009). This would build on the well-known U.S. examples of Creative Commons, the Electronic Frontier Foundation, Free Software Foundation, Center for Democracy and Technology, and Free Press, and consider how such civil society groups could be better represented in the European standards sphere.

Governance policies involve a variety of actors operating at different layers, from physical infrastructure to content and behavior, including protocols and standards definition, as well as services and applications. Cross-mapping governance methodologies and policies can be carried out by crossing them with, on the one hand, the categories of human and nonhuman actors defining and executing them and, on the other hand, the layer at which they operate. Each element of the resulting three-dimensional matrix can then be analyzed and assessed with respect to its compliance (or lack thereof) with democratic values, such as transparency, legitimacy, accountability, and fundamental rights. The case studies we have presented demonstrate the approach.

We argue that transdisciplinary research following the type of methodology we have outlined can make a better effort at solving the following agendas:

• Assessing the impact of different market structures and their dynamics

• Developing the pioneering international political economy work of the 1970s for the Internet, compared to energy, transport, health care, and pharmaceutical sectors that Drahos and Braithwaite (2002) began

• Predicting how new minnows and gorillas (e.g., Facebook) are likely to affect regulation such as the Data Protection Directive and its 2009 revision, to be implemented in 2015–2016

• Helping governments in effective impact assessments for policy and legislation in the ICT field.

The answer to these research grand challenges is essential not only to the future study of regulation of the Internet but also to good policymaking under the U.S. and European requirements for impact assessment and better regulation. It is therefore critical to all future regulation of code.

Glossary of Abbreviations and Terms

3G   Third-generation mobile networks, providing voice and data capacity above 128 kilobits per second.

3GPP   3rd Generation Partnership Project, a collaboration between telecommunications associations to make a globally applicable 3G mobile phone system specification within the scope of the International Telecommunication Union.

ACTA   Anti-Counterfeiting Trade Agreement, an international agreement on trademark and copyright infringement heavily criticized for bias toward producers' interests, rejected as "undemocratic" by the European Parliament in July 2012.

APIs   Application programming interfaces allow software application programmers to use functionality in operating systems such as Windows, Mac OS, and Android.

BEREC   Body of European Regulators of Electronic Communications, a regulatory body to help implement 2009 EU telecoms laws.

BT   British Telecommunications plc, a major global telephony and Internet Service Provider privatized by the UK government in 1984.

CDN   Content Distribution Network, a technical method of efficiently distributing large media files across the Internet using servers hosted in multiple well-connected parts of the network.

CoE   Council of Europe, a sociocultural organization established in 1948 that in part seeks to uphold human rights in the wider Europe of both EU member states and nonmembers to the east and north, with currently forty-seven members. It is responsible for the Cybercrime Convention of 2001, ETS No. 185. See also ECHR.

CRTC   Canadian Radio-Television and Telecommunications Commission, the converged federal regulator of broadcasting and telecoms for federal Canada.

CSISAC   Civil Society Information Society Advisory Council; one of the stakeholder groups advising the Organization for Economic Co-operation and Development's Committee on Information, Communications and Computer Policy.

DMCA   Digital Millennium Copyright Act 1998 in the United States, a statute that obliges Internet service provides to take down material whenever they are notified of copyright infringement, under the notice and takedown procedure.

DPD   Data Protection Directive 1995/46/EC, which harmonizes EU privacy standards.

DPI   Deep Packet Inspection: means by which Internet service providers can read into the packets of data they carry to analyze the contents as well as the header, in order to prioritize, deprioritize, or even block the packets.

DRM   Digital rights management, a method of embedding content standards and policy into computer-readable form; used to enforce copyright conditions.

E2E   End-to-end, the dominant Internet design philosophy which emphasizes computing capability at the "end points" of the network in servers, personal computers and smart phones.

EC   European Commission, the executive body of the EU, responsible for developing and implementing the *acquis communitaire*, the body of EU law.

ECD   Electronic Commerce Directive, 2000/31/EC, which limits Internet Service Provider liability for data hosted or carried over their networks without knowledge of the content.

ECHR   European Convention of Human Rights, more formally the Convention for the Protection of Human Rights and Fundamental Freedoms, signed in 1950 by member states of the Council of Europe.

EDPS   European Data Protection Supervisor, the official responsible for overseeing the EU institutions' compliance with data privacy rules.

EDRi   European Digital Rights Initiative, a nonprofit lobbying group on behalf of national privacy and Internet rights groups across Europe.

ETSI   European Telecommunications Standard Institute, a nonprofit member organization that defines communications standards—notably for mobile telephony. Recognized by the EU as a European Standards Organization.

EU	European Union, as established in the Treaty of Maastricht 1992. Formerly the European Economic Community (EEC).
European Council	The heads of state or government of EU member states, collectively responsible for defining the political direction and priorities of the EU.
FCC	Federal Communications Commission, the converged broadcast and telecoms regulator for the United States at the federal level.
FRAND	Fair, reasonable, and nondiscriminatory terms, where a monopoly provider of facilities (whether patents and other intellectual property or physical goods) provides access to its competitors.
FTA	Free Trade Agreement, regulating market access between two or more states. See also ACTA.
FTC	Federal Trade Commission, the U.S. federal regulator for consumer and competition protection.
HADOPI	Haute autorité pour la diffusion des oeuvres et la protection des droits sur internet (High Authority of Diffusion of the Art Works and Protection of the (Copy)Rights on Internet), an agency established under the 2009 French law against copyright infringement (formerly the Loi favorisant la diffusion et la protection de la création sur Internet).
ICANN	Internet Corporation for Assigned Names and Numbers; the nonprofit multistakeholder organization responsible for overseeing the Internet's Domain Name System, addresses, and other unique naming and numbering systems.
ICCPR	The United Nations' International Covenant on Civil and Political Rights, adopted by the General Assembly on December 16, 1966.
ICRA	Formerly the Internet Content Rating Association; develops tools and standards to rate digital content so that it can be blocked by filtering software. Now part of the nonprofit Family Online Safety Institute.
ICT	Information and Communication Technology.
IETF	Internet Engineering Task Force, a self-regulating technical standards body.
IGF	Internet Governance Forum: annual United Nations multistakeholder discussion forum initially held in Athens 2006.
IMS	IP Multimedia Subsystem, a set of standards for next-generation networks.
IP	Internet Protocol.
IPR	Intellectual property rights.

IPTV	Internet Protocol television: video programming delivered over IP rather than broadcast (cable, terrestrial, and satellite) networks.
ISP	Internet service provider, a company providing access to the Internet for consumers and businesses. The largest ISP in many states is the incumbent telecommunications company. ISPs often provide content, with portal pages that offer news, weather, and video reports; dating; chat; search; and other functions. Mobile networks with data services are also ISPs.
ITU	International Telecommunication Union, a United Nations body established to coordinate global telecommunications; successor to International Telegraph Union founded in 1865.
IWF	Internet Watch Foundation: the U.K. hotline for illegal content reporting established in 1996.
MPLS	Multiprotocol Label Switching, a standard set for next-generation networks.
NGNs	Next-generation networks: all-Internet Protocol networks.
NRA	National regulatory authority, in reference to independent national bodies established under national law of the member states of the EU, which implement the European communications framework; can also be used generically to refer to any national authority.
NTD	Notice and takedown: regime by which ISPs can avoid liability for potentially damaging content by removing such content on receipt of notice from a third party.
OECD	Organization for Economic Cooperation and Development: Think tank formed in 1961 for developed nations, with Israel joining as the thirtieth national member in 2010; membership requires commitment to a market economy and a pluralistic democracy.
Ofcom	Office of Communications Regulation: U.K.-converged regulator of broadcasting and telecoms established in 2002 and operational in December 2003.
ONA	Open network architecture: the principle behind interconnection of telephone networks that helped liberalize U.S. and European data networks in the late 1990s.
OSI	Open Systems Interconnection; a pre-Internet series of networking standards defined by the International Organization for Standardization and the International Telecommunication Union.

P2P	Peer-to-peer: usually used in reference to file sharing among many peers, an efficient form of many-to-many information sharing as compared to a broadcast model using a central server. P2P is the method of distribution used by Skype, BitTorrent, and many other information-sharing programs.
P3P	Platform for Privacy Preferences, a largely defunct standard that allows Web sites to describe their privacy policies to Web browsers in machine-readable form.
PET	Privacy-enhancing technology, a technical method for reducing the amount of personal information required in a system or transaction.
Petabyte	1,000 terabytes (1 million gigabytes).
PICS	Platform for Internet Content Selection, a World Wide Web Consortium standard for labeling Web pages according to their suitability for children.
QoS	Quality of service. Protocols and standards designed to offer guaranteed QoS have been mooted for many years, but none has yet been successfully marketed on the public Internet.
RFID	Radio Frequency Identification, a cheap, low-power tag that can be read remotely over short distances for object identification and tracking purposes.
SNS	Social networking system, such as Facebook or LinkedIn.
SOPA	Stop Online Piracy Act, a bill introduced in the U.S. House of Representatives that was stalled indefinitely after widespread protests by Internet users and sites such as Wikipedia and Reddit.
SSL	Secure Sockets Layer, a technical standard to allow data communications to be encrypted and/or authenticated to protect the confidentiality and integrity of information such as credit card numbers. See also TLS.
TLS	Transport Layer Security, a more recent version of the Secure Sockets Layer standard. See also SSL.
ToU	Terms of use, the contract presented to users by Web sites and software that is the main private governance mechanism for these services.
TPM	Technological protection measure, a technical means for controlling the use of copyrighted works given specific legal protection by the World Intellectual Property Organization's "Internet treaties" of 1996. See also DRM, WIPO.

UDHR   The United Nations' Universal Declaration of Human Rights, adopted by the General Assembly on December 10, 1948.

UGC   User-generated content, online media such as blogs and product reviews, created often without specific compensation by individual users, rather than commercial authors and media companies. See also Web 2.0.

URL   Uniform resource locator, a unique address for Internet resources such as Web pages and images.

VoIP   Voice over Internet protocol: technology to digitize sound in packets sent over the Internet. Its primary advantage is that distance does not affect the cost of the call between two VoIP-enabled phones (or PCs attached to the phone or a data system).

W3C   World Wide Web Consortium, a nonprofit organization responsible for Web technical standards.

Web 2.0   Social networking applications using blogs, podcasts, wikis, social networking Web sites, search engines, auction Web sites, games, voice over Internet Protocol, and peer-to-peer services. These services makes user-generated and distributed content central to consumers' Internet experiences.

WIPO   World Intellectual Property Organization, a United Nations agency established in 1970 that is responsible for numerous treaties related to patents, copyrights, and other forms of intellectual property.

References

A&M Records v Napster. 2001. 239 F.3d 1004.

Australian Associated Press. 2010. Facebook adviser critical of mandatory ISP filter. June. http://www.theaustralian.com.au/australian-it/facebook-adviser-critical-of-filter/story-e6frgakx-1225878605455.

Acquisti, A. 2002. Protecting privacy with economics: Economic incentives for preventive technologies in ubiquitous computing environments. In Workshop on Socially-Informed Design of Privacy-Enhancing Solutions, Fourth International Conference on Ubiquitous Computing.

Acquisti, A., A. Friedman, and R. Telang. 2006. Is there a cost to privacy breaches? An event study. In *Proceedings of the Fifth Workshop on the Economics of Information Security,* Cambridge, U.K.

Ahlert, C., C. Marsden, and C. Yung. 2004. How "liberty" disappeared from cyberspace: The mystery shopper tests Internet content self-regulation. http://www.rootsecure.net/content/downloads/pdf/liberty_disappeared_from_cyberspace.pdf.

Akdeniz, Yaman. 2008. *Internet child pornography and the law: National and international responses.* Aldershot: Ashgate.

Akdeniz, Yaman. 2011. Freedom of expression on the Internet: Study of legal provisions and practices related to freedom of expression, the free flow of information and media pluralism on the Internet in OSCE participating states. Office of the Representative on Freedom of the Media, Organization for Security and Co-Operation in Europe, Vienna. http://www.osce.org/fom/80723.

American Civil Liberties Union v. *Reno.* 1997. 21 U.S. 844.

American Civil Liberties Union. 2004. The surveillance-industrial complex. http://www.aclu.org/FilesPDFs/surveillance_report.pdf.

Anderson, Nate. 2011. "Very bold or very dumb": Data caps don't apply to ISP's own movie service." *Ars Technica* (July). http://arstechnica.com/tech-policy/news/2011/07/very-bold-or-very-dumb-data-caps-dont-apply-to-isps-own-movie-service.ars.

Anderson, R., I. Brown, T. Dowty, P. Inglesant, W. Heath, and A. Sasse. 2009. Database state. York: Joseph Rowntree Reform Trust.

Arthur, C. 2011a. Vodafone's Egypt texts may do them lasting damage. *Guardian*, February 3. http://www.guardian.co.uk/commentisfree/2011/feb/03/vodafone-egypt -text-messages.

Arthur, C. 2011b. Sony suffers second data breach with theft of 25m more user details. *Guardian*, May 3. http://www.guardian.co.uk/technology/blog/2011/may/03/ sony-data-breach-online-entertainment.

Article 29 Working Party. 2011a. Privacy and data protection impact assessment framework for RFID applications.

Article 29 Working Party. 2011b. Opinion 16/2011 on EASA/IAB best practice recommendation on online behavioural advertising.

Article 29 Working Party. 2011c. Opinion 9/2011 on the revised industry proposal for a privacy and data protection impact assessment framework for RFID applications.

Australian Government Department of Broadband, Communications and Digital Economy. 2010. Strategy papers. http://www.dbcde.gov.au/__data/assets/pdf _file/0019/131275/Strategy_papers.pdf.

Australian Privacy Charter Council. 1994. Australian Privacy Charter. http://www .privacy.org.au/apcc/.

Australian Tape Manufacturers Association Ltd v. *Commonwealth of Australia*. 1993. 25 IPR 1.

Ayres, I., and J. Braithwaite. 1992. *Responsive regulation: Transcending the deregulation debate*. New Haven, CT: Yale University Press.

Baird, Zoe. 2002. Governing the Internet: Engaging government, business, and nonprofits. *Foreign Affairs* 81 (6): 15–20.

Baldwin, R., C. Hood, and C. Scott. 1998. *Socio-legal reader on regulation*. New York: Oxford University Press.

Balkin, J. M., and B. S. Noveck, eds. 2006. *The state of play: Law and virtual worlds*. New York: New York University Press.

Ball, K., and F. Webster. 2003. *The intensification of surveillance: Crime, terrorism and warfare in the information age*. London: Pluto.

Balleisen, Edward, J. 2010. The prospects for effective co-regulation in the United States: A historian's view from the twenty-first century. In *Government and markets: Toward a new theory of regulation*, ed. Edward J. Balleisen and David A. Moss, 443–481. Cambridge: Cambridge University Press.

Balleisen, Edward J., and Marc Eisner. 2009. The promise and pitfalls of co-regulation: How governments can draw on private governance for public purpose. In *New perspectives on regulation*, ed. David A. Moss and John A. Cisternino, 127–150. New York: The Tobin Project.

Balleisen, Edward J., and David A. Moss. 2010. *Government and markets: Toward a new theory of regulation*. Cambridge: Cambridge University Press.

Bar, F., M. Borrus, and R. Steinberg. 1995. Islands in the bit-stream: mapping the NII interoperability debate. Working Paper 79, Berkeley Roundtable on the International Economy. http://brie.berkeley.edu/publications/WP%2079.pdf.

Bar, F., S. Cohen, P. Cowhey, B. DeLong, M. Kleeman, and J. Zysman. 2000. Access and innovation policy for the third-generation Internet. *Telecommunications Policy* 24 (6/7): 489–518.

Baran, Paul. 1964. *Introduction to distributed communications networks*. Santa Monica, CA: RAND.

Barlow, John Perry. 1996. A declaration of the independence of cyberspace. https://projects.eff.org/~barlow/Declaration-Final.html.

Barnes, Fod. 2000. Commentary: When to regulate in the GIS? A public policy perspective. In *Regulating the global information society*, ed. Chris Marsden. London: Routledge.

Barnett, Jonathan M. 2011. The host's dilemma: Strategic forfeiture in platform markets for informational goods. *Harvard Law Review* 124:1861.

Barton, John H. 1997. The balance between intellectual property rights and competition: Paradigms in the information sector. *European Competition Law Review Issue* 7:440–445.

Bauer, Johannes M., Jonathan A. Obar, and Taejin Koh. 2011. Reconciling economic and political goals in the Internet ecosystem. Paper presented to 39th Research Conference on Communication, Information and Internet Policy, Arlington, VA. http://www.tprcweb.com/jdownloads/2011/Network%20Management/tprc-2011 -nm-2.pdf.

BBC. 2006. Kazaa site becomes legal service. *BBC News*, July 27. http://news.bbc .co.uk/2/hi/science/nature/5220406.stm.

BBC. 2010. China Green Dam Web filter teams face funding crisis. *BBC News*, July 13. http://www.bbc.co.uk/news/10614674.

Bender, G. 1998. Bavaria v. Felix Somm: The pornography conviction of the former CompuServe manager. *International Journal of Communications Law and Policy* 1: 1–4.

Benkler, Y. 1998. Communications infrastructure regulation and the distribution of control over content. *Telecommunications Policy* 22 (3): 183–196.

Benkler, Y. 2002. Coase's penguin: Or Linux and the nature of the firm. *Yale Law Journal* 112 (3): 429.

Benkler, Y. 2006. *The wealth of networks: How social production transforms markets and freedom.* New Haven, CT: Yale University Press.

Benkler, Y. 2011a. A free irresponsible press: WikiLeaks and the battle over the soul of the networked fourth estate. *Harvard Civil Rights–Civil Liberties Law Review* 46: 311–397.

Benkler, Y. 2011b. Network theory: Networks of power, degrees of freedom. *International Journal of Communication* 5. http://ijoc.org/ojs/index.php/ijoc/article/view/ 1093.

Bennett, C. 2008. *The privacy advocates: Resisting the spread of surveillance.* Cambridge, MA: MIT Press.

Bennett, Colin, and Charles Raab. 2006. *Global privacy protection.* Cheltenham: Elgar.

Berman, Jerry, and Daniel J. Weitzner. 1995. Abundance and user control: Renewing the democratic heart of the First Amendment in the age of interactive media. *Yale Law Journal* 104:1626–1629.

Berners-Lee, Tim. 2006. Net neutrality: This is serious. June 21. http://dig.csail.mit .edu/breadcrumbs/node/144.

Berners-Lee, Tim. 2010. Long live the Web: A call for continued open standards and neutrality. *Scientific American Magazine*, November.

Berners-Lee, Tim, and Mark Fischetti. 2000. *Weaving the Web: The original design and ultimate destiny of the World Wide Web.* New York: HarperCollins.

Bernstein, G. 2006. When technologies are still new: Windows of opportunity for privacy protection. *Villanova Law Review* 51:921-949.

Beydogan, Turgut Ayhan. 2010. Interoperability-centric problems: New challenges and legal solutions. *International Journal of Law and Information Technology* 18 (4): 301–331.

Bick, Jonathan D. 1998. Why should the Internet be any different? *Pace Law Review* 91:41-67.

Birnhack, M. 2003. Acknowledging the conflict between copyright law and freedom of expression under the Human Rights Act. *Entertainment Law Review* 24. http:// works.bepress.com/michael_birnhack/9.

Bishop, J., J. Kay, and C. Mayer. 1995. *The regulatory challenge.* New York: Oxford University Press.

Bits of Freedom. 2011. Netherlands launches Internet freedom legislation. June. https://www.bof.nl/2011/06/22/netherlands-launches-internet-freedom -legislation/.

Black, Ian. 2010. How Arab governments tried to silence WikiLeaks: An appetite for state secrets led to bans on western newspapers and hacked news websites across the Middle East. *e Guardian*. http://www.guardian.co.uk/world/2010/dec/17/ arab-governments-silenced-wikileaks.

Blackman, Colin. 1998. Convergence between telecommunications and other media. How should regulation adapt? *Telecommunications Policy* 22 (3): 163–170.

Blom-Hansen, J. 1997. A "new institutionalist" perspective on policy networks. *Public Administration* 75:669–693.

Blumenthal, M., and D. Clark. 2001. Rethinking the design of the Internet: The end to end arguments vs. the brave new world. *ACM Transactions on Internet Technology* 1 (1): 70–109.

Boddewyn, J. J. 1988. *Advertising self-regulation and outside participation*. Westport, CT: Greenwood Press.

Body of European Regulators of Electronic Communications. 2010. Response to the European Commission's consultation on the open Internet and net neutrality in Europe. http://www.erg.eu.int/doc/berec/bor_10_42.pdf.

Body of European Regulators of Electronic Communications. 2011a. BoR(11) 44 draft guidelines on transparency as a tool to achieve net neutrality. http://erg.eu. int/doc/berec/bcn_bor_agenda.pdf.

Body of European Regulators of Electronic Communications. 2011b. Guidelines on transparency as a tool to achieve net neutrality. erg.eu.int/documents/berec_docs/ index_en.htm.

Berne Convention for the Protection of Literary and Artistic Works. 1886.

Botgirl. 2011. Executive Chairman Eric Schmidt admits Google+ is Essentially a trojan horse (identity platform). August. http://botgirl.blogspot.com/2011/08/ executive-chairman-eric-schidt-admits.html.

Boyd, Danah, and N. Ellison. 2007. Social network sites, definition, history and scholarship. *Journal of Computer Mediated Communication* 13 (1), article 11. http:// jcmc.indiana.edu/vol13/issue1/boyd.ellison.html.

Boyd, D., and E. Hargittai. 2010. Facebook privacy settings: Who cares? *First Monday*, August 2. http://www.uic.edu/htbin/cgiwrap/bin/ojs/index.php/fm/article/view/ 3086/2589.

Boyle, J. 2008. *Public domain: Enclosing the commons of the mind*. New Haven, CT: Yale University Press.

Boyle, Kevin. 2001. Hate speech: The United States versus the rest of the world? *Maine Law Review* 53:487–502.

Braithwaite, J., and P. Drahos. 2000. *Global business regulation.* Cambridge: Cambridge University Press.

Braman, Sandra. 2009. *Change of state: Information, policy, and power.* Cambridge, MA: MIT Press.

Braman, Sandra, and Stephanie Lynch. 2003. Advantage ISP: Terms of service as media law. *New Media and Society* 5:422–448.

Brand, Stewart. 1985. Report of the First Hacker's Conference. *Whole Earth Review,* May: 49.

Bresnahan, T., S. Greenstein, and R. Hendersen. 2011. *Schumpeterian competition and diseconomies of scope: Illustrations from the histories of Microsoft and IBM.* Cambridge, MA: National Bureau of Economic Research. http://www.nber.org/chapters/c12354 .pdf.

Briscoe, Bob. 2008. A fairer, faster Internet Protocol. *IEEE Spectrum* (December): 38–43.

Broadband Industry Technical Advisory Group. 2011. By-laws of Broadband Industry Technical Advisory Group. http://members.bitag.org/kwspub/background_docs/ BITAG_Bylaws.pdf.

Brown, Abbe. 2010. Access to essential technologies: The role of the interface between intellectual property, competition and human rights. *International Review of Law Computers and Technology* 24 (1): 51–61.

Brown, Abbe, and Charlotte Waelde. 2005. Intellectual property, competition and human rights: The past, the present and the future. *SCRIPT-ed* 2 (4):450–454.

Brown, Ian. 2003. *Implementing the European Union Copyright Directive.* London: Foundation for Information Policy Research.

Brown, Ian. 2009. Regulation of converged communications surveillance. In *New directions in privacy and surveillance,* ed. B. Goold and D. Neyland, 39–73. Exeter, UK: Willan.

Brown, Ian, ed. 2013. *Research handbook on governance of the Internet.* London: Edward Elgar

Brown, Ian, David Clark, and Dirk Trossen. 2011. Should specific values be embedded in the Internet architecture? In *Proceedings of the Re-Architecting the Internet workshop.* New York: ACM Press.

Brown, Ian, Lilian Edwards, and Christopher T. Marsden. 2006. Legal and institutional responses to Denial of Service Attacks. Communications Research Network/

Department for Trade and Industry joint seminar on Spam/DDoS. November. http://www.communicationsresearch.net/events/article/default.aspx?objid=1464.

Brown, Ian, Lilian Edwards, and Christopher T. Marsden. 2009. Information security and cybercrime. In *Law and the Internet*, 3rd ed., ed. L. Edwards and C. Waelde. Oxford: Hart.

Brown, Ian, and Douwe Korff. 2011. *Social media and human rights*. In *Human Rights and a Changing Media Landscape*. Strasbourg: Council of Europe Publications, 175–206.

Brown, Ian, and Douwe Korff. 2012. Digital Freedoms in International Law: Practical Steps to Protect Human Rights Online. Washington, DC: Global Network Initiative. http://globalnetworkinitiative.org/news/new-report-outlines-recommendations-governments-companies-and-others-how-protect-free.

Brown, Ian, and Christopher T. Marsden. 2008. Social utilities, dominance and interoperability: A modest proposal. Presentation to GikIII [Geek Law], Oxford. http://www.slideshare.net/blogzilla/social-networks-dominance-and-interoperability-presentation.

Brownsword, R. 2005. Code, control and choice: Why East is East and West is West. *Legal Studies* 25:1–21.

Brownsword, Roger. 2008. *Rights, regulation, and the technological revolution*. New York: Oxford University Press.

Brownsword, Roger, and Karen Yeung, eds. 2008. *Regulating technologies*. Oxford: Hart:

Brynjolfsson, E., M. D. Smith, and Y. Hu. 2003. Consumer surplus in the digital economy: Estimating the value of increased product variety at online booksellers. Working Paper 4305–03, MIT, Sloan, June. http://ssrn.com/abstract=400940.

Budde, P. 2011. *Broadband: A platform for progress*. New York: Broadband Commission for Digital Development, United Nations. http://www.broadbandcommission.org/Reports/Report_2_Executive_Summary.pdf.

Bundesamt für Sicherheit in der Informationstechnik. 2010. Technical guidelines for the secure use of RFID (TG RFID). Technical Guideline TR-03126.

Burk, Dan L. 1999. Virtual exit in the global information economy. *Chicago-Kent Law Review* 73:943–995.

Burstein, D. 2008. Comcast's fair 250 gig bandwidth cap. *DSL Prime*. October. http://www.dslprime.com/docsisreport/163-c/53-comcasts-fair-250-gig-bandwidth-cap.

Bygrave, L. A. 2010. Privacy and data protection in an international perspective. *Scandinavian Studies in Law* 56:165–200.

Caddick, Anna, and Hugh Tomlinson. 2010. Norwich Pharmacal orders: An effective global remedy. *New Law Journal* 160 (7404). http://www.newlawjournal.co.uk/nlj/content/effective-global-remedy.

Cairncross, Frances. 1997. *The death of distance: How the communications revolution will change our lives.* Cambridge, MA: Harvard Business School Press.

Camp, L., and C. Vincent. 2004. Setting standards: Looking to the Internet for models of governance. http://papers.ssrn.com/sol3/papers.cfm?abstract_id=615201.

Cannon, Robert. 2003. The legacy of the FCC's computer inquiries. *Federal Communications Law Journal* 55:167–205.

Carnoy, M., M. Castells, S. S. Cohen, and F. H. Cardoso. 1993. *The new global economy in the information age: Reflections on our changing world.* New York: Macmillan.

Carrier, Michael A. 2010. The Pirate Bay, Grokster, and Google. *Journal of Intellectual Property Rights* 15:7–18.

Cave, Jonathan. 2005. The economics of cyber-trust among cyber-partners. In *Trust and crime in information societies,* ed. R. Mansell and B. Collins. Cheltenham: Edward Elgar.

Cave, Martin. 2004. Economic aspects of the new regulatory regime for electronic communication services. In *The economics of antitrust and regulation in telecommunications,* ed. P. Buiges and P. Rey, 27–41. Cheltenham: Edward Elgar..

Cave, Martin. 2011. Directorate for Financial and Enterprise Affairs: Competition Committee Working Party No. 2 on Competition and Regulation: Hearing on Network Neutrality Paper by Mr. Martin Cave. DAF/COMP/WP2(2011)4.

Cavoukian, A. 2009. *Privacy by design . . . Take the challenge.* Ontario: Information and Privacy Commissioner.

CBS Songs Ltd v. *Amstrad Consumer Electronics plc.* 1988. 11 IPR 1.

Center for Democracy and Technology. 2011. Account deactivation and content removal: Guiding principles and practices for companies and users. http://cdt.org/blogs/erica-newland/219dilemma-deactivation-networked-public-sphere.

Center for Democracy and Technology v. *Pappert.* 2004. 337 F.Supp.2d 606.

Cerf, Vint. 1994. Guidelines for conduct on and use of Internet, Draft v0.1. http://catbib.cm-beja.pt/MULTIMEDIA/ASSOCIA/CDU/6813TECNOINFORM/GUIDELINEUSEINTERNET.PDF.

CETS No.108. 1981. *Council of Europe Convention for the Protection of Individuals with Regard to Automatic Processing of Personal Data.*

CETS No.181. 2001a. *Additional protocol to the Convention for the Protection of Individuals with Regard to Automatic Processing of Personal Data, Regarding Supervisory Authorities and Transborder Data Flows.*

CETS No.185. 2001b. *Council of Europe Convention on Cybercrime* of Nov. 23

Chen, Peter. 2002. Lust, greed, sloth: The performance and potential of Internet coregulation in Australia. *Griffith Law Review* 11:465–496.

Cherry, Barbara. 2006. Misusing network neutrality to eliminate common carriage threatens free speech and the postal system. *Northern Kentucky Law Review* 33 (483):505–510.

Cherry, Barbara. 2008. Back to the future: How transportation deregulatory policies foreshadow evolution of communications policies. *Information Society* 24: (5), 273–291 .

Child Exploitation and Online Protection Centre. 2007. *Strategic review (2006–2007)*.

Children's Charities' Coalition on Internet Safety. 2010. Briefing on the Internet, e-commerce, children and young people. November 8. http://www.chis.org .uk/2010/11/08/briefing-on-the-internet-e-commerce-children-and-young-people.

Children's Online Privacy Protection Act 1998. 15 U.S.C. sec. 6501–6506.

China People's Daily. 2006. Online video boom raises concerns. July 13. http:// english.people.com.cn/200607/13/eng20060713_282632.html.

Christou, George, and Seamus Simpson. 2009. New modes of regulatory governance for the Internet? Country code top level domains in Europe. http://regulation.upf .edu/ecpr-07-papers/ssimpson.pdf.

Cisco Systems. 2011. Visual Networking Index (VNI) global mobile data traffic forecast. http://www.cisco.com/en/US/solutions/collateral/ns341/ns525/ns537/ns705/ ns827/white_paper_c11-520862.html.

Civil Society Information Society Advisory Committee. 2011. CSISAC statement on OECD communique on Internet policy-making principles. http://www.statewatch .org/news/2011/jun/internet-CSISAC-statement.pdf.

Clark, C. 1996. The answer to the machine is in the machine. In *The future of copyright in a digital environment*, ed. P. B. Hugenholtz, 139–148. Hague: Kluwer Law International.

Clark, David. D. 1988. The design philosophy of the DARPA Internet protocols. *Computer Communication Review* 18 (4): 106–114.

Clark, David D. 2005. FIND and architecture: A new NSF initiative. http://find.isi .edu/presentation_files/Clark_Arch_Security.pdf.

Clark, David D., and Marjory S. Blumenthal. 2011. The end-to-end argument and application design: The role of trust. *Federal Communications Law Journal* 63:357–390.

Clark, David. D., Frank Field, and Richard Marr. 2010. Computer networks and the Internet: A brief history of predicting their future. http://groups.csail.mit.edu/ana/People/DDC/Working%20Papers.html.

Clark, David D., William Lehr, and Steve Bauer. 2011. Interconnection in the Internet: The policy challenge. Paper presented to 39th Research Conference on Communication, Information and Internet Policy, September 25. http://www.tprcweb.com/images/stories/2011%20papers/Clark-Lehr-Bauer_2011.pdf.

Clark, David D., John Wroclawski, Karen R. Sollins, and Robert Braden. 2002. Tussle in cyberspace: Defining tomorrow's Internet. In *Proceedings of ACM Special Interest Group on Data Communications.* www.sigcomm.org/sigcomm2002/papers/tussle.pdf.

Clark, David D., John Wroclawski, Karen R. Sollins, and Robert Braden. 2005. Tussle in cyberspace: Defining tomorrow's Internet. *IEEE/ACM Transactions on Networking* 13 (3): 462–475.

Clayton, Richard. 2005. Anonymity and traceability in cyberspace. Technical Report 653, Cambridge University Computer Laboratory. http://www.cl.cam.ac.uk/techreports/UCAM-CL-TR-653.pdf.

Clayton, Richard. 2008a. Technical aspects of the censoring of Wikipedia. *Light Blue Touchpaper* (December). http://www.lightbluetouchpaper.org/2008/12/11/technical-aspects-of-the-censoring-of-wikipedia/.

Clayton, Richard. 2008b. The Phorm\Webwise system. http://www.cl.cam.ac.uk/~rnc1/080518-phorm.pdf.

Clayton, Richard, S. J. Murdoch, and R. N. M. Watson. 2006. Ignoring the great firewall of China. Paper presented to the Sixth Workshop on Privacy Enhancing Technologies, Cambridge, U.K., June. http://www.cl.cam.ac.uk/~rnc1/ignoring.pdf.

Clinton, H. 2010. Remarks on Internet freedom. Speech at the Newseum, January 21. http://www.state.gov/secretary/rm/2010/01/135519.htm.

Clinton, H. 2011. Internet rights and wrongs: Choices and challenges in a networked world. February. t http://www.state.gov/secretary/rm/2011/02/156619.htm.

Coates, Kevin. 2011. *Competition law and regulation of technology markets.* New York: Oxford University Press.

COD. 2011. European standardisation (COD/2011/0150:) (amending Directives 89/686/EEC, 93/15/EEC, 94/9/EC, 94/25/EC, 95/16/EC, 97/23/EC, 98/34/EC, 2004/22/EC, 2007/23/EC, 2009/105/EC and 2009/23/EC) Dossier of the committee IMCO/7/06240 at http://www.europarl.europa.eu/oeil/FindByProcnum.do?lang=2&procnum=COD/2011/0150.

Cohen-Almagor, Raphael. 2011. Internet history. *International Journal of Technoethics* 2 (2): 45–64.

Collins, R. 2010. *Three myths of cyberspace: Making sense of networks, governance and regulation*. Bristol: Intellect.

Columbus, S. 2011. France to disconnect first Internet users under three strikes regime. *OpenNet Initiative blog*. http://opennet.net/blog/2011/07/france-disconnect -first-internet-users-under-three-strikes-regime.

Comcast v. *FCC*. 2010. No. 08–1291, 600 F.3d 642.

Commission on Child Online Protection. 2000. Final report of the COPA Commission, presented to Congress. http://www.copacommission.org/report/.

Committee of Experts on New Media. 2011. MC-NM(2011)013_en. Report on the 4th meeting April: http://www.coe.int/t/dghl/standardsetting/media/mc-nm/ MC-NM(2011)013_en%20Report%204th%20meeting.asp#TopOfPage.

ComScore. 2011. M metrics. June. http://advertising.microsoft.com/uk/quick-stats?s _cid=uk_MSAHP_quick_3.

Constine, J. 2010. Facebook proposes minor changes to its governing documents. September. http://www.insidefacebook.com/2010/09/17/facebook-proposes-minor -changes-to-its-governing-documents/.

Cooper, Alissa, Andrea Soppera, and Arnaud Jacquet. 2011. Bandwidth usage and management: A UK case study. Paper presented to 39th Research Conference on Communication, Information and Internet Policy, Arlington, VA. http://www .tprcweb.com/images/stories/2011%20papers/alissacooper_2011.pdf.

Cornford, Tom. 2008. *Towards a public law of tort*. London: Ashgate Publishing.

Council of Europe. 2003. *Additional protocol to the Convention on Cybercrime, concerning the criminalisation of acts of a racist and xenophobic nature committed through computer systems*. Strasbourg, January 28.

Council of Europe. 2008. Human rights guidelines for Internet service providers. http://www.coe.int/t/dghl/standardsetting/media/Doc/H-Inf%282008%29009_en .pdf.

Council of Europe. 2010. Draft recommendation on the protection of human rights with regard to search engines. http://www.coe.int/t/dghl/standardsetting/media/ mc-nm/MC-NM_2010_004%20Draft%20Rec%20%20Search%20engines.pdf.

Council of Europe. 2011a. Proposal for draft guidelines for social network providers. http://www.coe.int/t/dghl/standardsetting/media/mc-nm/MC-NM_2011_008 _enGuidelines%20for%20soc%20Netw%20prov.pdf.

Council of Europe. 2011b. Recommendation CM/Rec (2011)8 on the protection and promotion of the universality, integrity and openness of the Internet http://www .assembly.coe.int/CommitteeDocs/2011/State%20secrecy_MartyE.pdf.

Council of Europe. Committee of Ministers. 2008. Recommendation CM/Rec(2008)6 on measures to promote the respect for freedom of expression and information with regard to Internet filters. Adopted at the 1022nd meeting of the Ministers' Deputies.

Cowhey, P., J. Aronson, and D. Abelson. 2009. *Transforming global information and communication markets: The political economy of innovation.* Cambridge, MA: MIT Press.

Cowie, C., and C. Marsden. 1999. Convergence: Navigating bottlenecks in digital pay-TV. *Info* 3 (1): 53–67.

Craven, S. A., M. Wu, B. Liu, A. Stubblefield, B. Swartzlander, D. S. Wallach, D. Dean, and E. W. Felten. 2001. Reading between the lines: Lessons from the SDMI challenge. In *Proceedings of the 10th USENIX Security Symposium.*

Crawford, Susan. 2011. The communications crisis in America. *Harvard Law and Policy Review* 5:244–263.

Crowcroft, Jon. 2009. An un-governating principle for the Internet. *Computers and Law* 19 (6): 8–10. http://www.scl.org/site.aspx?i=ca0&r=2&x=pf2cvbgh.

Crowcroft, J. 2011. The affordance of asymmetry or a rendezvous with the random? *Communications and Convergence Review* 3 (1): 40–56.

Canadian Radio-television and Telecommunications Commission. 2011. Telecoms Decision 2011-44, Ottawa, 25 January 2011, Usage-based billing for gateway access services and third-party Internet access services. File number:8661-C12-201015975. http://www.crtc.gc.ca/eng/archive/2011/2011-44.htm.

Cukier, Kenn. 2004. Multilateral control of Internet infrastructure and its impact on U.S. Sovereignty. October. http://www.tprc.org.

Cunard, J. P., K. Hill, and C. Barlas. 2003. Current developments in the field of digital rights management. Prepared for World Intellectual Property Organization Standing Committee on Copyright and Related Rights Tenth Session. http://www.wipo.int/meetings/en/doc_details.jsp?doc_id=29478.

Curtis, Polly. 2011. Will the government crackdown on internet porn work? *Guardian* (October 11). http://www.guardian.co.uk/politics/reality-check-with-polly-curtis/2011/oct/11/internet-pornography.

Darlin, Damian. 2010. Google settles suit over buzz and privacy. *New York Times,* November 3. http://bits.blogs.nytimes.com/2010/11/03/google-settles-suit-over-buzz-and-privacy/.

David, Paul. 2001. The evolving accidental information super-highway. *Oxford Review of Economic Policy* 17 (2): 159–187.

Davies, Howard. 2010. *The financial crisis—Who is to blame?* Cambridge: Polity Press.

Davies, T., and B. Noveck, eds. 2006. *Online deliberation: Design, research, and practice.* Chicago: CSLI Publications/University of Chicago Press.

De Beer, J. 2009. *Net neutrality in the Great White North (and its impact on Canadian culture).* Telecommunications Journal of Australia 59 (2): 24.1–24.19.

de Sola Pool, I. 1983. *Technologies of freedom.* Cambridge, MA: Belknap.

Deibert, R. J., J. G. Palfrey, R. Rohozinski, and J. Zittrain, eds. 2008. *Access denied: The shaping of power, rights, and rule in cyberspace.* Cambridge, MA: MIT Press.

Deibert, R. J., J. G. Palfrey, R. Rohozinski, and J. Zittrain, eds. 2010. *Access controlled: The shaping of power, rights, and rule in cyberspace.* Cambridge, MA: MIT Press.

DeNardis Laura, E. 2009. *Protocol politics: The globalization of Internet governance.* Cambridge, MA: MIT Press.

DiPerna. Paul. 2006. The Connector Website model: New implications for social change. Paper presented at the Annual Meeting of the American Sociological Association, Montreal, August.

Directive 95/46/EC of the European Parliament and of the Council of 24 October 1995 on the protection of individuals with regard to the processing of personal data and on the free movement of such data. 1995. OJ L 281/31 OJ L 281, of October 24, 1995.

Directive EC/2000/31. 2000. Directive on Electronic Commerce. OJ L 178/1, 17.07.2000.

Directive 2001/29/EC. 2001. Copyright in the Information Society Directive. OJ L 167, of May 22, 2001, 22/06/2001.

Directive 2002/58. 2002. Directive on Privacy and Electronic Communications. OJ L 201/37, 31.7.2002.

Directive 2004/18/EC. 2004. Directive on the Coordination of Procedures for the Award of Public Works Contracts, Public Supply Contracts and Public Service Contracts. OJ L 134, 30.4.2004, 114.

Directive 2006/24/EC. 2006. Directive on the Retention of Data Generated or Processed in Connection with the Provision of Publicly Available Electronic Communications Services or of Public Communications Networks and Amending Directive 2002/58/EC, OJ L105/54.

Directive 2007/65/EC. 2007. Amending Council Directive 89/552/EEC on the Coordination of Certain Provisions Laid Down by Law, Regulation or Administrative Action in Member States Concerning the Pursuit of Television Broadcasting Activities. OJ L332.

Directive 2009/140/EC. 2009a. Better Regulation Directive. OJ L. 337/37 18.12.2009.

Directive 2009/136/EC. 2009b. Citizens' Rights Directive. OJ L. 337/11 18.12.2009.

Directive 2011/92/EU. 2011. Combating the Sexual Abuse and Sexual Exploitation of Children and Child Pornography, and Replacing Council Framework Decision 2004/68/JHA, OJ L335/1.

Doctorow, Cory. 2007. Online censorship hurts us all. *Guardian*, October 2.

Dolmans, Maurits. 2010. A tale of two tragedies: A plea for open standards. *International Free and Open Source Software Law Review* 2 (2):115–136. http://www.ifosslr.org/ifosslr/article/view/46/72.

Dommering, E. J. 2006. Regulating technology: Code is not law. In *Coding regulation: Essays on the normative role of information technology*, ed. E. J. Dommering and L. F. Asscher, 1–17. The Hague: T.M.C. Asser Press.

Donahue, H. 2010. The network neutrality inquiry. *Info* 12 (2):3–8.

Donoso, V. 2011. Results of the assessment of the implementation of the Safer Social Networking Principles for the EU. Luxembourg: European Commission. http://ec.europa.eu/information_society/activities/social_networking/docs/final_report_11/part_two.pdf.

Drahos, Peter, and John Braithwaite. 2002. *Information feudalism: Who owns the knowledge economy?* New York: Free Press.

Drake, William J. 2000. The rise and decline of the international telecommunications regime. In *Regulating the global information Society*, ed. Chris Marsden. London: Routledge.

Drake, William J., ed. 2005. Reforming Internet governance: perspectives from the Working Group on Internet Governance. U.N. ICT Task Force Series 12. http://www.wgig.org/book-Launch.html.

Drake, William J., and Ernest J. Wilson III, eds. 2008. *Governing global electronic networks: International perspectives on policy and power*. Cambridge, MA: MIT Press.

Dramatico Entertainment Ltd & Ors v. British Sky Broadcasting Ltd & Ors. 2012. EWHC 1152 (Ch).

Economides, N., and J. Tåg. 2007. Net neutrality on the Internet: A two-sided market analysis. Working Paper, NYU Center for Law and Economics.

Edwards, L. 2004. The problem with privacy: A modest proposal. *International Review of Law, Computer, and Technology* 18 (3): 263–294.

Edwards, Lilian. 2013. Privacy, Law, Code and Social Networking Sites. In *Research handbook on governance of the Internet*, ed. Ian Brown. Cheltenham: Edward Elgar.

Edwards, Lilian, and Ian Brown. 2009. Data control and social networking: Irreconcilable ideas? In *Harboring data: Information security, law and the corporation*, ed. A. Matwyshyn. Palo Alto, CA: Stanford University Press.

Electronic Frontier Foundation. 2010. Unintended consequences: Twelve years under the DMCA. http://www.eff.org/wp/unintended-consequences-under-dmca.

Electronic Privacy Information Center. 2000. Pretty poor privacy: An assessment of P3P and Internet privacy. http://epic.org/reports/prettypoorprivacy.html.

Ellickson Robert C. 1991. *Order without law: How neighbors settle disputes*. Cambridge, MA: Harvard University Press.

Elmer-DeWitt, P., D. Jackson, and W. King. 1993. First nation in cyberspace. *Time Magazine* (December 6).

ENISA. 2007. European Network and Information Security Agency. Report on security issues and recommendations for online social networks. http://ec.europa.eu/information_society/activities/social_networking/docs/enisa_report.pdf.

ENISA. 2008. Technology-induced challenges in privacy and data protection in Europe. http://www.enisa.europa.eu/activities/risk-management/files/deliverables/technology-induced-challenges-in-privacy-data-protection-in-europe.

European Advertising Standards Alliance. 2011. EASA best practice recommendation on online behavioural advertising. http://www.easa-alliance.org/page.aspx/386.

European Commission. IP/07/139. 2007. Mobile operators agree on how to safeguard children using mobile phones.

European Commission. 2008. Public consultation on online social networking. http://ec.europa.eu/information_society/activities/sip/docs/pub_consult_age_rating_sns/summaryreport.pdf.

European Commission. 2009a. Recommendation on the implementation of privacy and data protection principles in applications supported by radio-frequency identification. http://ec.europa.eu/information_society/policy/rfid/documents/recommendationonrfid2009.pdf.

European Commission. IP/09/232. 2009b. Social networking: Commission brokers agreement among major Web companies.

European Commission. 2010a. Communication: Towards interoperability for European public services. December. http://ec.europa.eu/isa/documents/isa_iop_communication_en.pdf.

European Commission. 2010b. Consultation on the future of the universal service obligation. http://ec.europa.eu/information_society/policy/ecomm/library/public_consult/universal_service_2010/index_en.htm.

European Commission. 2010c. Web browser choice for European consumers. http:// ec.europa.eu/competition/consumers/web_browsers_choice_en.html.

European Commission. 2010d. A digital agenda for Europe. COM 245. http://ec .europa.eu/information_society/digital-agenda/documents/digital-agenda -communication-en.pdf.

European Commission. 2010e. A comprehensive approach on personal data protection in the European Union. COM 609 final. http://ec.europa.eu/justice/news/ consulting_public/0006/com_2010_609_en.pdf.

European Commission. IP/11/402. 2011a. Digital Agenda/Trade: EU and US agree trade-related information and communication technology principles to be promoted world-wide date.

European Commission. IP/11/479. 2011b. Digital Agenda: Children using social networks at a younger age; many unaware of basic privacy risks, says survey.

European Commission. IP/11/762. 2011c. Digital Agenda: Only two social networking sites protect privacy of minors' profiles by default.

European Commission. 2011d. Guidelines on the applicability of Article 101 of the Treaty on the Functioning of the European Union to horizontal co-operation agreements. *Official Journal of the European Union*, C 11 of 14.1.2011. http://eur-lex.europa .eu/LexUriServ/LexUriServ.do?uri=OJ:C:2011:011:0001:0072:EN:PDF.

European Commission. 2011e. Synthesis of the comments on the Commission Report on the Application of Directive 2004/48/EC of 29 April 2004 on the Enforcement of Intellectual Property Rights. COM/2010/779 final. July. http://ec.europa.eu/ internal_market/consultations/docs/2011/intellectual_property_rights/summary _report_replies_consultation_en.pdf.

European Commission. 2012. A coherent framework for building trust in the Digital Single Market for e-commerce and online services. COM/2011/942. January. http:// ec.europa.eu/internal_market/e-commerce/docs/communication2012/COM2011 _942_en.pdf.

European Data Protection Supervisor. 2010. Opinion on the current negotiations by the European Union of an Anti-Counterfeiting Trade Agreement (ACTA). O.J.C. (147). http://eur-lex.europa.eu/LexUriServ/LexUriServ.do?uri=OJ:C:2010:147:0001:0 013:EN:PDF.

European Data Protection Supervisor. 2011a. Opinion on net neutrality, traffic management and the protection of privacy and personal data. http://www.edps.europa .eu/EDPSWEB/webdav/site/mySite/shared/Documents/Consultation/Opinions/ 2011/11-10-07_Net_neutrality_EN.pdf.

European Data Protection Supervisor. 2011b. Do not track or right on track?—The privacy implications of online behavioural advertising. Lecture delivered at University of Edinburgh, School of Law, July 7. http://www.edps.europa.eu/EDPSWEB/webdav/site/mySite/shared/Documents/EDPS/Publications/Speeches/2011/11-07-07_Speech_Edinburgh_EN.pdf.

European Digital Rights Initiative. 2008. Google reduces search data retention time to 9 months, but not enough. September 24. http://www.edri.org/edrigram/number6.18/google-search-retention.

European Digital Rights Initiative. 2011. Internet blocking: Crimes should be punished and not hidden. http://www.edri.org/files/blocking_booklet.pdf.

European Digital Rights Initiative. 2012. Thank you SOPA, Thank you ACTA. http://www.edri.org/edrigram/number10.13/good-bye-acta.

European Network and Information Security Agency. 2008. *Technology-induced challenges in privacy and data protection in Europe*. Heraklion: ENISA.

European Parliament. 2010. Friends and foes of the Internet and human rights, information. 09–06–2010–14:33. http://www.europarl.europa.eu/sides/getDoc.do?language=EN&type=IM-PRESS&reference=20100607STO75582.

European Parliament. 2011. 2011/0150(COD) Committee on the Internal Market and Consumer Protection 9.2.2012: Amendments 66–276 to draft report of Lara Comi (PE478.420v01-00).

European Union. 2007. Mobile operators agree on how to safeguard children using mobile phones. Press release, IP/07/139.

European Union. 2009. Social networking: Commission brokers agreement among major Web companies. Press release, IP/09/232.

European Union. 2011a. Digital agenda/trade: EU and US agree trade-related information and communication technology principles to be promoted world-wide date. Press release, IP/11/402.

European Union. 2011b. Digital agenda: Children using social networks at a younger age; many unaware of basic privacy risks, says survey. Press release, IP/11/479.

European Union. 2011c. Digital agenda: Only two social networking sites protect privacy of minors' profiles by default. Press release, IP/11/762.

Evangelista, B. 2002. Napster runs out of lives: Judge rules against sale. *San Francisco Chronicle*, September 4. http://www.sfgate.com/cgi-bin/article.cgi?file=/chronicle/archive/2002/09/04/BU138263.DTL.

Facebook. 2010. Statement of rights and responsibilities Update, requesting comments by 30 September. http://www.facebook.com/fbsitegovernance?v=app_4949752878.

Facebook. 2012. Form S-1 Registration Statement under the Securities Act of 1933, Facebook, Inc. Washington DC: Securities and Exchange Commission.http://sec .gov/Archives/edgar/data/1326801/000119312512034517/d287954ds1.htm.

Faratin, P., David D. Clark, S. Bauer, W. Lehr, P. W. Gilmore, and A. Berger. 2008. The growing complexity of Internet interconnection. *Communications and Strategies* (72): 51–72.

Faulhaber, Gerald R. 2002. Network effects and merger analysis: Instant messaging and the AOL–Time Warner case. *Telecommunications Policy* 26 (5–6): 311–333.

Faulhaber, Gerald R. 2010. Transparency and broadband Internet Service Providers. *International Journal of Communication* 4:738–757.

Federal Communications Commission. 2005. Appropriate framework for broadband access to the Internet over wireline facilities et al. Policy Statement, 20 FCC Rcd 14986 (Internet Policy Statement).

Federal Communications Commission. 2008. Formal complaint of free press and public knowledge against Comcast Corp. for secretly degrading peer-to-peer applications; broadband industry practices; Petition of Free Press et al. for declaratory ruling that degrading an Internet application violates the FCC's Internet policy statement and does not meet an exception for "reasonable network management." Memorandum Opinion and Order. 23 FCC Rcd. (13028).

Federal Communications Commission. 2010. In the matter of preserving the open Internet broadband industry practices. Report and Order. GN Docket No. 09-191 WC Docket (07–52). Adopted: December 21, 2010.

Federal Register. 2011. Preserving the open Internet. Federal Communications Commission 47 CFR Parts 0 and 8 [GN Docket No. 09–191; WC Docket No. 07–52; FCC 10–201] September. http://www.gpo.gov/fdsys/pkg/FR-2011-09-23/pdf/2011-24259 .pdf.

Federal Trade Commmission. 2005. *Effectiveness and enforcement of the CAN-SPAM Act.* Federal Trade Commission Report to Congress, December. http://www.ftc.gov/ reports/canspam05/051220canspamrpt.pdf.

Federal Trade Commmission. 2007. *Report to Congress on Implementing the Children's Online Privacy Protection Act.* www.ftc.gov/reports/coppa/07COPPA_Report_to _Congress.pdf.

Federal Trade Commmission. 2010a. *Docket No. 9341 In the Matter of Intel Corporation. File No.: 061 0247.* Decision and Order of November 2. http://www.ftc.gov/os/ adjpro/d9341/101102inteldo.pdf.

Federal Trade Commmission. 2010b. *Protecting consumer privacy in an era of rapid change: A proposed framework for businesses and policymakers.* Preliminary. http://www. ftc.gov/os/2010/12/101201privacyreport.pdf.

Federal Trade Commmmission. 2011. *Google, Inc., FTC File No. 102 3136G. March 30 (consent order accepted for public comment).* http://www.ftc.gov/opa/2011/03/google.shtm.

Felten, Edward W. 2002. The Digital Millennium Copyright Act and its legacy: A view from the trenches. *Illinois Journal of Law Technology & Policy* 2002 (2): 289–294.

Felten, Edward W. 2006. Nuts and bolts of network neutrality. July. http://dreadedmonkeygod.net/home/attachments/neutrality.pdf.

Fernandez-Barrera, Meritxell. 2011. *Legal prosumers: How can government leverage user-generated content?* Ithaca, NY: Legal Information Institute, Cornell University. Vox Populii, November 17. http://blog.law.cornell.edu/voxpop/2011/11/17/legal-prosumers-how-can-government-leverage-user-generated-content/.

Ficsor, Mihály. 2002. *The law of copyright and the Internet: The 1996 WIPO treaties, their interpretation and implementation.* New York: Oxford University Press.

Fitzgerald, Brian, ed. 2010. *Access to public sector information: Law, technology and policy.* Sydney: Sydney University Press.

Ford, Richard. 2004. Beware rise of Big Brother state, warns data watchdog. *The Times*, August 16.

FreedomBox. 2011. IRC chatlog 2011-08-15 15:00UTC generated by irclog-xml.pl alpha-0.04 on Mon Aug 15 09:52:03 PDT 2011. https://freedomboxfoundation.org.

Frieden, R. 2010a. *Winning the Silicon sweepstakes: Can the United States compete in global telecommunications?* New Haven, CT: Yale University Press.

Frieden, Rob. 2010b. Invoking and avoiding the First Amendment: How Internet Service Providers leverage their status as both content creators and neutral conduits. *University of Philadelphia Journal of Constitutional Law* 12 (5): 1279–1324.

Frieden, Rob. 2011. Rationales for and against FCC involvement in resolving ISP interconnection disputes. Paper presented to 39th Research Conference on Communication, Information and Internet Policy, Arlington, VA. http://www.tprcweb.com/images/stories/2011%20papers/freiden_2011.pdf.

Froomkin, A. M. 1995. The metaphor is the key: Cryptography, the clipper chip and the Constitution. *University of Pennsylvania Law Review* 143 (3): 709–897.

Froomkin, A. M. 2000. Wrong turn in cyberspace: Using ICANN to route around the APA and the Constitution. *Duke Law Journal* 50 (1): 17–186.

Frydman, B., L. Hennebel, and G. Lewkowicz. 2008. Public strategies for Internet co-regulation in the United States, Europe and China. http://papers.ssrn.com/sol3/papers.cfm?abstract_id=1282826.

Frydman, B. and Rorive, I. 2002. Regulating Internet content through intermediaries in Europe and the USA. *Zeitschrift fur Rechtssoziologie* Bd.23/H1, July. http://www.droit-technologie.org/upload/dossier/doc/92-1.pdf.

Gaines, S. E., and C. Kimber. 2001. Redirecting self-regulation. *Environmental Law* (Northwestern School of Law) 13 (2): 157–184.

Ganslandt, Mattias. 2010. Completing the internal market. December. http://www.talkstandards.com/completing-the-internal-market/.

Gasser, Urs, and Silke Ernst. 2006. *EUCD best practice guide: Implementing the EU Copyright Directive in the digital age.* Cambridge, MA: Berkman Center.

Gasser, Urs, and John Palfrey. 2012. *Interop: The promise and perils of highly interconnected systems.* New York: Basic Books.

Geist, Michael. 2011. Unpacking the policy issues behind bandwidth caps and usage based billing. February. http://www.michaelgeist.ca/content/view/5611/99999/.

Georgieva, Kristalina. 2011. ASEAN and the European Union—new strategies and cooperation in disaster management. Public speech during visit in Jakarta/Indonesia, European Commission SPEECH/11/569, September 12. http://europa.eu/rapid/pressReleasesAction.do?reference=SPEECH/11/569&format=HTML&aged=0&language=EN&guiLanguage=en.

Ginsburg, Jane C. 2001. Copyright and control over new technologies of dissemination. *Columbia Law Review* 101 (7): 1613–1647.

Ginsburg, Jane C. 2008. Separating the Sony sheep from the Grokster goats: Reckoning the future business plans of copyright-dependent technology entrepreneurs. *Arizona Law Review.* 50:577–609.

Ginsburg, Jane C., and Sam Ricketson. 2006. Inducers and authorisers: A comparison of the US Supreme Court's Grokster decision and the Australian federal court's Kazaa ruling. *Media and Arts Law Review* 11 (1): 1–25.

Global Network Initiative. 2011. Statement on Internet shutdown in Egypt. January. http://www.globalnetworkinitiative.org/newsandevents/Global_Network_Initiative_Statement_on_Internet_Shutdown_in_Egypt.php.

Goldsmith, Jack. 1998. What Internet gambling legislation teaches about Internet regulation. *International Lawyer* 32:1115–1119.

Goldsmith, Jack, and Tim Wu. 2006. *Who controls the Internet? Illusions of a borderless world.* New York: Oxford University Press.

Gould, Mark. 2000. Locating Internet governance: Lessons from the standards process. In *Regulating the global information society*, ed. Chris Marsden. New York: Routledge.

Gowers, Andrew. 2006. *Gowers review of intellectual property*. London: Stationary Office.

Gowers, Andrew. 2008. Copyright extension is out of tune with reality. *Financial Times*, December 14.

Grabowsky, P. 1995. Using non-governmental resources to foster regulatory compliance. *Governance: An International Journal of Policy, Administration and Institutions* 8:527–550.

Greenleaf, Graham. 2011. Asia-Pacific data privacy: 2011, year of revolution. University of New South Wales Law Research Paper No. 2011-29. http://papers.ssrn.com/sol3/papers.cfm?abstract_id=1914212.

Greenleaf, Graham. Forthcoming. Global data privacy in a networked world. In *Research handbook on governance of the Internet*, ed. Ian Brown. Cheltenham: Edward Elgar.

Greenstein, Shane. 2010. Standardisation and coordination. *IEEE Micro* 30 (3): 6–7.

Grewlich, K. 1999. *Governance in "cyberspace": Access and public interest in communications*. Amsterdam: Kluwer.

Griffiths, J. 2011. Criminal liability for intellectual property infringement in Europe: The role of fundamental rights. In *Criminal enforcement of intellectual property: A blessing or a curse?* ed. C. Geiger. Cheltenham: Edward Elgar.

Gross, P. 1986. *Proceedings of the DARPA Gateway Algorithms and Data Structures Task Force*. January.

Gross, R. 2007. World Intellectual Property Organisation, Global Information Society Watch. http://www.giswatch.org/institutional-overview/civil-society-participation/world-intellectual-property-organisation-wipo.

Group of 8. 2011. *G8 Declaration: Renewed Commitment for Freedom and Democracy*. G8 Summit of Deauville, May 26–27. http://www.g20-g8.com/g8-g20/g8/english/live/news/renewed-commitment-for-freedom-and-democracy.1314.html.

GS1 and Logica CMG. 2007. *European passive RFID Market Sizing 2007 –2022: Report of the BRIDGE Project*. February.

Guadamuz, Andres. 2009. Free and open source software. In *Law and the Internet*, 3rd ed., ed. L. Edwards and C. Waelde. Oxford: Hart Publishing.

Haddadi, Hamed, D. Fay, S. Uhlig, A. Moore, R. Mortier, and A. Jamakovic. 2009. Analysis of the Internet's structural evolution. UCAM-CL Technical Report 756, Computer Laboratory.

Hahn, Robert, and Scott Wallsten. 2006. *The economics of net neutrality*. Washington, DC: AEI Brookings Joint Center for Regulatory Studies. http://papers.ssrn.com/sol3/papers.cfm?abstract_id=943757.

Halderman, J. A., and E. Felten. 2006. Lessons from the Sony CD DRM episode. In *Proceedings of the USENIX Security Symposium*. August.

Hall, Chris, Richard Clayton, Ross Anderson, and Evangelos Ouzounis. 2011. *Inter-X: Resilience of the Internet interconnection ecosystem. Summary report*. Brussels: ENISA.

Halliday, Josh. 2011. Facebook to transform into an entertainment hub. *Guardian*. September. http://www.guardian.co.uk/technology/2011/sep/22/facebook -transform-entertainment-hub?intcmp=239.

Hammarberg, Thomas. 2011. Speech by Council of Europe commissioner. CommDH/ Speech (1), Budapest, January 27.

Handley, M. 2011. Network neutrality and the IETF. In *Proceedings of 75th IETF Meeting*. http://www.ietf.org/proceedings/75/slides/plenaryt-4.pdf.

Hargreaves, I. 2011a. *Digital opportunity: A review of intellectual property and growth*. London: UK Intellectual Property Office.

Hargreaves, I. 2011b. *Data on the prevalence and impact of piracy and counterfeiting*. London: UK Intellectual Property Office.

Hart, Jeffrey A. 2011. The net neutrality debate in the United States. *Journal of Information Technology and Politics* (1):1.

Hartje, James. 2011. QQ: China's Facebook—but bigger. August. http://seekingalpha .com/article/290092-qq-china-s-facebook-but-bigger?source=yahoo.

Hassanabadi, Amir. 2011. *Viacom v. YouTube*: All Eyes Blind—the Limits of the DMCA in a Web 2.0 World. *Berkeley Technology Law Journal* 26:405–440.

Helfer, L. R.., and G. W. Austin. 2011. *Human rights and intellectual property: Mapping the global interface*. Cambridge: Cambridge University Press.

Helft, Miguel. 2008. Yahoo limits retention of search data. *New York Times*, December 18. http://www.nytimes.com/2008/12/18/technology/internet/18yahoo .html?_r=1&em.

Hert, Paul de, and Vagelis Papakonstaninou. 2010. The EU PNR framework decision proposal: Towards completion of the PNR processing scene in Europe. *Computer Law and Security Review* 28:368–376.

Hodgson, Geoffrey M. 1988. *Economics and institutions: A manifesto for a modern institutional economics*. Cambridge: Polity Press.

Hoffman, J. 2005. Internet governance: A regulative idea in flux. Paper presented to European Consortium of Political Research, September.

Hoofnagle, C. 2010. New Challenges to Data Protection Study—Country Report: United States. European Commission DG Freedom, Security and Justice. http:// papers.ssrn.com/sol3/papers.cfm?abstract_id=1639161.

Hornle, J. 2010. *Cross-border online gambling law and policy*. Cheltenham: Edward Elgar.

Horten, Monica. 2011. *The copyright enforcement enigma: Internet politics and the telecoms package*. Basingstoke: Palgrave Macmillan.

House of Lords. 2008. *Personal Internet Security 4th Report*. HL Paper 131, Science and Technology Committee Report. http://www.parliament.uk/business/committees/committees-archive/lords-s-t-select/internet/.

House of Lords. 2011. *Behaviour change*. HL Paper, Science and Technology Committee Report. http://www.publications.parliament.uk/pa/ld201012/ldselect/ldsctech/179/17902.htm.

Howard, Alex. 2011. At the eG8, 20th century ideas clashed with the 21st century economy. *O'Reilly Radar*, May 27. http://radar.oreilly.com/2011/05/eg8-2011-internet-freedom-ip-copyright.html.

Hu, Kunming. 2007. A history of the China incident. *HRI China*. http://hrichina.org/sites/default/files/oldsite/PDFs/CRF.1.2008/CRF-2008-1_Yahoo.pdf.

Hugenholtz, P. B. 2000. Why the copyright directive is unimportant, and possibly invalid. *European Intellectual Property Review* 11:499–505.

Hugenholtz, P. B. 2002. Copyright and freedom of expression. In *The commodification of information*, ed. N. Elkin-Koren and N. W. Netanel. Amsterdam: Kluwer.

Hugenholtz, P. B. 2008. Open letter concerning European Commission's Intellectual Property Package. August. http://www.ivir.nl/news/Open_Letter_EC.pdf.

Hüpkes, Eva. 2009. Regulation, self-regulation or co-regulation? Journal of Business Law 5:427–446.

Hustinx, P. 2011. Public lecture, University of Edinburgh School of Law, July. http://www.edps.europa.eu/EDPSWEB/webdav/site/mySite/shared/Documents/EDPS/Publications/Speeches/2011/11-07-07_Speech_Edinburgh_EN.pdf.

Hyoungshick, Kim, John Tang, and Ross Anderson. 2012. Social authentication: Harder than it looks. Paper presented at the Sixteenth International Financial Cryptography and Data Security Conference.

I v. *Finland*. 2008. Application No. 20511/03. European Court of Human Rights.

IEEE. 2011. Network: Future Internet. http://dl.comsoc.org/livepubs/ci1/public/2011/jul/index.html.

Index on Censorship. 2011. South Korea: plans to scrap real-name system. August. http://www.indexoncensorship.org/2011/08/south-korea-plans-to-scrap-real-name-system/.

Industry Canada. 2006. Assessing the economic impacts of copyright reform on Internet Service Providers. http://www.ic.gc.ca/eic/site/ippd-dppi.nsf/eng/ip01083.html.

Infonetics. 2011. *Report: Service provider deep packed inspection products.* http://www.infonetics.com.

Ingram, Mathew. 2011. Clinton: We love Net freedom, unless it involves WikiLeaks. GigaOM, February 15. http://gigaom.com/2011/02/15/clinton-we-love-net-freedom-unless-it-involves-wikileaks.

Intellectual Property Rights Working Group. 1995. *Report on National Information Infrastructure (NII) Task Force on Intellectual Property and the National Information Infrastructure.* September.

International Standards Organization. 2009. Guidance on social responsibility. International Standard ISO/DIS 26000.

International Telecommunications Union. 2005. Initial comments by the European Union and the acceding countries Romania and Bulgaria, on the report of the Working Group on Internet Governance. WSIS-II/PC-3/CONTR/19-E. August.

International Telecommunications Union. 2010. FG-FN Output Document 77. Focus Group on Future Networks 8th FG-FN meeting, November 28–December 3.

International Telecommunications Union. 2005. Initial comments by the European Union and the acceding countries Romania and Bulgaria, on the report of the Working Group on Internet Governance. WSIS-II/PC-3/CONTR/19-E. August.

International Telecommunications Union. 2010. FG-FN Output Document 77. Focus Group on Future Networks. 8th FG-FN meeting, November 28–December 3.

Internet Engineering Task Force. 2006. MPLS Charter. http://www.ietf.org/html.charters/mpls-charter.html.

Internet Governance Forum. 2008. Network neutrality: Examining the issues and implications for development. Workshop. December. http://www.intgovforum.org/cms/index.php/2008-igf-hyderabad/event-reports/72-workshops/370-workshop-58-network-neutrality-examining-the-issues-and-implications-fordevelopment.

Internet Governance Forum. 2009. Programme, format and schedule for the 2009 meeting. Revision of June 4. http://www.intgovforum.org/cms/2009/postings/ProgrammePaper.04.06.2009.rtf.

IP Multimedia Subsystem (IMS). 2006. Technical specification group services and system aspects. 2006. Stage 2, TS 23.228, 3rd Generation Partnership Project.

IPSphere. 2006. Creating a commercially sustainable framework for IP services realizing next generation revenues. IPsphere Forum Work Program Committee Ver-

sion 1b.0. May. http://www.autonomic-communication.org/web/bodies/ipsphere/
IPsphere_CommercialPrimerExec050806.pdf.

Jefferson, T. 1854. *Writings of Thomas Jefferson*, ed. H. A. Washington, 6:180–181. Washington, DC: Taylor and Maury.

Jennings, Kevin. 2011. The White House Blog: Add your voice to the White House Conference on Bullying Prevention. http://www.whitehouse.gov/blog/2011/03/10/ add-your-voice-white-house-conference-bullying-prevention.

Johnson D., and D. Post. 1996. Law and borders: The rise of law in cyberspace. *Stanford Law Review* 48:1367–1402.

Johnson, D. R., S. P. Crawford, and J. G. Palfrey. 2004. The accountable Net: Peer production of Internet governance. *Virginia Journal of Law and Technology* 9 (9): 1–32.

Jones, C., and W. S. Hesterly. 1993. *Network organization: An alternative governance form or a glorified market?* Atlanta, GA: Academy of Management Meetings.

Jordana, Jacint, and David Levi-Faur. 2004. *The politics of regulation*. Cheltenham: Edward Elgar.

JWZ. 2011. Surprise! Facebook doesn't like privacy countermeasures. *JWZ Blog*. September. http://www.jwz.org/blog/2011/09/surprise-facebook-doesnt-like-privacy -countermeasures/.

Kahin, B., and J. Abbate, eds. 1995. *Standards policy for information infrastructure*. Cambridge, MA: MIT Press.

Kahin, B., and C. Nesson, eds. 1997. *Borders in cyberspace: Information policy and the global information infrastructure*. Cambridge, MA: MIT Press.

Kahn, Robert E., and Vinton Cerf. 1999. *What is the Internet (and what makes it work)*. Washington, DC: Internet Policy Institute http://www.policyscience.net/cerf.pdf.

Karagiannis, Thomas, Pablo Rodriguez, and Dina Papagiannaki. 2005. Should Internet Service Providers fear peer-assisted content distribution? Paper presented at the Internet Measurement Conference, Berkeley, CA.

Katz v. *United States*. 1967. 389 U.S. 347.

Kaul, I., I. Grunberg, and M. Stern, eds. 1999. *Global public goods: International cooperation in the 21st century*. New York: Oxford University Press.

Keller, Perry. 2000. China's impact on the global information society. In *Regulating the global information society*, ed. C. Marsden. London: Routledge.

Kerr, Ian. 2010. Digital locks and the automation of virtue. In *From "radical extremism" to "balanced copyright": Canadian copyright and the digital agenda*, ed. Michael Geist. Toronto: Irwin Law.

Kiedrowski, T. 2007. Net neutrality: Ofcom's view. http://www.wwww.radioauthority.org.uk/media/speeches/2007/02/net_neutrality.

Kierkegaard, Sylvia. 2005. How the cookies (almost) crumbled: Privacy and lobbyism. *Computer Law and Security Report* 21 (4): 310–322.

Kingma, Sytze. 2008. The liberalization and (re)regulation of Dutch gambling markets: National consequences of the changing European context. *Regulation and Governance* 2 (4): 445–458.

Kleinrock, Leonard. 2010. An early history of the Internet. *IEEE Communications Magazine* 48 (8): 26–36.

Kleinwächter, Wolfgang. 2004. Internet co-governance: Towards a multilayer multiplayer mechanism of consultation, coordination and cooperation. Paper presented at the informal consultation of the Working Group on Internet Governance, September, Geneva, Switzerland.

Kleinwächter, Wolfgang. 2011. Internet principle hype: How soft law is used to regulate the Internet. http://news.dot-nxt.com/2011/07/27/internet-principle-hype-anon.

Kleist, T., and C. Palzer. 2007. Co-regulation as an instrument of modern regulation. Paper presented at EU Media Experts Conference, Leipzig.

Kohler-Koch, B., and R. Eising, eds. 1999. *The transformation of governance in the European Union.* London: Routledge.

Komaitis, Konstantinos. 2010. *The current state of domain name regulation: Domain names as second class citizens in a mark-dominated world.* London: Routledge.

Kooiman, J. 2003. *Governing as governance.* Thousand Oaks, CA: Sage.

Korff, D., and I. Brown. 2010. New challenges to data protection. European Commission DG Freedom, Security and Justice. http://papers.ssrn.com/sol3/papers.cfm?abstract_id=1636706.

Kreimer, Seth. 2006. Censorship by proxy: The First Amendment, Internet intermediaries, and the problem of the weakest link. *University of Pennsylvania Law Review* 155:11–101.

Kroes, N. 2010a. Address at Open Forum Europe 2010 Summit: Openness at the heart of the EU digital agenda. Brussels. Speech 10/300.

Kroes, N. 2010b. Towards more confidence and more value for European digital citizens. European Roundtable on the Benefits of Online Advertising for Consumers Brussels. SPEECH/10/452.

Kroes, N. 2011a. Internet essentials. SPEECH/11/479.

Kroes, N. 2011b. Privacy: Reinforcing trust and confidence. Online Tracking Protection and Browsers Workshop. SPEECH/11/461.

Kummer, M. 2004. The results of the WSIS negotiations on Internet governance. In *Internet governance: A grand collaboration,* ed. Don MacLean, 53–57. New York: U.N. Information and Communications Technology Task Force.

La Rue, Frank. 2011. *Report of the special rapporteur on the promotion and protection of the right to freedom of opinion and expression.* Human Rights Council Seventeenth session agenda item 3, A/HRC/17/27, May 2011. http://www2.ohchr.org/english/bodies/hrcouncil/docs/17session/A.HRC.17.27_en.pdf.

Labovitz, C., S. Iekel-Johnson, D. McPherson, D. Oberheide, F. Jahanian, and M. Karir. 2009. ATLAS Internet Observatory annual report and presentation. North American Network Operators Group. http://www.nanog.org/meetings/nanog47/presentations/Monday/Labovitz_ObserveReport_N47_Mon.pdf.

Laffont, J.-J., and J. Tirole. 2001. *Competition in telecommunications.* Cambridge, MA: MIT Press.

Lardner, James. 1987. *Fast forward: Hollywood, the Japanese, and the onslaught of the VCR.* New York: Norton.

Laurie, B. 2000. *An expert's apology.* http://www.apache-ssl.org/apology.html.

Leader, Sheldon. 1982. Free speech and the advocacy of illegal action in law and political theory. *Columbia Law Review* 82 (3): 412–443.

Leader, Sheldon. 2005. Human rights and international trade. In *Understanding the World Trade Organization: Perspectives from law, economics and politics,* ed. P. Macrory, A. Appleton, and M. Plummer. 664–695. New York: Springer.

Leeds, J. 2005. Grokster calls it quits on sharing music files. *New York Times,* November 8. http://www.nytimes.com/2005/11/08/technology/08grokster.html.

Leiner, Barry, M. Vinton G. Cerf, David D. Clark, R. Kahn, L. Kleinrock, D. Lynch, J. Postel, L. Roberts, and S. Wolff. 1998. A brief history of the Internet. http://www.internetsociety.org/internet/internet-51/history-internet/brief-history-internet.

Lemley, Mark A. 1999. Standardizing government standard-setting policy for electronic commerce. *Berkeley Technology Law Journal* 14:745–758.

Lemley, Mark A. 2007. Rationalizing ISP safe harbors. *Journal on Telecommunications and High Technology Law* 6:101–120.

Lemley, Mark A., and L. Lessig, 1999. Ex parte declaration of Professor Mark A. Lemley and Professor Lawrence Lessig in the Matter of: Application for Consent to the Transfer of Control of Licenses of MediaOne Group, Inc. to AT&T Corp CS. Federal Communications Commission. Docket No. 99–251.

Lemley, Mark A., and David McGowan. 1998. Legal implications of network economic effects. *California Law Review* 86:479–611.

Lesk, Michael. 2003. Chicken Little and the Recorded Music Crisis. *IEEE Spectrum* 1(5):73–75.

Lessig, L. 1998. The New Chicago School. *Journal of Legal Studies* 2: 661–690.

Lessig, L. 1999. *Code and other laws of cyberspace.* New York: Basic Books.

Lessig, L. 2006. *Code version 2.0.* New York: Basic Books.

Lessig, L. 2008. *Remix: Making art and commerce thrive in the hybrid economy.* London: Bloomsbury Academic.

Lessig, L., and P. Resnick. 1998. The architectures of mandated access controls. In *Proceedings of the 1998 Telecommunications Policy Research Conference.* http://groups.csail.mit.edu/mac/classes/6.805/articles/cda/lessig-resnick-access-controls.pdf.

Lessig, L., and T. Wu. 2003. Letter to the FCC Ex parte. August. http://timwu.org/wu_lessig_fcc.pdf.

Leucio, A. Cutillo, R. Molva, and M. Önen. 2011. Safebook: A distributed privacy preserving online social network. Paper presented at the IEEE International Symposium on a World of Wireless Mobile and Multimedia Networks, Lucca, Italy.

Levy, Brian, and Pablo Spiller. 1994. The institutional foundations of regulatory commitment: A comparative analysis of telecommunications regulation. *Journal of Law, Economics and Organization* 10:201–246.

Lewis, T. 2009. *Network science: Theory and practice.* Hoboken, NJ: Wiley.

Lievens, E., J. Dumortier, and P. S. Ryan. 2006. The co-protection of minors in new media: A European approach to co-regulation. *University of California Davis Journal of Juvenile Law and Policy* 10 (1): 97–151.

Litman, J. 2001. *Digital copyright: Protecting intellectual property on the Internet.* New York: Prometheus Books.

Litman, J. 2009. The politics of intellectual property. *Cardozo Arts and Entertainment Law Journal* 27:313–320.

Livingstone, S., L. Haddon, A. Görzig, and K. Ólafsson. 2010. *Risks and safety on the Internet: The perspective of European children, initial findings.* London: London School of Economics. http://www2.lse.ac.uk/media@lse/research/EUKidsOnline/Initial_findings_report.pdf.

London Economics. 2010. Study on the economic benefits of privacy enhancing technologies (PETs), European Commission DG Justice, Freedom and Security. http://ec.europa.eu/justice/policies/privacy/docs/studies/final_report_pets_16_07_10_en.pdf.

Longstaff, Patricia H. 2003. The puzzle of competition in the communications sector: Can complex systems be regulated or managed? Working Paper 9, Harvard University Program on Information Resources Policy. http://www.pirp.harvard.edu/ pubs_pdf/longsta/longsta-p03-1.pdf.

Love, J. 2009. Obama administration rules texts of new IPR agreements are state secrets. *Huffington Post*, March 12.

Lusoli, Wainer, and Caroline Miltgen. 2009. Young people and emerging digital services: An exploratory survey on motivations, perceptions and acceptance of risks. Joint Research Centre Institute for Prospective Technological Studies. http://ipts.jrc .ec.europa.eu/publications/pub.cfm?id=2119.

MacAskill, Ewen. 2010. US blocks access to WikiLeaks for federal workers: Employees unable to call up WikiLeaks on government computers as material is still formally classified, says US. *Guardian,* December 3. http://www.guardian.co.uk/world/2010/ dec/03/wikileaks-cables-blocks-access-federal.

Machill, M., and C. Ahlert. 2001. Wer regiert das Internet? ICANN als Fallbeispiel fuÈr neue Formen der Kommunikationsregulierung (Who governs the Internet? ICANN as a case study for new forms of communications regulation). *Publizistik* 46 (3): 295–316.

Machill, M., T. Hart, and B. Kaltenhauser. 2003. Structural development of Internet self-regulation: Case study of ICRA. *Info* 4 (5): 39–55.

MacKinnon, Rebecca. 2012. *Consent of the networked: The worldwide struggle for Internet freedom.* New York: Basic Books.

MacLean, Don, ed. 2004a. *Internet governance: A grand collaboration.* New York: United Nations.

MacLean, Don. 2004b. "Herding Schrödinger's cats": Some conceptual tools for thinking about Internet governance. In *Internet governance: A grand collaboration,* ed. Don MacLean, 73–99. New York: United Nations.

Manne, Geoffrey A., and Joshua D. Wright. 2011. Google and the limits of antitrust: The case against the antitrust case against Google. *Harvard Journal of Law and Public Policy* 34 (1). http://papers.ssrn.com/sol3/papers.cfm?abstract_id=1577556.

Marcus, J. Scott, Neil Robinson, Joel Reidenberg, Yves Poullet, Adam Peake, Kenneth Carter, Lisa Klautzer, Chris Marsden, Florence De Villenfagne, Franck Dumortier, Camilla Abder, et al. 2007. Comparison of privacy and trust policies in the area of electronic communications. http://ec.europa.eu/information_society/policy/ ecomm/doc/library/ext_studies/privacy_trust_policies/final_report_20_07_07_pdf .pdf.

Marsden, C., ed. 2000. *Regulating the global information society.* New York: Routledge.

Marsden, C. 2004. Hyperglobalized individuals: The Internet, globalization, freedom and terrorism. *Foresight* 6 (3): 128–140.

Marsden, C. 2008. Beyond Europe: The Internet, regulation, and multi-stakeholder governance—Representing the consumer interest? *Journal of Consumer Policy* 31 (1): 115–132.

Marsden, C. 2010. *Net neutrality: Towards a co-regulatory solution.* London: Bloomsbury Academic.

Marsden, C. 2011. *Internet co-regulation: European law and regulatory legitimacy in cyberspace.* Cambridge: Cambridge University Press.

Marsden, C. 2012. Regulation of information society service providers. In *Telecommunications Law and Regulation*, 4th ed., ed. I Walden. New York: Oxford University Press.

Marsden, C. 2013. Network neutrality: A research guide. In *Research handbook on governance of the Internet*, ed. Ian Brown. London: Edward Elgar.

Marsden, C., and J. Cave. 2006. *Better re-use of public sector information: Evaluating the proposal for a government data mashing lab.* San Mateo, CA: Rand.

Marsden, C., J. Cave, E. Nason, A. Parkinson, C. Blackman, and J. Rutter. 2006. Assessing indirect impacts of the EC proposals for video regulation. In *TR-414 for Ofcom*. Santa Monica, CA: RAND.

Marsden, Christopher T., Steve Simmons, Ian Brown, Lorna Woods, Adam Peake, Neil Robinson, Stijn Hoorens, and Lisa Klautzer. 2008. Options for and effectiveness of Internet self- and co-regulation phase 2: Case study report. European Commission DG Information Society and Media. http://ssrn.com/abstract=1281374.

Marsh v. *Alabama.* 1946. 326 U.S. 501.

Mayer, Jonathan. 2012. *Setting the record straight on Google's Safari tracking.* http://webpolicy.org/2012/02/20/setting-the-record-straight-on-googles-safari-tracking.

Mayer-Schönberger, Viktor. 2008. Demystifying Lessig. *Wisconsin Law Review* 4:713–746.

Mayer-Schönberger, Viktor. 2009. *Delete: The virtue of forgetting in the digital age.* Princeton, NJ: Princeton University Press.

Mayer-Schönberger, Viktor, and J. Crowley. 2005. Napster's second life? The regulatory challenges of virtual worlds. Working Paper Series RWP05–052KSG, Faculty Research, September.

Mayer-Schönberger, Viktor, and Malte Ziewitz. 2007. Jefferson rebuffed. *Columbia Science and Technology Law Review* 8:188–238.

McCahery, J., W. W. Bratton, S. Piciotto, and C. Scott, eds. 1996. *International regulatory competition and coordination.* New York: Oxford University Press.

McCullagh, D. 2005. US reasserts control over the Internet. *Zdnet.* July. http://news.zdnet.co.uk/Internet/0,39020369,39206653,00.htm.

McIntyre, T. J. 2013. Child abuse images and Cleanfeeds: Assessing Internet blocking systems. In *Research handbook on governance of the Internet,* ed. Ian Brown. Cheltenham: Edward Elgar.

McIntyre, T. J. 2010. Blocking child pornography on the Internet: European Union developments. *International Review of Law Computers & Technology* 24 (3): 209–221.

McIntyre, T. J. 2011. Data protection commissioner investigating Eircom's "three strikes" system. http://www.tjmcintyre.com/2011/06/300-false-accusations-data-protection.html.

McIntyre, T. J., and C. Scott. 2008. Internet filtering: rhetoric, legitimacy, accountability and responsibility. In *Regulating technologies,* ed. R. Brownsword and K. Yeung. Oxford: Hart Publishing.

McKay, Jennifer M. 1994. Classification of Australian corporate and industry based codes of conduct. *International Business Law* 22:507–514.

McStay, Andrew. 2011. Profiling Phorm: An autopoietic approach to the audience-as-commodity. *Surveillance and Society* 8 (3): 310–322.

Mehra, Salil K. 2011. Paradise is a walled garden? Trust, antitrust and user dynamism. *George Mason Law Review* 18:889–952.

Meisel, J. P. 2010. Trinko and mandated access to the Internet. *Info* 12 (2): 9–27.

Metro-Goldwyn-Mayer Studios, Inc. v. Grokster. 2005. 545 U.S. 900.

Mikler, John. 2008. Sharing sovereignty for global regulation: The cases of fuel economy and online gambling. *Regulation and Governance* 2 (4): 383–404.

Mill, John Stuart. 1869. *On liberty.* London: Longman, Roberts & Green.

Mims, Christopher. 2011. How carriers hamstring your smart phone: "Middlebox" study reveals slow downloads, battery drains, and security flaws. *MIT Technology Review* (August). http://www.technologyreview.com/communications/38435/page1/.

Moe, Terry. 1997. The positive theory of public bureaucracy. In *Perspectives on public choice: A handbook,* ed. Dennis C. Mueller. Cambridge: Cambridge University Press.

Moglen, Eben. 2003. The dotCommunist Manifesto. http://emoglen.law.columbia.edu/publications/dcm.html.

Moody, Glyn. 2010. European interoperability framework v2: The great defeat. *Computerworld* 17. http://blogs.computerworlduk.com/open-enterprise/2010/12/european-interoperability-framework-v2---the-great-defeat/index.htm.

Morozov, Evgeny. 2011. *The Net delusion: The dark side of Internet freedom.* New York: Public Affairs Press.

Morris, John, and Cynthia Wong. 2009. Revisiting user control: The emergence and success of a First Amendment theory for the Internet age. *First Amendment Law Review* 8: 109–137.

Morrison, P. D., J. H. Roberts, and E. von Hippel. 2000. Determinants of user innovation and innovation sharing in a local market. *Management Science* 46 (12): 1513–1527.

Morth, U., ed. 2004. *Soft law in governance and regulation: An interdisciplinary analysis.* Cheltenham: Edward Elgar.

Mosco, V. 2004. *The digital sublime: Myth, power and cyberspace.* Cambridge, MA: MIT Press.

Moss, David A., and John A. Cisternino. 2009. *New perspectives on regulation.* New York: Tobin Project.

Mueller, Milton. 1998. *Universal service: Competition, interconnection, and monopoly in the making.* Washington, DC: AEI Press.

Mueller, Milton. 2000. Technology and institutional innovation: Internet domain names. *International Journal of Communications Law and Policy* 5: 1–32. http://ijclp.net/old_website/5_2000/pdf/ijclp_webdoc_1_5_2000.pdf.

Mueller, Milton. 2002. *Ruling the root: Internet governance and the taming of cyberspace.* Cambridge, MA: MIT Press.

Mueller, Milton. 2007. Net neutrality as global principle for Internet governance. Internet Governance Project Paper IGP07–003. http://www.internetgovernance.org/wordpress/wp-content/uploads/NetNeutralityGlobalPrinciple.pdf.

Mueller, Milton. 2010. *Networks and states: The global politics of Internet governance.* Cambridge, MA: MIT Press.

Mueller, M., J. Mathiason, and L. McKnight. 2004. Making sense of "Internet governance": Defining principles and norms in a policy context. In *Internet governance: A grand collaboration,* ed. Don MacLean, 100–121. New York: United Nations.

Mulligan, D., and A. Perznowski. 2007. The magnificence of the disaster: Reconstructing the Sony Rootkit incident. *Berkeley Technology Law Journal* 22:1157–1232.

Murray, Andrew. 2006. *The regulation of cyberspace: Control in the online environment.* London: Routledge.

Murrey, A., and Matthias Klang, eds. 2005. *Human rights in the digital age*. London: Glasshouse Press.

Napoli, L. 1999. Yahoo angers GeoCities members with copyright rules. *New York Times*, June 30. http://emoglen.law.columbia.edu/LIS/archive/webright/geocities -changes.html.

New Jersey Coalition Against War in the Middle East v. *J.M.B. Realty Corp.* 1994. 650 A.2d 757 (N.J.)

New York Times Co. v. *United States* 1971 403 U.S. 713.

Noam, Eli M. 1983. Federal and state roles in telecommunications: The effects of deregulation. *Vanderbilt Law Review* 36:949–955.

Noam, E. M. 1994. Beyond liberalization II: The impending doom of common carriage. *Telecommunications Policy* 18 (6):435–452.

Noam, E. M. 2008. Beyond Net neutrality: Enduser sovereignty. Columbia University draft paper, 34th Telecoms Policy Research Conference, August.

Noam Eli, M. 2011. "Let them eat cellphones": Why mobile wireless is no solution for broadband. *Journal of Information Policy* 1:470–485.

North, Douglass C. 1990. *Institutions, institutional change and economic performance*. Cambridge: Cambridge University Press.

Norwegian Code. 2009. Guidelines for net neutrality. http://www.npt.no/ikbViewer/ Content/109604/Guidelines%20for%20network%20neutrality.pdf.

Noveck, Beth. 2009. *Wiki government: How technology can make government better, democracy stronger, and citizens more powerful*. Washington, DC: Brookings Institution Press.

National Telecommunications and Information Administration. 2005. US domain name system principles. Speech at Wireless Communications Association. June. http://www.ntia.doc.gov/ntiahome/domainname/USDNSprinciples_06302005.htm.

O'Connell. Rachel. 2009. Safer social networking principles for the EU. http://ec .europa.eu/information_society/activities/social_networking/docs/sn_principles .pdf.

O'Reilly. Tim. 2005. What is Web2.0? http://oreilly.com/web2/archive/what-is -web-20.html.

Odlyzko, Andrew, and David Levinson. 2007. Too expensive to meter: The influence of transaction costs in transportation and communication. http://www.dtc.umn .edu/~odlyzko/doc/metering-expensive.pdf.

OECD. 1980. *Guidelines on the protection of privacy and transborder flows of personal data*. Paris: OECD

OECD. 2007. *Report: Participative Web and user-created content: Web 2.0, Wikis and social networking.* Paris: OECD.

OECD. 2008. OECD broadband portal, Table 5(m): Time to reach bit/data caps at advertised speeds. http://www.oecd.org/dataoecd/11/15/39575302.xls.

OECD. 2010. OECD broadband portal, Table 1l: Percentage of fibre connections in total broadband among countries reporting fibre subscribers June. http://www.oecd.org/dataoecd/21/58/39574845.xls.

OECD. 2011a. Communiqué on principles for Internet policy-making. OECD High Level Meeting on the Internet Economy. June. http://www.oecd.org/dataoecd/40/21/48289796.pdf.

OECD. 2011b. *Guidelines for multinational enterprises.* Paris: OECD.

OECD. 2011c. The role of Internet intermediaries in advancing public policy: Forging partnerships for advancing policy objectives for the Internet economy, Part II. DSTI/ICCP(2010)11/FINAL. http://www.oecd.org/dataoecd/8/9/48685066.pdf.

Ofcom. 2006. Market impact assessment: BBC new on-demand video proposals. http://stakeholders.ofcom.org.uk/market-data-research/tv-research/bbc-mias/ondemand/bbc-ondemand/.

Ofcom. 2008. Social networking: A quantitative and qualitative research report into attitudes, behaviours and use. Ofcom research document .April. http://stakeholders.ofcom.org.uk/binaries/research/media-literacy/report1.pdf.

Office of the Data Protection Commissioner. Ireland. 2011. Data protection audit of Facebook Ireland. December 21. http://dataprotection.ie/viewdoc.asp?m=f&fn=/documents/Facebook%20Report/report.pdf/report.pdf.

Oftel. 2000. Draft Direction under Condition 45 of the Public Telecommunications Licence granted to British Telecommunications plc of a dispute between BT and MCI Worldcom concerning the provision of a Flat Rate Internet Access Call Origination product (FRIACO). http://www.ofcom.org.uk/static/archive/oftel/publications/internet/fria0400.htm.

Ogus, A. I. 1994. *Regulation: Legal form and economic theory.* London: Hart.

Ohm, Paul. 2008. The myth of the superuser: Fear, risk, and harm online. *University of California Davis Law Review* 41:1327–1402.

Ohm, Paul, and James Grimmelmann. 2010. Dr. Generative or: How I learned to stop worrying and love the iPhone. *Maryland Law Review* 69:910–953.

Olmstead v. *United States.* 1928. 277 U.S. 438.

Omand, David. 2009. *The national security strategy: Implications for the UK intelligence community.* London: Institute for Public Policy Research.

OpenNet Initiative. 2011. France to disconnect first Internet users under three strikes regime. *OpenNet Initiative blog*, July 27. http://opennet.net/blog/2011/07/france-disconnect-first-internet-users-under-three-strikes-regime.

O'Rourke Sam. 2009. The fight goes on. August–October. https://blog.facebook.com/blog.php?post=58219622130.

Oxman, Jason. 1999. The FCC and the Unregulation of the Internet. Office of Plans and Policy, Federal Communications Commission. http://www.fcc.gov/Bureaus/OPP/working_papers/oppwp31.pdf.

Palfrey, J., and U. Gasser. 2008. *Born digital: Understanding the first generation of digital natives*. New York: Basic Books.

Palfrey, J., U. Gasser, and D. Boyd. 2010. Response to FCC Notice of Inquiry 09–94. Working paper series paper no. 10–19. Harvard Law School, Public Law and Legal.

Palmera, Ian. 1989. Images of regulation: Travel agent legislation and the deregulation debate. *Politics* 24 (2): 13–22.

Parr, Ben. 2011. U.S. government wins access to Twitter accounts of WikiLeaks supporters. *Mashable* (March). http://mashable.com/2011/03/11/twitter-wikileaks-doj/.

Patry, W. 2009. *Moral panics and the copyright wars*. New York: Oxford University Press.

Pattberg, Philip. 2005. The institutionalization of private governance: How business and nonprofit organizations agree on transnational rules. *Governance: An International Journal of Policy, Administration and Institutions* 18:589–610.

People's Republic of China. 2010. "The Internet in China, Information Office of the State Council of the People's Republic of China." White Paper, section III. http://china.org.cn/government/whitepaper/2010-06/08/content_20207994.htm.

Peracchio. Tom. 2011. Why is WikiLeaks more popular than net neutrality? Important issues to the future of the Internet. *Yahoo! Contributor Network* (February). http://www.associatedcontent.com/article/7803238/why_is_wikileaks_more_popular_than_pg2.html?cat=15.

Perfect 10, Inc. v. *CCBill LLC.* 2007. 488 F.3d 1102 (9th Cir.).

Pfleeger, Charles, and Shari L. Pfleeger. 2006. *Security in computing*. Englewood Cliffs, NJ: Prentice Hall Pearson.

Pierre, J. 2000. Introduction: Understanding governance. In *Debating governance, authority, steering and democracy*, ed. J. Pierre. New York: Oxford University Press.

Pitofsky, Robert. 1998. Self regulation and antitrust. Prepared remarks of the chairman, Federal Trade Commission, D.C. Bar Association Symposium, February. http://www.ftc.gov/speeches/pitofsky/self4.shtm.

Pollett, T. V., S. Roberts, and R.I.M. Dunbar. 2011. Use of social network sites and instant messaging does not lead to increased offline social network size, or to emotionally closer relationships with offline network members. *Cyberpsychology, Behavior and Social Networking* 14:253–258.

Porter, Michael, and Mark Kramer. 2006. Strategy and society: The link between competitive advantage and corporate social responsibility. *Harvard Business Review* (December): 78–93.

Posner, R. A. 1984. Theories of economic regulation. *Bell Journal of Economics and Management Science* 5:335–358.

Post, David. 2009. *In Search of Jefferson's moose: Notes on the state of cyberspace*. New York: Oxford University Press.

Poullet, Y. 2007. Internet governance: Some thoughts after the two WSIS. In *The information Society: Innovation, legitimacy, ethics and democracy*, ed. Philippe Goujon, Sylvain Lavelle, Penny Duquenoy, Kai Kimpa, and Veronique Laurent, 201–224. New York: Springer.

Powell, Alison, and Alissa Cooper. 2011. Net neutrality discourses: Comparing advocacy and regulatory arguments in the United States and the United Kingdom. *Information Society* 27:311–325.

Powell, Alison, and Michael Hills. 2010. Child protection and free speech: Mapping the territory. Discussion forum paper 17, Oxford Internet Institute. http://www.oii.ox.ac.uk/news/?id=405.

Preibusch, Sören, and Joseph Bonneau. 2011. The privacy landscape: Product differentiation on data collection. Washington, DC, June 14.

Preuschat, Archibald. 2011. KPN admits to using deep packet inspection. *Wall Street Journal,* May 12, Tech Europe. http://blogs.wsj.com/tech-europe/2011/05/12/kpn-admits-to-using-deep-packet-inspection/.

Price, M., and S. Verhulst. 2004. *Self-regulation and the Internet*. Amsterdam: Kluwer.

Priest, Margot. 1997. The privatisation of regulation: Five models of self-regulation. *Ottawa Law Review* 29:233–301.

Raab, Charles. 1993. The governance of data protection. In *Modern governance*, ed. J. Kooiman, 89–103. Thousand Oaks, CA: Sage.

Ramstad, Evan. 2011. Hackers breach South Korean database. *Wall Street Journal,* July 28. http://online.wsj.com/article/SB10001424053111904888304576473744264486236.html.

Reding, Viviane. 2005. Opportunities and challenges of the ubiquitous world and some words on Internet governance. Speech to Global Business Dialogue on e-Society October.

Reding, Viviane. 2007. Better regulation for a single market in telecoms. Plenary meeting of the European Regulators Group, Athens. SPEECH/07/624.

Reding, Viviane. 2008. Social networking in Europe: Success and challenges. SPEECH 08/465.

Reding, Viviane. 2009. Freedom of speech: ICT must help, not hinder. EP Plenary Session, Strasbourg. http://ec.europa.eu/commission_barroso/reding/docs/speeches/2009/strasbourg-20090203.pdf.

Reding, Viviane. 2010. Privacy: The challenges ahead for the European Union. Keynote speech at the Data Protection Day, European Parliament, Brussels, January. SPEECH/10/16.

Reding, Viviane. 2012. Statement by Viviane Reding on freedom of expression and information via the Internet, attempts to block websites, "three-strikes-laws," and ACTA. http://ec.europa.eu/commission_2010-2014/reding/pdf/quote_statement_en.pdf.

Reed, C. 2007. Taking sides on technology neutrality. *SCRIPTed* 4: 263–284.

Regulation EC/1177/2009. 2009. Application thresholds (contracts for public works, public supply and public service). OJ L 314/64, November 30.

Regulation EU/1251/2011. 2011. Amending Directives 2004/17/EC, 2004/18/EC and 2009/81/EC in respect of their application thresholds for the procedures for the awards of contract. OJ L319/43, November 30.

Reidenberg, J. 1993. Rules of the road for global electronic highways: Merging the trade and technical paradigms. *Harvard Journal of Law and Technology* 6:287, 301–304.

Reidenberg, J. 1998. Lex informatica: The formulation of information policy rules through technology. *Texas Law Review* 76:553–593.

Reidenberg, J. 1999. Restoring Americans' privacy in electronic commerce. *Berkeley Technology Law Journal* 14:771–792.

Reidenberg, J. 2002. Yahoo and democracy on the Internet. *Jurimetrics* 42:261, 265–266.

Reidenberg, J. 2004. States and law enforcement. *University of Ottawa Law and Technology Journal.* 213:225–229.

Reidenberg, J. 2005. Technology and Internet jurisdiction. *University of Pennsylvania Law Review* 153:1951-1959.

Reidenberg, Joel R. 2006. Privacy wrongs in search of remedies. *Hastings Law Journal* 54:877–881.

Republic of Iceland. 2011. A proposal for a new constitution for the Republic of Iceland. March. English translation http://www.stjornlagarad.is/other_files/stjornlagarad/Frumvarp-enska.pdf.

Resnick, P., and J. Miller. 1996. PICS: Internet access controls without censorship. *Association for Computing Machinery* 39(10): 87–93. http://www.w3.org.PICS.iacwcv2.htm.

Reuters. 2011. EU wants Facebook, Google to comply with new data rules. March 16. http://www.reuters.com/article/2011/03/16/us-eu-data-privacy-idUSTRE72F69S20110316.

RFC 2543. 1999. *SIP: Session initiation protocol, IETF*, ed. M. Handley, H. Schulzrinne, E. Schooler, and J. Rosenberg. http://www.ietf.org/rfc/rfc2543.txt.

RFC 5670. 2009. Proposed standard: Metering and marking behaviour of PCN-nodes, ed. P. Eardley. http://tools.ietf.org/html/rfc5670.

Rooney, Ben. 2011. Net neutrality debate in Europe is "over." *Wall Street Journal*, February 28. http://blogs.wsj.com/tech-europe/2011/02/28/net-neutrality-debate-in-europe-is-over/?mod=google_news_blog.

Rosston, G. I., and M. D. Topper. 2010. An anti-trust analysis of the case for wireless net neutrality. *Information Economics and Policy* 22 (10): 103–119.

Rubinstein, I. 2012. Regulating privacy by design. *Berkeley Technology Law Journal* 46:1409–1456.

Ruggie, John. 2011. Guidelines for multinational enterprises on human rights. Special Representative to United Nations Human Rights Council. http://www.business-humanrights.org/media/documents/ruggie/ruggie-guiding-principles-21-mar-2011.pdf.

S and Marper v. *UK*. 2008. Application No. 30562/04. ECHR 1581 of 4 December.

SABAM v. *Netlog*. Case C-360/10. http://curia.europa.eu/juris/document/document.jsf?text&docid=119512&pageIndex=0&doclang=EN&mode=req&dir&occ=first&part=1&cid=158253.

Sabbagh, Dan. 2011a. Google evangelist warns Facebook could be the next AOL or IBM. *Guardian*, September. http://www.guardian.co.uk/technology/2011/sep/21/google-facebook-vint-cerf.

Sabbagh, Dan. 2011b. Tories torn over regulating social media. *Guardian*, August 24. http://www.guardian.co.uk/uk/2011/aug/24/cameron-twitter-regulation.

Sahel, Jean-Jacques. 2006. Multistakeholder governance and Internet regulation: A new policy-making paradigm for the information society. Telecommunications Policy Research Conference. October.

Sahel, Jean-Jacques. 2011. Final act: The few more steps needed to restore and protect net neutrality in Europe. *Communications and Strategies* 84:15–34.

Saltzer, J., D. Reed, and D. Clark. 1984. End-to-end arguments in system design. *ACM Transactions on Computer Systems* 2:277–288.

Samuelson, P. 1997. The U.S. digital agenda at WIPO. *Virginia Journal of International Law* 37:369–439.

Samuelson, P. 2001. Anticircumvention rules: Threat to science. *Science* 293 (5537): 2028–2031.

Samuelson, P. 2006. Three reactions to MGM v. Grokster. *Michigan Telecommunications Technology Law Review* 13:177–196.

Santo, Alysia. 2011. Behind the news: A Q&A with Icelandic parliamentarian Birgitta Jónsdóttir. *Columbia Journalism Review.*

Santucci, Gérald. 2011. The privacy and data protection impact assessment framework for RFID applications: A defining moment in the modern epic of co-regulation in ICT. *European Commission Digital Agenda Blog.* http://blogs.ec.europa.eu/digital -agenda/the-privacy-and-data-protection-impact-assessment-framework-for-rfid -applications-a-defining-moment-in-the-modern-epic-of-co-regulation-in-ict/.

Sarkozy, N. 2010. Speech to the Embassy of France to the Holy See.

Scarlet Extended SA v. *SABAM (Société Belge des auteurs, compositeurs et éditeurs).* 2011. Case C-70/10 OJ C 113, 1.5.2010: 20–20, OJ C 25/6, 28.1.2012.

Schneider, Volker, and Johannes M. Bauer. 2007. Governance: Prospects of complexity theory in revisiting system theory. Paper presented at the annual meeting of the Midwest Political Science Association, Chicago. http://www.uni-konstanz.de/FuF/ Verwiss/Schneider/ePapers/MPSA2007Paper_vs_jmb.pdf.

Schulz, W., and T. Held. 2001. *Regulated self-regulation as a form of modern government.* Bloomington: Indiana University Press.

Scott, Colin. 2004. Regulation in the age of governance: The rise of the post-regulatory State. In *The politics of regulation,* ed. Jacint Jordana and David Levi-Faur. Cheltenham: Edward Elgar.

Scott, Colin. 2005. Between the old and the new: Innovation in the regulation of Internet gaming. In *Regulatory innovation: A comparative analysis,* ed. Julia Black, Martin Lodge, and Mark Thatcher. Cheltenham: Edward Elgar.

Scott, Colin. 2007. Innovative regulatory response. *Risk and Regulation Magazine* (Summer). http://www.lse.ac.uk/resources/riskAndRegulationMagazine/magazine/ summer2007/innovativeRegulatoryResponses.htm.

Scribbins, K. 2001. Privacy@net: An international comparative study of consumer privacy on the Internet. Consumers International. http://www .consumersinternational.org/news-and-media/publications/privacy@net-an -international-comparative-study-of-consumer-privacy-on-the-internet.

Searls, Doc. 2011. Circling around your wallet. *Harvard Law Blog* (August). http:// blogs.law.harvard.edu/vrm/2011/08/28/circling-around-your-wallet/.

Staff Working Document. 2009. Impact assessment on proposal for a directive on combating the sexual abuse, sexual exploitation of children and child pornography.

Security Blog. 2011. Facebook to prevent third party apps from seeing your information. http://www.thesecurityblog.com/2011/09/facebook-to-prevent-3rd-party-apps -from-seeing-your-information-via-your-friends/?utm_source=pulsenews&utm _medium=referral&utm_campaign=Feed%3A+TheSecurityBlog+%28The+Security +Blog%29.

Seltzer, W. 2010. Free speech unmoored in copyright's Safe Harbor: Chilling effects of the DMCA on the First Amendment. *Harvard Journal of Law and Technology* 24 (1):171–232.

Senden, L. 2005. Soft law, self-regulation and co-regulation in European law: Where do they meet? *Electronic Journal of Comparative Law* 9 (1) 1–27.

Shah, Rajiv C., and Kesan, Jay P. 2003. Manipulating the governance characteristics of code. *info* 5 (4) 3–9.

Shannon, Claude E. 1948. A mathematical theory of communication. *Bell System Technology Journal* 27:379–423, 623–656.

Shannon, Claude E. 1949. Communication in the presence of noise. *Proceedings of the IRE* 37(1):10–21.

Shirkey, C. 2003. Power laws, Weblogs, and inequality. http://www.shirky.com/ writings/powerlaw_weblog.html.

Sinclair, Darren. 1997. Self-regulation versus command and control? Beyond false dichotomies. *Law and Policy* 19:529–559.

Sluijs, Jasper P. 2010. Network neutrality between false positives and false negatives: Introducing a European approach to American broadband markets. *Federal Communications Law Journal* 62:77–117.

Smith, Gerry. 2011. US State Department official Philip Crowley forced to resign after criticizing treatment of Manning. March. http://assangewatch.blogspot.com.

Smith, J. 2009. Canada wins Facebook fight. *Toronto Star*, August 28. http://www .thestar.com/news/canada/article/687719.

Smythe, Dallas. 1977. Communications: blindspot of western Marxism. *Canadian Journal of Political and Social Theory* 1:1–27.

Soghoian, Chris. 2011. Interest-based advertising: in whose interest? Paper presented at Do Not Track or Right on Track? Privacy and Consumer Protection Implications of Online Behavioural Advertising, Edinburgh University.

Soghoian, C., and S. Stamm. 2010. Certified lies: Detecting and defeating government interception attacks against SSL. Working paper. http://papers.ssrn.com/sol3/papers.cfm?abstract_id=1591033.

Sommer, Peter, and Ian Brown. 2011. *Reducing systemic cybersecurity risk.* Paris: Organisation for Economic Cooperation and Development.

Sony Corp. of America v. *Universal City Studios, Inc.* 1984. 464 U.S. 417.

Sorrell v. *IMS Health.* 2011. 131 S. Ct. 2653.

Spar, Debora. 2001. *Pirates, prophets and pioneers: Business and politics along the technological frontier.* London: Random House.

Spiekermann, S. 2011. The RFID PIA: Developed by regulators, agreed by industry. In *Privacy impact assessment: Engaging stakeholders in protecting privacy*, ed. David Wright and Paul de Hert. Dordrecht: Springer.

Spulber, Daniel F., and Christopher S. Yoo. 2009. *Networks in telecommunications: Economics and law.* Cambridge: Cambridge University Press.

Stalla-Bourdillon, Sophie. 2010. The flip side of ISP's liability regimes: The ambiguous protection of fundamental rights and liberties in private digital spaces. *Computer Law and Security Report* 26:492–501.

Stiglitz, Joseph E. 1985. Information and economic analysis: A perspective. *Economic Journal* 95 (supplement):21–41.

Stiglitz, Joseph. 1999. Knowledge as a global public good. In *Global public goods: International Cooperation in the 21st Century*, ed. Inge Kaul, Isabelle Grunberg, and Marc A. Stein. New York: Oxford University Press.

Sui-Lee Wee. 2011. Insight: Cisco suits on China rights abuses to test legal reach. *Reuters Beijing.* September. http://www.reuters.com/article/2011/09/09/us-china-cisco-idUSTRE78809E20110909.

Sunstein, C. R. 2002. Switching the default rule. *New York University Law Review* 77:106–134.

Synovate. 2010. Summary: Music Matters/Synovate/MidemNet Global Survey. http://www.synovate.com/news/article/2010/01/global-survey-reveals-music-trends-rocking-fans-across-the-world.html.

Talbot, D. 2006. Toward a high-definition YouTube. *MIT Technology Review*, October 26. http://www.technologyreview.com/read_article.aspx?id=17654&ch=biztech&sc=&pg=2.

Tambini, Damian, Leonardi Danilo, and Chris Marsden. 2007. *Codifying cyberspace: Self regulation of converging media.* London: Routledge.

Teubner, G. 1986. The transformation of law in the welfare state. In *Dilemmas of law in the welfare state*, ed. G. Teubner. Berlin: W. de Gruyter.

Thaler, Richard H., and Cass R. Sunstein. 2009. *Nudge: Improving decisions about health, wealth, and happiness.* New Haven, CT: Yale University Press.

Thierer, A. 2007. Social networking and age verification: Many hard questions; no easy solutions. Progress and Freedom Foundation. http://www.technewsreview.com.au/article.php?article=1430.

Thierer, A., and Clyde W. Crews, eds. 2003. *Who rules the Net? Internet governance and jurisdiction.* Washington, DC: Cato Institute.

Tiebout, C. 1956. A pure theory of public expenditures. *Journal of Political Economy* 64:416–424.

Alvin, Toffler. 1980. *The third wave.* New York: Bantam.

TorrentFreak. 2012. Pirate Bay founders' prison sentences final, supreme court appeal rejected. February 1. http://torrentfreak.com/pirate-bay-founders-prison-sentences-final-supreme-court-appeal-rejected-120201/.

Twentieth Century Fox Film Corporation and Others v. *British Telecommunications Plc (No.2)* 2011. EWHC 2714 (Ch).

UEJF et LICRA v. *Yahoo! Inc. et Yahoo France.* Tribunal de Grande Instance de Paris, May 22, 2000, No. RG 00/05308.

U.K. Children's Charities' Coalition on Internet Safety. 2008. Guidance on best practice for the providers of social networking services used by children and young people. http://media.education.gov.uk/assets/files/industry%20guidance%20%20%20social%20networking.pdf.

U.K. Data Protection Registrar. 1999. The Fifteenth Annual Report of the Data Protection Registrar. In *HC (575)*. London: Stationary Office.

U.K. Department for Business. 2009. Digital Economy Bill impact assessments. http://www.ialibrary.bis.gov.uk/uploaded/DEB-Impact-Assessments.pdf..

Ungerer, H. 2000. Access issues under EU regulation and anti-trust law: The case of telecommunications and Internet markets. http://conferences.wcfia.harvard.edu/fellows/files/ungerer.pdf .

Ungerer, H. 2005. Competition in the media sector—how long can the future be delayed? *info* 7 (5): 52–60.

U.N. Economic and Social Council. 2006. Agenda item 5: Compendium of basic terminology in governance and public administration. Committee of Experts on Public Administration: Fifth session. E/C.16/2006/4, March 27–31.

U.N. Human Rights Committee. 1988. General Comment 16. Twenty-third session.

U.N. Human Rights Council. 2011. Human rights and transnational corporations and other business enterprises. Resolution 17/4, A/HRC/RES/17/4. (June). http://www.business-humanrights.org/media/documents/un-human-rights-council-resolution-re-human-rights-transnational-corps-eng-6-jul-2011.pdf.

U.N. Special Rapporteur. 2005. Joint Declaration by the U.N. Special Rapporteur on Freedom of Opinion and Expression, the OSCE Representative on Freedom of the Media and the OAS Special Rapporteur on Freedom of Expression, International Mechanisms for Promoting Freedom of Expression. http://www.article19.org/data/files/pdfs/standards/three-mandates-dec-2005.pdf.

U.S. Department of Justice. 2012. Justice Department charges leaders of Megaupload with widespread online copyright infringement. Office of Public Affairs.

U.S. Government. 2005. State Department Comments of the United States of America on Internet governance. August.

U.S. Government. 2009. Affirmation of commitments by the United States Department of Commerce and the Internet Corporation for assigned names and numbers. http://www.icann.org/en/about/agreements/aoc/affirmation-of-commitments-30sep09-en.htm.

U.S. Government. 2012. *Consumer data privacy in a networked world: A framework for protecting privacy and promoting innovation in the global digital economy.* February 23. http://www.whitehouse.gov/sites/default/files/privacy-final.pdf.

U.S. Government Accountability Office. 2010. *Observations on efforts to quantify the economic effects of counterfeit and pirated goods.* Washington, DC: Government Accountability Office.

U.S. Mission to the EU. 2009. The many sides of data privacy: Managing rising tensions. http://wikileaks.org/cable/2009/08/09USEUBRUSSELS1140.html.

Vallejo, A., A. Zaballos, X. Canaleta, and J. Dalmau. 2008. End-to-end QoS management proposal for the ITU-T IMS/NGN architecture. Paper presented at 16th International Conference on Software, Telecommunications and Computer Networks.

Van Oranje, C., S. Simmons, J. Kahan, M. Botterman, and P. Lundin. 2005. *The Spring Council Review: Implications for information society policy options.* Report for the European Commission, DG Information Society.

Van Schewick, Barbara. 2010. *Internet architecture and innovation*. Cambridge, MA: MIT Press.

Verizon v. Trinko. 2004. 540 U.S. 398.

Viacom et al. v. YouTube, Inc. et al. 2010. 718 F. Supp. 2d 514.

Von Hippel, E. 1976. The dominant role of users in the scientific instrument innovation process. *Research Policy* 5 (3): 212–239.

Waclawsky, J. G. 2005. IMS 101: What you need to know. http://109.69.9.58/wp -content/uploads/2011/10/03_waclawsky-18_Jun05.pdf.

Wang, Zhaoguang, Z. Qian, Q. Xu, Z. Mao, and M. Zhang. 2011. An untold story of middleboxes in cellular networks. *SIGCOMM*. http://web.eecs.umich.edu/~zmao/ Papers/netpiculet.pdf.

Warren, Samuel, and Louis Brandeis. 1890. The right to privacy. *Harvard Law Review* 4:193–220.

Waters, D. 2007. DRM group vows to fight bloggers. *BBC News*, May 4. http://news. bbc.co.uk/1/hi/technology/6623331.stm

Weber, R., and M. Grosz. 2009. Legitimate governing of the Internet. *International Journal of Private Law* 2:316–330.

Weinberg, J. 1997. Rating the Net. *Hastings Communications and Entertainment Law Journal* 19:453–482.

Weiser, P. 2009. The future of Internet regulation. *University of California Davis Law Review* 43:529–590.

Weiser, Phil. 2010. Towards an international dialogue on the institutional side of antitrust. *NYU Annual Survey of American Law*, 66 (1): 101–113.

Werbach, Kevin. 1997. Digital tornado: The Internet and telecommunications policy, Office of Plans and Policy. Federal Communications Commission. http:// transition.fcc.gov/Bureaus/OPP/working_papers/oppwp29pdf.html.

Werbach, Kevin. 2002. A layers model for Internet policy. *Journal on Telecommunications and High Technology Law* 1:37–67.

Werbach, Kevin. 2005. The Federal Computer Commission. *North Carolina Law Review* 84 (1): 21.

Weitzner, Daniel J. 2007. Free speech and child protection on the Web. *IEEE Internet Computing* 11 (3): 86–89.

Werbach, Kevin. 2010. Off the hook. *Cornell Law Review* 95:535.

Westin, Alan. 1967. *Privacy and Freedom*. New York: Atheneum.

Winn, J. K. 2010. Technical standards as data protection regulation. http://dx.doi .org/10.2139/ssrn.1118542.

Working Group on Internet Governance. 2005. *Report of the Working Group on Internet Governance. Transmitted to the President of the Preparatory Committee of the World Summit on the Information Society.* July. http://www.wgig.org/WGIG-Report.html.

Williams, Martyn, and Angela Gunn. 2007. EMI to ditch DRM, offer improved sound on iTunes. *Computerworld,* April 2. http://www.computerworld.com/s/article/ 9015282/EMI_to_ditch_DRM_offer_improved_sound_on_iTunes.

Williamson, O. E. 1975. *Markets and hierarchies: Analysis and antitrust implications.* New York: Free Press.

Williamson, O. E. 1985. *The economic institutions of capitalism: Firms, markets and relational contracting.* New York: Free Press.

Williamson, O. E. 1994. Transaction cost economics and organization theory. In *The handbook of economic sociology,* ed. N. J. Smelser and R. Swedberg, 77–107. Princeton, NJ: Princeton University Press.

Wohl, Isaac. 2009. The Antigua-United States online gambling dispute. *Journal of International Commerce and Economics* 332:1–22.

World Privacy Forum. 2011. Comments on EASA best practice recommendation on behavioural advertising. http://www.worldprivacyforum.org/pdf/WPF_EASA _comment_2011fs.pdf.

Wright, Jane. 2001. *Tort law and human rights.* Oxford: Hart.

Wright, Tim. 2006. Next Generation Networks: The interconnect challenges. Paper presented at the Thirteenth European Conference of Postal and Telecommunications Administrations. October.

World Trade Organization. 2005. *United States—Measures affecting the cross-border supply of gambling and betting services.* WT/DS285/AB/R.

Wu, T. 2003a. When code isn't law. *Virginia Law Review* 89:679.

Wu, T. 2003b. Network neutrality, broadband discrimination. *Journal on Telecommunications and High Technology Law*: 2:141–172.

Wu, Tim. 2006. The world trade law of internet filtering. *Chicago Journal of International Law* 7:263.

Wu, T. 2007. Wireless net neutrality: Cellular Carterfone and Consumer Choice in Mobile Broadband. http://www.newamerica.net/files/WorkingPaper17 _WirelessNetNeutrality_Wu.pdf.

Wu, T. 2010. *The master switch: The rise and fall of digital empires.* New York: Knopf.

Xinhua. 2011a. Baidu makes deal with world music giants. July 19. http://news .xinhuanet.com/english2010/china/2011-07/19/c_13995900.htm.

Xinhua. 2011b. S Korea plans to scrap online real-name system. *China Daily*, August 11. http://www.chinadaily.com.cn/world/2011-08/11/content_13095102.htm.

Yen, A. 2000. Internet Service Provider liability for subscriber copyright infringement, enterprise liability and the First Amendment. *Georgetown Law Journal* 88:1833–1889.

Yeung, Karen. 2012. Nudge as fudge. *Modern Law Review* 75:122–148.

Yoo, C. S. 2005. Beyond network neutrality. *Harvard Journal of Law and Technology* 19:20.

Yoo, C. 2010. The changing patterns of Internet usage. *Federal Communications Law Journal* 63 (1): 67–90.

York, Jillian C. 2010. Policing content in the quasi-public sphere. *Open Net Initiative Bulletin*. http://opennet.net/sites/opennet.net/files/PolicingContent.pdf.

York, J. 2012. Thoughts on Twitter's latest move. http://jilliancyork.com/2012/01/26/thoughts-on-twitters-latest-move/.

Yu, Peter K. 2010. The graduated response. *Florida Law Review* 62:1373–1430.

Zetter, Kim. 2011. DoJ's WikiLeaks probe widens to include Gmail, ISP. *Threat Level blog* (October). http://www.wired.com/threatlevel/2011/10/doj-wikileaks-probe/.

Ziewitz, Malte, and Ian Brown. 2013. A prehistory of Internet governance. In *Research handbook on governance of the Internet*, ed. Ian Brown. Cheltenham: Edward Elgar.

Zittrain, J. 2003. Be careful what you ask for: Reconciling a global Internet and local law. In *Who Rules the Net?* ed. A. Thierer and C. Crews. Washington, DC: Cato Institute.

Zittrain, Jonathan. 2006. The generative Internet. *Harvard Law Review* 119:1974–2040.

Zittrain, J. 2008. *The future of the Internet and how to stop it*. New Haven, CT: Yale University Press.

Zuckerberg, Mark. 2009. On Facebook, people own and control their information. February. https://blog.facebook.com/blog.php?post=54434097130.

Zysman, J., and S. Weber. 2000. Governance and politics of the Internet economy: Historical transformation or ordinary politics with a new vocabulary? In *International encyclopedia of the social and behavioral sciences*, ed. N. J. Smelser. Oxford: Elsevier Science Limited.

Index